Discourse, Interpretation, Organization

This much-needed systematic exploration of the emerging field of organizational discourse addresses both scholarly perspectives and empirical applications of the concepts. The interpretive, functional, critical, and structurational perspectives are examined in detail. Issues discussed include the constructive potential of discourse; prominent interpretive approaches; the role of discourse, in particular metaphor, in fostering certain organizational outcomes; a critical view addressing the power and political dimensions of discourse; and the dual aspects of discourse as both communicative action and deep structures, interrelated through the modality of interpretive schemes. Application chapters illustrate how discourse theory can be employed in field research, aiding the analyst in gaining a deeper understanding of the social context and of the effects of discourse on that context. In particular, a view of discourse as situated symbolic action, and a structurational view of discourse are illustrated empirically, using examples from a major IT organization and a global consulting firm.

LOIZOS HERACLEOUS is Reader in Strategy at the Saïd Business School and an Official Fellow of Templeton College, Oxford University.

Discourse, Interpretation, Organization

LOIZOS HERACLEOUS

CAMBRIDGE
UNIVERSITY PRESS

CAMBRIDGE UNIVERSITY PRESS
Cambridge, New York, Melbourne, Madrid, Cape Town, Singapore,
São Paulo, Delhi, Dubai, Tokyo, Mexico City

Cambridge University Press
The Edinburgh Building, Cambridge CB2 8RU, UK

Published in the United States of America by Cambridge University Press, New York

www.cambridge.org
Information on this title: www.cambridge.org/9780521181426

First published 2006
First paperback edition 2010

A catalogue record for this publication is available from the British Library

ISBN 978-0-521-84402-4 Hardback
ISBN 978-0-521-18142-6 Paperback

Cambridge University Press has no responsibility for the persistence or
accuracy of URLs for external or third-party internet websites referred to in
this publication, and does not guarantee that any content on such websites is,
or will remain, accurate or appropriate.

To all the people who make my life meaningful; you know who you are

Contents

Figures

Tables

Preface

This book is based on my research in organizational discourse over the last decade. Starting with my doctoral research, I have conducted theoretical and empirical studies, employing aspects of the four approaches or paradigms that are discussed in this book (interpretive, functional, critical and structurational). Even though what is presented here is far from a comprehensive discussion of the available approaches to understanding and researching discourse (something unlikely to be achieved in a single volume), I have nevertheless endeavoured to present a structured exposition that addresses the main streams of research in organizational discourse and conveys the variety of options, vibrancy and promise of this emerging field.

Chapter 1 underlines the increased attention to discourse in social science, and more particularly in organization theory since the late 1970s. It then addresses the important role of context in understanding discourse; outlines some key features of organizational texts; discusses the role of empirical discourse analysis; outlines the variety of ways in which discourse has been conceptualized and employed; and finally offers some thoughts on what makes a discourse lens for the study of organizations distinctive and fruitful.

Chapters 2–5 then expand on the interpretive, functional, critical and structurational streams to organizational discourse. In chapter 2 interpretivism is outlined as encompassing the commitment to in-depth understanding of actors' first-order interpretations, and distinguished from subjectivism in terms of interpretivism's acceptance of the desirability of more general frameworks derived inductively from data. Then an understanding of discourse as constructive of social reality is developed, where discourse is viewed as situated symbolic action (a view further discussed and employed empirically in chapter 6). Finally, five interpretive approaches to organizational discourse (hermeneutics, rhetoric, metaphor, symbolic interactionism and story-telling) are discussed and their analytical implications outlined.

Chapter 3 addresses the functional approach to organizational discourse where discourse is viewed as language-based communication employed by managerial and social actors for achieving particular ends. Empirical research is drawn on to clarify the importance of understanding and taking account of the soft aspects of organizations in the context of organizational change and development, and the role of discourse, particularly metaphor, in this process. This chapter draws on an organization development intervention where a process involving the construction of "embodied" metaphors was employed to facilitate more effective debate and understanding of a new strategic concept.

Chapter 4 outlines the critical approach to organizational discourse, where discursive social reality construction is seen as imbued with power and interest considerations, where dominant groups attempt to shape reality, social practices, and even subjects' identities in ways that perpetuate these groups' own interests. The chapter addresses the work of Michel Foucault, a prominent social theorist who has been particularly influential in critical approaches. It traces Foucault's conceptions of discourse in his archaeological and genealogical periods, offers a constructive critique of archaeological conceptions of discourse, traces Foucault's conceptual shifts and concerns in his genealogical period, and finally outlines implications for organizational discourse analysis.

In the context of long-standing divisions in sociology between action and structure-oriented theories, interpretive and functional conceptions of discourse tend to privilege the former, whereas critical approaches tend to privilege the latter. As a basis for a more encompassing understanding of organizational discourse chapter 5 draws on the work of the sociologist Anthony Giddens to propose a structurational conceptualization where discourse is viewed as a duality of communicative actions and deep structures, recursively linked through the modality of actors' interpretive schemes. Relevant implications of this conceptualization are then outlined in terms of placing alternative approaches in context, extending current theoretical perspectives, and having methodological implications in terms of context and temporality.

The final two chapters are then devoted to empirical illustrations of organizational discourse. Chapter 6 presents a conceptualization of organizational discourse as situated symbolic action, drawing from the fields of speech act theory, rhetoric, ethnography of communication and social constructionism. This conceptualization is then illustrated through analysis of an episode of negotiated order, a meeting of senior managers of a major IT organization where a new business model for its advanced consulting division is being debated. Three complementary and additive levels of analysis are employed: discourse as action, examining what participants said and what they may have intended to achieve through their communicative actions; discourse as situated action, examining the added value that arises from a knowledge of different levels of context; and discourse as symbolic action, involving considerations of how discourse frames, constructs, and represents issues in particular ways. This perspective helps to respond to some of the key challenges facing the organizational discourse field in terms of developing more structured and clearly specified conceptualizations of discourse that are appropriate to the organizational level of analysis; achieving a more holistic and discourse-sensitive understanding of empirical contexts by organizational researchers; and lastly illustrating that organizational discourse analysis is not simply an intellectual luxury but can have pragmatic, relevant implications.

Chapter 7 illustrates an empirical employment of a structurational view of discourse, in combination with an analytical approach based on rhetoric and hermeneutics. The study analyzes the discourses operating in the UK operations of a global consulting firm in the context of its organizational change program. This research clarifies the nature of "modes of discourse" in specific organizational settings; investigates how modes of discourse in such settings can be interrelated; and finally explores the constructive potential of modes of discourse. This research suggests that modes of discourse can be usefully conceptualized as rhetorical enthymemes constituted of relatively stable, normative structures and flexible, action-oriented structures; that modes of discourse can interrelate through their deeper structural features, and can have mutually co-optive or antagonistic relationships; and that the constructive potential of discourse is based primarily on its deeper structures, and on the consonance of surface communicative actions with these structures.

A lot of the research reported in this book has benefited from interactions and collaborations with several research associates over the years, some still ongoing: Michael Barrett, Andrew Chan, John Hendry, Claus Jacobs, and Robert Marshak; I thank all of them for making the ideas pool richer than it would have been. I would also like to thank Chris Harrison and his colleagues at Cambridge University Press for their professionalism in dealing with all publication aspects of this work, and for putting up with my more flexible and idiosyncratic view of deadlines. Finally, my gratitude goes to my wife for providing an environment where I could spend time with my thoughts without worrying about the need to be sociable.

Loizos Heracleous
Oxford, 4 July 2006

1 | Images of Discourse: Interpretive, Functional, Critical, and Structurational[1]

T HE linguistic turn of the later twentieth century has led to a widespread and growing interest in discourse, both in organization studies and in the social sciences more generally. Since the late 1970s, organization scholars have began to move beyond a conception of language as a functional, instrumental conduit of information, and drew attention to its symbolic and metaphorical aspects as constructive of social and organizational reality (Dandridge, Mitroff and Joyce, 1980: Manning, 1979), constitutive of theory (Morgan, 1980, 1983), and enabling of shared meanings, co-ordinated action, and even organization itself (Daft and Wiginton, 1979; Louis, 1983; Pondy and Mitroff, 1979; Smircich, 1983). Subsequent scholars have adopted a wide range of approaches to the analysis of organizational discourses and have conceptualized discourse itself, and its relevance to organizational interpretations, actions and subjectivity, in a variety of ways (Grant, Keenoy and Oswick, 1998; Heracleous and Hendry, 2000; Mumby and Stohl, 1991; Phillips and Hardy, 2002).

Discourse analysis, in the broad sense of utilizing textual data in order to gain insights to particular phenomena, has had a rich and varied heritage in the social sciences, spanning the fields of sociology, anthropology, psychology, political science and history (OConnor, 1995), and this same richness and diversity is evident in the organizational sciences. Approaches include hermeneutics (Kets de Vries and Miller, 1987; Phillips and Brown, 1993; Thachankary, 1992), ethnomethodology (Atkinson, 1988), rhetorical analysis (Alvesson, 1993; Keenoy, 1990; Watson, 1995), deconstruction (Kilduff, 1993; Noorderhaven, 1995), metaphorical analysis (Jacobs

---

[1] This chapter draws from Heracleous and Hendry (2000), Heracleous and Barrett (2001), and Heracleous (2004).

1

and Heracleous, 2006; Lakoff and Johnson, 1980; Ortony, 1979), critical discourse analysis (van Dijk, 1993; Garnsey and Rees, 1996; du Gay and Salaman, 1992; Knights and Morgan, 1991, 1995), narrative analysis (Barry and Elmes, 1997; Manning and Cullum-Swan, 1994), and semiotic analysis (Barley, 1983; Fiol, 1989).

Both discourse and related terms, such as language, text or narrative, have been conceptualized and categorized in diverse ways in organization theory (van Dijk, 1997; Grant, Keenoy and Oswick, 1998; Grant et al., 2004). In my work, I have employed the term "discourse" to mean collections of texts, whether oral or written, located within social and organizational contexts that are patterned by certain structural, inter textual features and have both functional and constructive effects on their contexts. In this sense, language can be seen as the raw material of discourse, and individual texts are both manifestations, and constitutive, of broader discourses (Heracleous, 2004 and Hendry, 2000).

In spite of the variety of conceptualizations and operationalizations, three dominant approaches to the study of organizational discourse can be discerned interpretive, functional, and critical (Heracleous, 2006; Heracleous and Barrett, 2001; Heracleous and Hendry, 2000). These approaches are not mutually exclusive, but they can be seen as analytically distinct. A key distinction has been made between interpretive and critical approaches to discourse (Mumby and Clair, 1997) that parallels the related distinction of research focusing on meaning construction processes or on issues of power (Oswick, Keenoy and Grant, 1997), as well as the distinction between monological accounts presenting the perspective of a dominant group and dialogical accounts presenting a multiplicity of conflicting perspectives and multiple realities (Boje, 1991; Grant, Keenoy and Oswick, 1998; Keenoy, Oswick and Grant, 1997).

Interpretive approaches conceptualize discourse as communicative action that is constructive of social and organizational realities. Functional approaches view discourse as a tool at actors' disposal, to be employed for facilitating managerially relevant processes and outcomes such as effective leadership, employee motivation, and organizational change. Critical approaches conceptualize discourse as power knowledge relationships, constitutive of subjects' identities and of organizational and societal structures of domination. The emerging structurational approach finally views discourse as a duality of communicative actions and deep structures, interrelated through the modality of interpretive schemes (Heracleous, 2006; Heracleous and Barrett, 2001; Heracleous and Hendry, 2000).

This conceptual diversity is symptomatic of a similar diversity of approaches to discourse in the social sciences more generally, and reflects long standing divisions between agent-centered and structuralist-oriented theories in sociology (Burrell and Morgan, 1979, Thompson, 1989). The interpretive and functional approaches to organizational discourse tend to privilege the action level, giving primacy to human agency, the hermeneutic nature of discourse at the individual and organizational levels, and how agents can employ discourse to shape their own or others' understandings of situations. The critical approach, on the other hand, tends to privilege the structural level, giving primacy to how human agency, identity and subjectivity are constituted, shaped, and may even be lost in the webs of discursive structures and the patterns of social domination that these structures surreptitiously help to legitimize and sustain. The structurational approach, in line with Giddens's efforts to transcend the structure/agency dualism, aims to address both communicative actions and discursive deep structures as inherently interlinked and mutually constituted levels via actors' interpretive schemes, in which communicative actions are both a manifestation and instantiation of deep structures.

Organizational Texts and Contexts

As noted earlier, organizational discourses can be seen as collections of texts, both spoken and written. The term "text" has been interpreted in a variety of ways, with texts viewed broadly as "all types of data that contain messages and themes that can be systematized" (Kets de Vries and Miller 1987: 235; Phillips and Brown, 1993), for example structured patterns of actions and interpretations, or even organizations (Putnam, Phillips and Chapman, 1996: 391; Thachankary, 1992); as well as in a more literal way as primarily language-based artifacts (Gephart, 1993; Giddens, 1979).

An understanding of context is crucial to the interpretive validity and potential insight afforded by discourse analyses. According to Cicourel, "the study of discourse and the larger context of social interaction requires explicit reference to a broader organizational setting and aspects of cultural beliefs often ignored by students of discourse" (1981: 102). Unfortunately, some approaches that began with interpretive or hermeneutic inspirations like ethnomethodology, stressing features of language such as indexicality (the notion that language use and interpretation depends on contextual features) and the temporality of social activity (where social action is understood and analyzed with regard to its temporal location), have gradually proceeded to restrict themselves to behaviorist straitjackets which can hinder them from grasping the richness of social life, as in the form most ethnomethodological conversation analysis has taken (Atkinson, 1988).

Fairclough has observed that in practice "analysis of text is perceived as frequently proceeding with scant attention to context discourse analysis needs a developed sense of and systematic approach to *both* context *and* text" (1992: 212–213). Fortunately, several useful approaches for integrating context in organizational discourse analysis have been developed. These include critical discourse analysis (van Dijk, 1993; Fairclough and Wodak, 1997) social semiotics (Hodge and Kress, 1988; Kress, Leite-Garcia and van Leeuwen, 1997); rhetorical analysis (Aristotle, 1991; Gill and Whedbee, 1997); or ethnography of communication (Hymes 1964, 1972; Gumperz and Levinson, 1991).

From a sociological perspective, Giddens has suggested that the influence of structuralist and post-structuralist thought has encouraged the neglect of context and temporality in discourse analysis, indicating that although structuralism and post-structuralism have brought to the fore of social theory important issues such as the importance of temporality as reversible time, the properties of signification systems as existing outside time-space, and the relevance of decentring the subject, they are fraught with theoretical difficulties that make them unsuitable theoretical traditions through which the themes they have highlighted can be pursued (Giddens, 1979; 1987).

Saussures (1983) basic distinction between langue and parole, for example, and the emphasis on langue, is deemed as inadequate because it isolates language from its social environments of use and therefore does not promote the need for a theory of the competent speaker or language-user (Giddens, 1979). As a result, a conception of human subjects as agents has not been reached in structuralism, and the theoretically decentered elements (such as the author) are not satisfactorily recombined in the analysis (Giddens, 1987).

Furthermore, because of the stress on form rather than substance, and because of the thesis of the arbitrary character of the sign (Saussure, 1983), structuralism and poststructuralism have promoted a "retreat into the code," where the aim was "to determine the forces operating permanently and universally in all languages, and to formulate general laws which account for all particular linguistic phenomena historically attested" (Saussure, 1983: 6). This "retreat into the code" means that structuralism and post-structuralism have been unable to provide satisfactory accounts of reference, or of meaning. Meaning, for example, is said to derive from the intra- or inter textual play of differences of the signifiers, ignoring the relationship of such signifiers with their contexts of use (Giddens, 1987). The focus on the signifier/signified distinction as arbitrary has led to an elision between the "signified" and the "object signified," the reality to which the sign is related (Giddens, 1979).

Further, Saussures theoretical distinction between synchrony and diachrony has been utilized by structuralism as a methodological division, which is deemed unjustifiable because one can often gain a deeper understanding of linguistic and social systems in longitudinal rather than cross-sectional study (Lewin, 1952). The general "repression of time" in social theory has been attributed to the maintenance of this distinction between synchrony and diachrony, or statics and dynamics (Giddens, 1979).

While structuralism isolates texts from their contexts, a tradition such as hermeneutics stress their essential contextuality and the role of context in valid textual interpretations (Giddens, 1979). Ricoeur has defined hermeneutics as "the theory of the operations of understanding in relation to the interpretation of texts," and posed as a key idea the transformation of spoken discourse in written text (1991: 53). Spoken discourse is seen as an event in that (1) it is realized temporally and in the present; (2) the "instance of discourse" is self-referential because it refers back to its speaker; (3) discourse is always about something: it refers to a world that it attempts to describe, express or represent; and (4) discourse is in practice addressed to an other (Ricoeur, 1991: 77–78).

Ricoeur argues, however, that as soon as discourse is "fixed" in writing as text, several hermeneutic issues emerge. First, whereas discourse is realized temporally as a speech event, the written text fixes, in decreasing order of susceptibility to such fixing, the locutionary, illocutionary and perlocutionary acts of spoken discourse and divorces them from their temporal and social contexts. Second, whereas spoken discourse is self-referential in that it refers back to its speaker, the intended meanings of the author and the semantic meanings of the text do not necessarily coincide when spoken discourse is fixed as a text, because the text is open to a potentially unlimited series of interpretations. Third, whereas spoken discourse displays ostensive references deriving from the common situation and context within which the interlocutors find themselves, texts, divorced from such conditions, display non ostensive references, ideally projecting new possibilities of being-in-the-world – a concept that is for Ricoeur the ultimate referent of all texts. Finally, whereas spoken discourse is addressed at a specific interlocutor, texts are in principle available to anybody who can read (Ricoeur, 1991: 146–150).

On the basis of Ricoeur's distinction between spoken discourse and written text, I would suggest that organizational texts (not only oral communicative actions but also those fixed in writing) can be seen as implicated in particular conditions and imperatives which necessitate that they are understood and analyzed as being ontologically closer to spoken discourse than written text. This proposal can be clarified through a comparison of Roland Barthes' (1972, 1977, 1994) early structuralist and later post-structuralist conceptions of text, with the particular conditions that *organizational* texts tend to be implicated in.

Some Features of Organizational Texts

Organizational texts are often bound up with and shaped by, imperatives such as rules of communicative appropriateness in particular organizations, and overarching purposes as espoused by dominant coalitions. Further, due to the need for co ordination and collective action, organizational texts most often aim to display unambiguous references that suppress the plurality of meanings that, according to Barthes' (1977: 155–164) suggestions, should characterize texts. The organizational imperative of effective cross-functional coordination fosters demands for such organizational texts to have a relatively unambiguous, representational (or informational) aspect, and to suppress the plurality of possible meanings.

The possibility of varying interpretations of organizational texts (or, in Barthian terms, a plurality of meanings) of course cannot be fully suppressed. But the imperatives of competitiveness and effective organizational processes tend to limit the signified. Time-starved, goal-oriented readers of organizational texts are usually not disposed in this context to write the text anew or metaphorically participate in textual production through active reading. The instance of the Barthian text is the signifier, but that of organizational texts is the signified. In this sense, organizational texts cannot practice "the infinite deferment of the signified" (Barthes, 1977: 158). They are thus potentially reducible, as opposed to Barthian text, which is not only plural but also irreducible (1977: 159).

The content of organizational texts, moreover, tends to be of a different, more intentional and indexical nature from that of other types of texts. Barthes (1994) does not make explicit to what types of narrative his structural analysis might apply, but the fleeting references to "the story," the previous research on which he draws (Propp, Bremond, Todorov, Greimas, Levi-Strauss), many of the examples he uses (e.g. from James Bond movies), and the important part played by the actional level in his mode of analysis make it clear that the structural analysis of narrative, as developed by him, would be more suited to stories (at the social system level), novels, or myths. Organizational texts may not exhibit similar discourse-level structures to those discovered for stories, myths, or novels, and thus a homology of textual ontology and the analytical process between these texts cannot be assumed.

From the perspective of Barthian structuralist analysis, textual content would be of interest merely as a manifestation of deeper structures due to the assumed supremacy of form over substance (an idea originating from Saussure, 1983). In interpretive-oriented studies of the constructive role of discourse in organizations, this structural-level perspective needs to be complemented with consideration of textual content in its own right, in the light of the particular context, since the meaning of texts does not reside solely in intra- or inter textual relations but also in the dynamic interaction of these domains with the social context within which agents act (Giddens, 1987: 91).

With regard to textual functions, Barthes (1994) does not make clear in his structural analyses what functions stories or novels might have in their wider social context. "Functions" in Barthes structuralism relate solely to signifying units within the text, and do not refer to the interrelation of text with its social context. Barthes draws an analogy between narrative and linguistics, viewing narrative as a "great sentence" (1994: 99–100), and between narrative analysis and linguistic analysis holding that "just as linguistics halts at the sentence, the analysis of narrative halts at discourse" (1994: 127). In *Mythologies* (1972) his narrative analyses revealed critical concerns, relating to the unmasking of ideological processes working in the interests of the bourgeoisie, while in his "post-structuralist" period the consumption of the text was bound to "a pleasure without separation" (1977: 164).

Organizational texts on the other hand, as argued earlier, in addition to their constructive potential, tend to be imbued by a functional, representational nature that suppresses an infinite plurality of meanings due to the imperatives of systemic co ordination, collective action, and organizational competitiveness. Organizational texts have particular functions in their social and organizational contexts; they are normally not concerned with the critical aims of unmasking social domination, and any pleasure they bring to the reader is incidental. The latitude of interpretation of organizational texts varies according to the type of text, but all texts have an underlyings purposive construction by agents who have specific intentions in producing them for particular audiences, and intentionally wish to limit the potential plurality of textual meanings (except in special cases in which, for example, metaphorical discourse can aid organizational change processes because of its wide latitude of interpretation).

With regard to textual authorship, the structuralist tendency to "equate the production of texts with their inner 'productivity'," the decentering of the author, ultimately derives from the preoccupation with signifiers rather than signifieds (or the emphasis on form over substance), and often leads to an impression that texts wrote themselves (Giddens, 1987: 94–95). Organizational texts, in line with Barthes concept of "work," however, are "caught up in a process of filiation" (1977: 160). Their authors are not "paper authors" (1977: 161) but flesh- and -blood individuals whom the audience knows and has opinions and thoughts about. Individuals referred to in organizational texts are not "paper beings" (1994: 123) but people bound up with the textual context. Various characteristics of the author are highly relevant for the interpretation and persuasive potency of a text (Burgoon, Hunsaker and Dawson, 1994; Petty and Cacioppo, 1986). This would not be the case for the kinds of stories, myths or novels that Barthian structuralist analysis was concerned with, however, where their interpretation (at least by readers if not by literary critics) does not depend on who the author is, and there is usually no immediate, context-dependent persuasive intention attached to them.

Temporality, in addition, is seen in structuralist approaches such as Barthes' (1994: 112) as "only a structural class of narrative," divorced from the texts social context. In analyzing organizational discourse to gain ideographic insights to social settings, however, temporality must ideally be considered in terms of real-time, recursive, and historical events. Organizational texts, especially intra-organizational ones, while "fixed" in writing (and thus according to Ricoeur available to anyone who can read and potentially subject to an unlimited series of interpretations), they are read, if at all, a relatively short amount of time after they are written and are usually read only once. Their functional, intentional relevance tends to diminish the longer they remain unread, and after a certain period of time the only individuals likely to have an interest in them are not organizational actors themselves but organizational researchers and historians. Such researchers, ironically, may themselves in fact be trying to utilize texts as a source of information in order to reconstitute retrospectively actual events or situations that they would have ideally preferred access to in real time but could not, because of various constraints.

The above discussion suggests that, because of the particular contextual conditions in which organizational texts are implicated, irrespective of whether they are spoken or written, they should be understood and analyzed more as spoken discourse or language-events (temporal, self-referential, representational, occurring among identifiable agents), rather than texts in a Ricoeurian or Barthian sense. This perspective, of course, does not discount or discourage a focus on such aspects as inter textual patterns and their constructive effects, or effects on agents' subjectivity. What the above discussion suggests, however, is that attention to the various dimensions of organizational context is indispensable for higher validity in textual interpretations.

Analyzing Organizational Discourse

Discourse analysis approaches, at least as employed in organization theory, sociology and literary studies, are not methods in the positivist sense of precisely defined sequential steps in search of universally applicable laws, but rather approaches emphasizing hermeneutic, iterative journeys of discovery by (re)reading individual texts in the context of the whole and their social context and then (re)considering the whole as manifested in individual texts. Several authors have drawn attention to the unstructured, interpretive nature of discourse analysis (Fairclough, 1992; Potter and Wetherell, 1987). Narrative analysis, for example, is said to be "rather loosely formulated, almost intuitive, using terms defined by the analyst" (Manning and Cullum-Swan, 1994: 465) discourse analysis is "neither systematic nor detailed" (Fairclough, 1992: 196) and deconstruction is "not reducible to a set of techniques, . . . [and] cannot be summarized as a mechanical series of operations to be applied to any piece of language" (Kilduff, 1993: 16). Barthes has on repeated occasions consciously refused to refer to his analyses as exemplifying a "method" which he saw as having positivistic connotations (Barthes, 1994: 223, 248, 263). Contrary to his early structuralist statements that narrative was to be studied in a deductive fashion, he later denounced an inductive deductive science of texts as illusory (Barthes, 1977: 159–160).

As discussed in more detail in chapter 2, this situation does not necessarily imply insufficient or inadequate methodological rigor, or degeneration to totally subjective opinions as a basis of textual interpretation. Rigor in organizational discourse analysis however has a different meaning than in positivism; replicability, especially in ethnograpically oriented studies is not possible, and the search is for broad principles relating to the nature and functioning of social systems rather than mechanistic "universal laws" that would foster the same outcome if the technologies they imply are implemented in different settings. Discourse analysis aiming to identify such entities as genre repertoires (Orlikowski and Yates, 1994; Yates and Orlikowski, 1992), generative metaphors (Schön, 1979) or deep structures (Heracleous, 2006; Heracleous and Barrett, 2001) as opposed to more narrowly defined discursive aspects (e.g. turntaking in conversational analysis) is necessarily a loosely structured, interpretive exercise in which the researchers own competencies and judgment are critical (Fairclough, 1992; Potter and Wetherell, 1987). Similarly to ethnography, the pivotal role of the researcher has emphasized reflexivity (Heracleous, 2001) in organizational discourse research; the ability to consciously reflect on and codify how one's personal interests, biases and evaluations may have influenced the research process, the findings, and the researchers' own narrative.

The Interpretive Approach: Discourse as Constructive of Social Reality[2]

In the interpretive approach language as the basic building block of texts and discourses has been viewed not merely as an instrumental, intentional means of information exchange (a "representational" or "correspondence" view of language as evident in the early Wittgenstein) but primarily as constructive of social and organizational reality, through its framing effects on actors' thoughts, interpretations and actions (as evident in the late Wittgenstein). Both organization theory (Pondy and Mitroff, 1979; Weick, 1977) and the sociology of knowledge (Berger and Luckmann, 1966; Moscovici, 1981, Ortony, 1979) have long recognized the constructive role of language in social life. After Pondy and Mitroff's (1979) call for the development of more complex understandings of organizations, researchers began to focus on interpretive frameworks emphasizing the social construction of meaning and the central role of language as a symbolic medium in constructing social reality (Donnellon, Gray and Bougon, 1986; Gray, Bougon and Donnellon, 1985; Pondy, 1983).

Even though a variety of theoretical traditions, with subtle differences, find a home under the umbrella of interpretivism, what they have in common is a commitment to an in-depth understanding of the actors' frame of reference, and a view of language as constructive rather than merely representational. Studies from an interpretive perspective have illustrated such issues as how language use as a

---

[2] Chapter 2 discusses a variety of prominent interpretive approaches to organizational discourse, as well as their analytical foci and implications.

symbolic process is central to the development and sustenance of shared meanings (Smircich, 1983) and a common identity for organizational members (Evered, 1983). The guiding motivation of the approach is to gain an in-depth understanding of the role of language in meaning construction processes, and to this end researchers have explored such elements or configurations of discourse as stories (Boje, 1991; Boyce, 1995; Hansen and Kahnweiler, 1993; Martin and Powers, 1983), humor (Hatch, 1997; Rodrigues and Collinson, 1995), and metaphor (Chilton and Ilyin, 1993; Crider and Cirillo, 1991, Tsoukas, 1991, 1993). To achieve these understandings, researchers in this tradition typically aim to study broader discourses (as collections of texts often exhibiting a variety of positions and voices) rather than just single texts (or sentences, a traditional concern of linguistics), with a concern of linking these discourses to their effects on agents' interpretations and actions within particular organizational and social settings.

The Functional Approach: Discourse as a Facilitator of Managerially Relevant Outcomes[3]

Building on insights of the interpretive approach to discourse, as well as on insights from a variety of other disciplines such as organization development and change management, researchers in the functional tradition have focused on how language can be applied to the facilitation of managerially relevant processes and outcomes such as the exercise of leadership (Pondy, 1978; Schein, 1992; Westley and Mintzberg, 1989), the emergence of effective and creative strategies (Heracleous and Jacobs, 2005; Liedtka and Rosenblum, 1996) and the management of organizational change (Barrett, Thomas and Hocevar, 1995; Ford and Ford, 1995; Westley and Vredenburg, 1996).

Ford and Ford (1995) for example, arguing that intentional change is based in and driven by particular types of linguistic communication, drew on speech act theory (Austin, 1961) to analyze the change process and its breakdown as a dynamic of conversations. Westley and Vredenburg (1996), drawing on theories of cultural change,

---

[3] Chapter 3 discusses functional approaches in more detail, focusing on the role of metaphor in facilitating organizational change and development processes.

focused on the need for a constant realignment of interpretation and action within intentionally managed change processes and explored the role of metaphor in mediating between these. Barrett, Thomas and Hocevar (1995), conceptualizing change processes in terms of the social construction of meaning, stressed in particular the importance of dialogue as providing a medium for the evolution of language and consequent reconstruction of meaning within an organization.

Various studies of the role of metaphor in facilitating organizational change (Cleary and Packard, 1992; Marshak, 1993; Pondy, 1983; Sackmann, 1989) have highlighted the creative potential of metaphorical statements in enabling organizational actors to re-perceive reality in novel ways that can bridge the old state with the new. Finally, storytelling advocates suggest that various types of stories can be employed by managers to achieve particular outcomes (Denning, 2004), for example engaging the emotional commitment of internal and external stakeholders (Kaufman, 2003; McKee, 2003) or developing high-potential managers into leaders (Ready, 2002).

The more sophisticated variants of these studies draw on aspects of the interpretive approach, but the emphasis is different. Whereas interpretive studies focus on the emergent nature and effects of discourse on agents and the social context, and on the mutual constitution of discourses and contexts, functional research focuses on how managers, consultants, facilitators, and other actors can employ language to achieve certain outcomes. The functional view thus emphasizes the instrumental use of language-based communication to achieve managerially relevant outcomes, with discourse seen not so much as a medium for the social construction of meaning as a communicative tool at the actors' disposal[4].

---

[4] We do not use the term "functional" in exactly the same manner as employed in sociology, where functionalism is a paradigm drawing on organic analogies, aiming to explain the existence of social institutions and their features as ways of fulfilling biological and social needs of individuals. However there is a broad similarity in the sense that discourse in the functional stream is seen as a tool for achieving desired ends, i.e. having specific functions.

The Critical Approach: Discourse as Constitutive of Structures of Domination[5]

Critical discourse analysis shares with the approaches the interpretive concern exploring the social construction of reality, and the role of discourse in this process. It emphasizes, however, that the social construction of reality is not neutral or unbiased. Symbolic universes function not only as communicational and sensemaking mechanisms but also as legitimating ones (Giddens, 1984), representing different and potentially conflicting views of reality. Confrontations of symbolic universes are thus in effect power confrontations, in which "he who has the bigger stick has the better chance of imposing his definitions of reality" (Berger and Luckmann, 1966: 127). Critical discourse analysis aims to demystify situations, perceptions, and social practices that may be viewed as "natural" or taken for granted, but that have in effect been discursively constructed over time by groups in power aiming to skew social reality and institutional arrangements to their own advantage (Barthes, 1972; Gramsci, 1971).

Critical discourse analysis consists of a variety of approaches drawing from strands of critical theory within Western Marxism (Fairclough and Wodak, 1997), as well as from other critical theorists such as Foucault, particularly his latter genealogical work (1980) focusing on the intimate links between discourse and power. Critical discourse analysis is ethically committed to unmasking the processes through which discourses promote social constructions that support and perpetuate the interests of dominant groups or classes (Fairclough and Wodak, 1997; Wodak, 1990). In this connection, discourses are not seen as neutral or unbiased, but as "sites of power" (Mumby and Stohl, 1991: 316) and as serving to entrench social practices (Fairclough and Wodak, 1997: 258) as well as organizational practices (Jacobs and Heracleous, 2001) that produce particular sorts of subjectivity and identity (du Gay and Salaman, 1992).

Discourses are thus seen as imbued with ideological hegemony, the process by which dominant classes and groups attempt to construct

---

[5] Chapter 4 offers an extended discussion of a Foucauldian critical approach, through a critical analysis of Foucault's conceptions of discourse and their implications for organizational discourse analysis.

and perpetuate belief systems that support their own interests, and make the *status quo* appear commonsensical and natural (Barthes, 1972; Gramsci, 1971). Critical discourse analysis assumes that social representations (or shared cognitions) are principally constituted through discourse, or more succinctly, that "managing the mind of others is essentially a function of text and talk" (van Dijk, 1993: 254).

Critical discourse analyses thus follow interpretive, context-sensitive, often historical methodologies to empirically analyze discourses, discover how ideologies permeate and manifest in these discourses, and highlight discourses' organizational and societal effects. In employing this approach, discourse analysts aim to bring about demystification and challenge of the *status quo* and thus, ideally, social change. The foci of analysis are often pressing social problems, such as racism, gender relations or ethnic tensions, not merely as a scholarly endeavor but as a committed form of social intervention.

Table 1.1 gives an outline of the three streams discussed, as well as of the structurational approach, as proposed by Heracleous and Hendry (2000), Heracleous and Barrett (2001), and Heracleous (2006).

The Structurational Approach: Discourse as a Duality of Communicative Actions and Deep Structures Interrelated Through Interpretive Schemes[6]

In tending to privilege the action level, interpretive and functional conceptions of discourse have constrained researchers from exploring the deeper discursive and social structures on which the very possibility of intentional communication depends, and through which that possibility is both enabled and constrained. The critical conceptualization of discourse as socially embedded power–knowledge relationships is much more sensitive to these aspects of social structure and context, but its decentering of the subject tends to downplay a view of the individual as an active agent, and affords little prospect of relating

---

[6] Chapter 5 develops the structurational approach to discourse in some detail. This section will therefore give just a brief outline.

Table 1.1. Streams of Organizational Discourse Research

Approach	Discourse seen as	Relation with the subject	Time frame and usual levels of application	Guiding motivation of approach
Functional	Language-based communication, used instrumentally by social and managerial actors to achieve their ends	Discourse is a communicative tool at actors' disposal. Subjects use discourse for their ends rather than being trapped in it	Shorter-term managerial time frame (months or a few years); application at the organizational level	To facilitate managerially relevant processes and outcomes such as organization change or effective leadership
Interpretive	Communicative action exhibiting structural properties, and constructive of social and organizational realities	Subjects' social realities are constructed through discourse as a symbolic medium in the context of social interaction	Medium-term organizational time frame (a few years or decades); application at the organizational, social group or societal levels	To gain an in-depth understanding of the actors' point of view, and of the role of language in meaning construction processes
Critical	Power–knowledge relations–linguistically communicated, historically located and embedded in social practices. Subjects	Subjects' identity and rationality constituted by effects of elite discourses and other "technologies of power".	Longer-term historical time frame (decades or centuries); application at the social group or societal levels	Aspiration for radical social change through critical understanding and demystification of relations of social domination

| | dominated by discursive structures and associated social practices | | | |
| **Structurational** | A duality of deep discursive structures and surface communicative actions, interrelated through modality of interpretive schemes | Actors are purposeful, knowledgeable agents, both enabled and constrained by discursive structures | Medium-term Organizational time frame (a few years or decades); application at the organizational, social group or societal levels | In addition to interpretive motivations as noted above, to bridge dualisms of structure and action in social analysis through an encompassing metatheoretical framework |

Source: Adapted from Heracleous and Barrett (2001).

the structural level to functional concerns or the understanding of everyday social practices from the agents' own first order perspective.

A structurational view of discourse based on the work of Giddens (1979, 1984, 1987, 1993), and especially his theory of structuration (1979, 1984), has the potential to address both the action and the structure levels and their dynamic interrelation. Giddens has written relatively little about discourse, which has not been developed as a central construct in his theory (Gadacz, 1987), but he has done more than anyone to integrate structure and agency within a single conceptual framework (Thompson, 1989).

Drawing on structuration theory, discourse is viewed as a duality constituted by two dynamically interrelated levels: the surface level of communicative action and the deeper level of discursive structures, recursively linked through the modality of actors interpretive schemes. This view of discourse, elaborated by Heracleous and Hendry (2000), Heracleous and Barrett (2001) and Heracleous (2006), goes beyond understandings of discourse that focus on either structure or action and tend to advance a monolithic view of the relationship between discourse and the subject, and is able to encompass the interrelated action–structure levels and offer a more nuanced view of the discourse–subject relationship.

At the level of *communicative action*, discourse is constituted of communicative statements that occur in the context of social interaction when an actors purpose, or one of an actors purposes, is linked to the achievement of passing on information to others (Giddens 1993:94; cf. Austin 1961). In addition to their symbolic nature, communicative actions have a functional, intentional dimension; in this sense discourses not only say things but also do things (Oswick, Keenoy and Grant, 1997). These broad types of aims or intentions, which Habermas (1984) has identified respectively with the teleological, normative and dramaturgical models of action, come together in his encompassing communicative model of action (Habermas 1984: 94–96). Thus, at this level, discourse can usefully be seen as *situated symbolic action*[7].

---

[7] Chapter 6 develops in more detail a view of discourse as situated symbolic action, and illustrates an application of this view in an organizational context.

Discursive deep structures on the other hand are relatively stable, mostly implicit, and continually recurring processes and patterns that underlay and guide surface, observable events and actions (Heracleous and Barrett, 2001). They are persistent features of discourse that transcend individual texts, speakers or authors, situational contexts and communicative actions, and pervade bodies of communicative action as a whole and in the long term (Heracleous and Hendry, 2000). Discursive deep structures can be interpreted and operationalized by researchers in different ways[8]. Discursive deep structures should be understood in a structurational and not a structuralist sense. In structuralist approaches such as Foucaults (1972) archaeology, subjects actions, identities, and even their reason are said to be determined by and caught in the webs of anterior, pervasive discursive structures (Heracleous, 2006; Jacobs and Heracleous, 2001). From a structurational viewpoint, however, the various types of structures are seen as the rules and resources that actors draw on and enact in their daily practices and which have no other ontological existence than their instantiation in action, and in agents' interpretive schemes. In line with Giddens's concept of the duality of structure therefore, social structures and the discursive structures they are linked to are not separate from and determinative of human actions, but are both the medium and the outcome of such actions (Giddens 1984).

Interpretive schemes from a structurational perspective are the modality through which discursive structures are instantiated, or manifested, at the level of communicative interaction, and through which communicative interaction can reproduce or challenge such structures. A schema is a cognitive structure that consists in part of the representation of some stimulus domain (Taylor and Crocker, 1981: 91). Schemata operate at various levels of detail or abstraction, and are both evaluative and descriptive, serving basic and vital functions in the interpretation of experience and indication of appropriate action (Taylor and Crocker, 1981). The interaction between communicative actions and interpretive schemes is central to the construction

---

[8] Chapter 7 presents a study that operationalized discursive structures as rhetorical strategies actualised through rhetorical enthymemes, or argumentations-in-action.

of social reality and to agents' actions based on their perceived reality (Gioia, 1986a,b). Shared cognitive schemes have a basic discursive aspect, as they are manifested, diffused and changed through 'text and talk' (van Dijk 1990:165).

Perhaps it would be useful at this point to briefly outline the distinctiveness and usefulness of the discourse lens for understanding organizations. Even though the book as a whole provides an answer to this question, we can say that firstly, the plethora of multi disciplinary antecedents to the field of organizational discourse (see e. g. Grant et al., 2004) provide a treasure trove of concepts, frameworks, and perspectives for organization studies. This becomes clear when one delves, for example, into the sociological literatures informing the interpretive approach, the managerial literatures informing the functional approach, or the literatures emerging from Western Marxism informing the critical approach. Secondly, through its focus on language in context, the discourse lens can provide rich access to the ideational, sense-making world of both individuals and organizations. Where as in-depth, qualitative research has necessarily been done with a high reliance on the medium of language (e.g. unstructured interviewing, field note-taking based on observations), what the discourse lens can add is theoretically informed, sophisticated frameworks for analyzing such textual data, with a conscious focus on the constructive role of language. Thirdly, a discursive approach, in common with other approaches such as ethnography, encourages researcher reflectivity. If researchers take seriously the idea that language as constructive, it becomes clear that research results do not simply report the data but also tell a story from the researcher's perspective and position; and the research process is itself selective, where the researcher's interests, biases, and views influence where attention is paid.

The field of organizational discourse is still young, but its appeal irresistible, its proponents productive, and its potential immense. Chapters 2–5 offer detailed discussions of the interpretive, functional, critical and structurational approaches to organizational discourse. Finally, chapters 6 and 7 offer illustrations of how specific approaches to discourse can be applied in empirical settings; in particular, a view discourse as situated symbolic action, and the structurational view of discourse.

References

Alvesson, M. 1993. Organizations as rhetoric: Knowledge-intensive firms and the struggle with ambiguity. *Journal of Management Studies*, **30**: 997–1015.

Aristotle. 1991. *On rhetoric*. Kennedy, G. A. (tansl.). Oxford: Oxford University Press

Atkinson, P. 1988. Ethnomethodology: A critical review. *Annual Review of Sociology*, **14**: 441–465.

Austin, J. L. 1961. *How to do things with words*. Oxford: Oxford University Press

Barley, S. R. 1983. Semiotics and the study of occupational and organizational cultures, *Administrative Science Quarterly*, **23**: 393–413.

Barrett, F. J., Thomas, G. F. and Hocevar, S. P. 1995. The central role of discourse in large-scale change: a social construction perspective. *Journal of Applied Behavioral Science*, **31**: 352–272.

Barry, D., and Elmes, M. 1997. Strategy retold: toward a narrative view of strategic discourse. *Academy of Management Review*, **22**: 429–452.

Barthes, R. 1972. *Mythologies*. A. Lavers, (trans.). London: Vintage.

1977. *Image, music, text*. London: Fontana.

1994. *The semiotic challenge*. Berkeley: University of California Press.

Berger, P. and Luckmann, T. 1966. *The social construction of reality*. London: Penguin.

Boje, D. M. 1991. The storytelling organization: A study of story performance in an office-supply firm. *Administrative Science Quarterly*, **36**: 106–126.

Bougon, M., Weick, K. and Binkhorst, D. 1977. Cognition in organizations: An analysis of the Utrecht jazz orchestra. *Administrative Science Quarterly*, **22**: 607–639.

Boyce, M. E. 1995. Collective centering and collective sense-making in the stories and storytelling of one organization. *Organization Studies*, **16** (1): 107–137.

Burgoon, M., Hunsaker, F. G. and Dawson, E. J. 1994. *Human communication*. (3rd ed.). London: Sage.

Burrell, G. and Morgan, G. 1979. *Sociological paradigms and organizational analysis*. Hants: Gower.

Chilton, P. and Ilyin, M. 1993. Metaphor in political discourse: The case of the "common European house". *Discourse and Society*, **4** (1): 7–31.

Cicourel, A. V. 1981. Three models of discourse analysis: The role of social structure. *Discourse Processes*, **3**: 101–131.

Cleary, C. and Packard, T. 1992. The use of metaphors in organizational assessment and change. *Group and Organization Management*, **17**: 229–241.

Crider, C. and Cirillo, L. 1991. Systems of interpretation and the function of metaphor. *Journal for the Theory of Social Behavior*, 21: 171–195.

Daft, R. L. and Wiginton, J. C. 1979. Language and organization. *Academy of Management Review*, 4: 179–191.

Dandridge, T. C., Mitroff, I. and Joyce, W. F. 1980. Organizational symbolism: A topic to expand organizational analysis. *Academy of Management Review*, 5: 77–82.

Denning, S. 2004. Telling tales. *Harvard Business Review*, May: 122–129.

van Dijk, T. A. 1988. Social cognition, social power and social discourse. *Text*, 8: 129–157.

   1990. Social cognition and discourse. In H. Giles and W. P. Robinson (eds.), *Handbook of language and social psychology*: 163–183. Chichester: Wiley.

   1993. Principles of critical discourse analysis. *Discourse and Society*, 4: 249–283.

   1997. The study of discourse. In T. A. van Dijk (ed.), *Discourse as structure and process*: 1–34. London: Sage.

Donnellon, A., Gray, B. and Bougon, M. G. 1986. Communication, meaning and organized action. *Administrative Science Quarterly*, 31: 43–55.

Evered, R. 1983. The language of organizations: the case of the navy. In L R. Pondy, P. J. Frost, G. Morgan, and T. C. Dandridge (eds.), *Organizational symbolism*: 109–121. Greenwich: JAI Press.

Fairclough, N. 1992. Discourse and text: linguistic and intertextual analysis within discourse analysis. *Discourse and Society*, 3: 193–217.

Fairclough, N. and Wodak, R. 1997. Critical discourse analysis. In T. A. van Dijk (ed.), *Discourse studies: A multidisciplinary introduction*, vol. 2: 258–284. Beverly Hills, CA: Sage.

Fiol, C. M. 1989. A semiotic analysis of corporate language: Organizational boundaries and joint venturing. *Administrative Science Quarterly*, 34: 277–303.

Ford, J. D. and Ford, L. W. 1995. The role of conversations in producing intentional change in organizations. *Academy of Management Review*, 20: 541–70.

Foucault, M. 1972. *The archaeology of knowledge*. London: Routledge.

   1980. *Power/Knowledge: selected interviews and other writings*, 1972–77. New York: Pantheon.

Gadacz, R. R. 1987. Agency, unlimited. *Canadian Journal of Political and Social Theory*, 11: 158–163.

Garnsey, E. and Rees, B. 1996. Discourse and enactment: Gender inequality in text and context. *Human Relations*, 49: 1041–1064.

du Gay, P. and Salaman, G. 1992. The cult(ure) of the customer. *Journal of Management Studies*, 29: 615–33.

du Gay, P., Salaman, G. and Rees, B. 1996. The conduct of management and the management of conduct: Contemporary managerial discourse and the constitution of the "competent" manager. *Journal of Management Studies*, 33: 263–282.

Gephart, R. P. 1993. The textual approach: Risk and blame in disaster sensemaking. *Academy of Management Journal*, 36: 1465–1514.

Giddens, A. 1979. *Central problems in social theory*. London: Macmillan.

1984. *The constitution of society*. Cambridge: Polity.

1987. *Social theory and modern sociology*. Cambridge: Polity.

1993. *New rules of sociological method* (2nd edn.). Stanford: Stanford University Press.

Gill, A. M. and Whedbee, K. 1997. Rhetoric. In T. A. van Dijk (ed.), *Discourse studies: A multidisciplinary introduction*, vol. 1: 157–183. Thousand Oaks, CA: Sage.

Gioia, D. A. 1986a. Symbols, scripts and sensemaking: Creating meaning in the organizational experience. In H. P. Sims, Jr. and D. A. Gioia (eds.). *The thinking organization*: 49–74. San Francisco: Josey-Bass.

1986b. The state of the art in organizational social cognition: A personal view. In H. P. Sims, Jr. and D. A. Gioia (eds.), *The thinking organization*: 336–356. San Francisco: Josey-Bass.

Gramsci, A. 1971. *Selections from the prison notebooks of Antonio Gramsci*. Q. Hoare and G. Nowell-Smith (eds.). London: Lawrence and Wishart.

Grant, D., Hardy, C., Oswick, C. and Putnam, L. 2004. *The Sage Handbook of Organizational Discourse*. London: Sage.

Grant, D., Keenoy, T. and Oswick, C. 1998. Organizational discourse: Of diversity, dichotomy and multi-disciplinarity. In D. Grant, T. Keenoy and C. Oswick, *Discourse and organization*: 1–13. London: Sage.

Gray, B., Bougon, M. G., and Donnellon, A. 1985. Organizations as constructions and destructions of meaning. *Journal of Management*, 11 (2): 77–92.

Gumperz, J. J. and Levinson, S. C. 1991. Rethinking linguistic relativity. *Current Anthropology*, 32: 613–623.

Hansen, C. D. and Kahnweiler, W. M. 1993. Storytelling: An instrument for understanding the dynamics of corporate relationships. *Human Relations*, 46: 1391–1409.

Hatch, M. J. 1997. Irony and the social construction of contradiction in the humor of a management team. *Organization Science*, 8: 275–288.

Habermas, J. 1984. *The theory of communicative action*, vol. 1. Boston: Beacon Press.

Heracleous, L. 2004. Interpretivist approaches to organizational discourse. In Grant, D., Phillips, N., Hardy, C., Putnam, L. and Oswick, C. *Handbook of Organizational Discourse*. Beverly Hills: Sage: 175–192.

2006. A tale of three discourses: The dominant, the strategic and the marginalized. *Journal of Management Studies*, 43: 1059–1087.

Heracleous, L. and Barrett, M. 2001. Organizational change as discourse: Communicative actions and deep structures in the context of IT Implementation. *Academy of Management Journal*, 44 (4): 755–778.

Heracleous, L. and Hendry, J. 2000. Discourse and the study of organization: Towards a structurational perspective. *Human Relations*, 53 (10): 1251–1286.

Heracleous, L. and Jacobs, C. 2005. The serious business of play. *MIT Sloan Management Review*, Fall: 19–20.

Hodge, R. and Kress, G. 1988. *Social semiotics*. Cambridge: Polity.

Hymes, D. 1964. Toward ethnographies of communication. *American Anthropologist*, 66 (6), part 2: 12–25.

1972. Models of the interaction of language and social life. In J. Gumperz and D. Hymes (eds.), *Directions in sociolinguistics: The ethnography of communication*: 35–71. New York: Holt, Rinchart and Winston.

Jacobs, C. and Heracleous, L. 2001. Seeing without being seen: Towards an Archaeology of Controlling Science. *International Studies of Management and Organization*, 31 (3): 113–135.

Jacobs, C. and Heracleous, L. 2006. Constructing shared understanding. The role of embodied metaphors in organization development. *Journal of Applied Behavioral Science*, 42: 207–226.

Kaufman, B. 2003. Stories that sell, stories that tell. *Journal of Business Strategy*, March-April: 11–15.

Keenoy, T. 1990. Human resource management: Rhetoric, reality and contradiction. *International Journal of Human Resource Management*, 1: 363–384.

Keenoy, T., Oswick, C. and Grant, D. 1997. Organizational discourses: Text and context. *Organization*, 4: 147–157.

Kets de Vries, M. F. R. and Miller, D. 1987. Interpreting organizational texts. *Journal of Management Studies*, 24: 233–247.

Kilduff, M. 1993. Deconstructing organizations. *Academy of Management Review*, 18: 13–27.

Knights, D. and Morgan, G. 1991. Corporate strategy, organizations and subjectivity: a critique. *Organization Studies*, 12: 251–273.

1995. Strategy under the microscope: Strategic management and IT in financial services. *Journal of Management Studies*, 32: 191–214.

Knights, D. and Willmott, H. 1989. Power and subjectivity at work: From degradation to subjugation in social relations. *Sociology*, 23: 535–558.

Kress, G., Leite-Garcia, R. and van Leeuwen, T. 1997. Discourse semiotics. In T. A. van Dijk (ed.), *Discourse studies: A multidisciplinary introduction*, vol. 1: 257–291. Beverly Hills, CA: Sage.

Lakoff, G. and Johnson, M. 1980. *Metaphors we live by*. Chicago: Chicago University Press.

Lewin, K. 1952. *Field theory in social science*. London: Tavistock.

Liedtka, J. M. and Rosenblum, J. W. 1996. Shaping conversations: Making strategy, managing change. *California Management Review*, 39 (1): 141–157.

Louis, M. R. 1983. Organizations as culture-bearing milieux. In L. R. Pondy, P. J. Frost, G. Morgan, and T. C. Dandridge (eds.), *Organizational symbolism*: 39–54. Greenwich: JAI Press.

Manning, P. K. 1979. Metaphors of the field: Varieties of organizational discourse. *Administrative Science Quarterly*, 24: 660–671.

Manning, P. K. and Cullum-Swan, B. 1994. Narrative, content, and semiotic analysis. In N. K. Denzin and Y. S. Lincoln (eds.). *Handbook of qualitative research*: 463–477. California: Sage.

Marshak, R. J. 1993. Managing the metaphors of change. *Organizational Dynamics*, 22: 44–56.

Martin, J. and Powers, M. E. 1983. Truth or corporate propaganda: The value of a good war story. In L. R. Pondy, P. J. Frost, G. Morgan, and T. C. Dandridge (eds.), *Organizational symbolism*: 93–107. Greenwich: JAI Press.

McKee, R. 2003. Storytelling that moves people. *Harvard Business Review*, June: 51–55.

Morgan, G. 1980. Paradigms, metaphor and puzzle solving in organization theory. *Administrative Science Quarterly*, 25: 660–671.

1983. More on metaphor: Why we cannot control tropes in administrative science. *Administrative Science Quarterly*, 28: 601–607.

Moscovici, S. 1981. On social representations. In J. P. Forgas (ed.), *Social congnition: Perspectives on everyday understanding*: 181–209. London: Academic Press.

Mumby, D. K. and Stohl, C. 1991. Power and discourse in organization studies: Absence and the dialectic of control. *Discourse and Society*, 2: 313–332.

Mumby, D. K. and Clair, R. P. 1997. Organizational Discourse. In T. A. van Dijk (ed.), *Discourse as social interaction*: 181–205. London: Sage.

Noorderhaven, N. 1995. The argumentational texture of transaction cost economics. *Organization Studies*, 16: 605–623.

O'Connor, E. S. 1995. Paradoxes of participation: Textual analysis and organizational change. *Organization Studies*, 16: 769–803.

Orlikowski, W. J. and Yates, J. 1994. Genre repertoire: The structuring of communicative practices in organizations. *Administrative Science Quarterly*, 39: 541–574.

Ortony, A. 1979. *Metaphor and thought.* Cambridge: Cambridge University Press.

Oswick, C., Keenoy, T. and Grant, D. 1997. Managerial discourses: Words speak louder than actions? *Journal of Applied Management Studies,* 6: 5–12.

Petty, R. E. and Cacioppo, J. T. 1986. The elaboration likelihood model of persuasion. In L. Berkowitz (ed.), *Advances in experimental social psychology,* vol. 19: 123–205. Orlando: Academic Press.

Phillips, N. and Brown, J. L. 1993. Analyzing communication in and around organizations: A critical hermeneutic approach. *Academy of Management Journal,* 36: 1547–1576.

Phillips, N. and Hardy, C. 2002. *Discourse analysis: Investigating processes of social construction.* London: Sage.

Pondy, L. R. 1978. Leadership as a language game. In M. W. McCall Jr. and M. M. Lombardo, M. M. (eds.), *Leadership: where else can we go?*: 87–101. Durham, NC: Duke University Press.

    1983. The role of metaphors and myths in organization and the facilitation of change. In L. R. Pondy, P. J. Frost, G. Morgan, and T. C. Dandridge (eds.), *Organizational symbolism:* 157–166. Greenwich: JAI Press.

Pondy, L. R. and Mitroff, I. I. 1979. Beyond open systems of organization. *Research in Organizational Behavior,* 1: 3–39.

Pondy, L. R., Frost, P. J., Morgan, G. and Dandridge, T. C. (eds.), 1983. *Organizational symbolism.* Greenwich: JAI Press.

Potter, J. and Wetherell, M. 1987. *Discourse and social psychology.* London: Sage.

Putnam, L. L., Phillips, N. and Chapman, P. 1996. Metaphors of communication and organization. In S. R. Clegg, Hardy, C., and Nord, W. R. *Handbook of organization studies:* 375–408. London: Sage.

Ready, D. A. 2002. How storytelling builds next-generation leaders. *MIT Sloan Management Review,* Summer: 63–69.

Ricoeur, P. 1991. *From text to action.* Illinois: Northwestern University Press.

Rodrigues, S. B. and Collinson, D. L. 1995. "Having fun?" Humor as resistance in Brazil. *Organization Studies,* 16: 739–768.

Sackmann, S. 1989. The role of metaphors in organization transformation. *Human Relations,* 42: 463–485.

de Saussure, F. 1983. *Course in general linguistics.* London: Duckworth.

Schein, E. 1992. *Organizational culture and leadership* (2nd ed.), San Francisco: Josey-Bass.

Schön, D. A. 1979. Generative metaphor. A perspective on problem-setting in social policy. In A. Ortony (ed.), *Metaphor and thought*: 254–283. Cambridge: Cambridge University Press.

Smircich, L., 1983. Organizations as shared meanings. In L. R. Pondy, P. J. Frost, G. Morgan, and T. C. Dandridge (eds.), *Organizational symbolism*: 55–65. Greenwich: JAI Press.

Taylor, S. E. and Crocker, J. 1981. Schematic bases of social information processing. In E. T. Higgins, C. P. Herman and M. P. Zanna (eds.), *Social cognition*: 89–134. Hillsdale, NJ: Erlbaum.

Thachankary, T. 1992. Organizations as 'texts': Hermeneutics as a model for understanding organizational change. *Research in Organization Change and Development*, 6: 197–233.

Thompson, J. B. 1989. The theory of structuration. In D. Held and J. B. Thompson (eds.), *Social theory of modern societies: Anthony Giddens and his critics*: 56–76. Cambridge: Cambridge University Press.

Tsoukas, H. 1991. The missing link: A transformational view of metaphors in organizational science. *Academy of Management Review*, 16: 566–585.

1993. Analogical reasoning and knowledge generation in organization theory. *Organization Studies*, 14: 323–346.

Watson, T. J. 1995. Rhetoric, discourse and argument in organizational sense making: A reflexive tale. *Organization Studies*, 16: 805–821.

Weick, K. 1977. Enactment processes in organizations. In B. M. Staw and G. R. Salancik (eds.), *New directions in organizational behavior*: 267–300. Chicago: St. Clair Press.

Westley, F. and Mintzberg, H. 1989. Visionary leadership and strategic management. *Strategic Management Journal*, 10: 17–32.

Westley, F. and Vredenburg, H. 1996. The perils of precision: Managing global tensions to achieve local goals. *Journal of Applied Behavioral Science*, 32: 143–159.

Wodak, R. 1990. Discourse analysis: Problems, findings, perspectives. *Text*, 10: 125–132.

Yates, J. and Orlikowski, W. J. 1992. Genres of organizational communication: A structurational approach to studying communication and media. *Academy of Management Review*, 17: 299–326.

2 | *Interpretive Approaches to Organizational Discourse*[1]

As discussed in chapter 1, interpretive approaches to organizational discourse view language as constructive of social and organizational reality, and seek to gain an in-depth understanding of this process and of the actors' own frame of reference. This chapter discusses the main tenets as well as analytical implications of five prominent interpretively oriented approaches to organizational discourse hermeneutics, rhetoric, metaphor, symbolic interactionism, and storytelling. Critical discourse analysis and the structurational approach, as further interpretively oriented approaches, are respectively discussed in detail in chapters 4 and 5.

Interpretivism and the Linguistic Turn

There is a broad range of theoretical approaches within the interpretive tradition[2] characterized by varying ontological and epistemological positions (Burrell and Morgan, 1979). However, a key unifying factor is their focus on achieving a *meaningful understanding* of the actors' frame of reference, which Weber (1922) referred to as *verstehen*. In Weber's view, this ability and desire to achieve an in-depth, first-order understanding is what distinguishes the social from the natural sciences. Meaningful understanding is often contrasted with *explanation* (Ricoeur, 1991), the search for causal, law-like deterministic regularities as in the positivist tradition—a tradition based on the methodology and ontology of the natural sciences. This simple contrast, however, does not do justice to the potential for meaningful understanding and explanation to operate in a complementary manner (notwithstanding the debate on paradigm incommensurability).

---

[1] This chapter is based on Heracleous (2004).
[2] For a more extended discussion of interpretive theory see Heracleous (2007a).

At the outset we must be clear that interpretivism should not be equated with subjectivism. This view is based upon the misconception that interpretivism lacks "objectivity" and instead affords primacy to the idiosyncratic, subjective meanings of single actors with no necessary relation to a more shared, inter subjective and verifiable reality. If interpretivism were to assume fully subjective properties, this would suggest a potential for unlimited interpretations of observations and textual data, with no means of verification or validation. Such a characterization is at the heart of Denzin's (1983) criticism that interpretivists reject generalization since each instance of observed social interaction is unique and social settings are complex and indeterminate.

Interpretive understanding does not however mean a degeneration to extreme subjectivism, unlimited interpretations and the inability to make any sort of generalizations, as several scholars emphasize. For Weber (1922), for example, the search for generalizations derived inductively from first-order data was compatible with, and indeed dependent on, the need for meaningful understanding of social action. His "ideal types" were aimed to inductively derive second-order frameworks based on regularities and patterns of empirically observed and theorized phenomena. Eco's (1990) "limits of interpretation" in addition, is an eloquent statement of the position that the potential for unlimited interpretations does not imply that all interpretations are equally likely or valid. Textual interpretations can be informed, limited or constrained by such features as the semantic meaning of the words used, the internal coherence of the text, its cultural context, and the interpreter's own frame of reference (Eco, 1990). Ricoeur (1991) and Giddens (1979, 1987) have also proposed criteria for validity of textual interpretations as a counter to extreme subjectivism and relativism, which will be discussed in the section on hermeneutics. Finally, Williams (2000) argues that interpretivists do in fact generalize, and that generalization in interpretive research is "inevitable, desirable and possible" He distinguishes between total generalizations (deterministic laws or axioms), statistical generalizations (where the probability of a situation or feature occurring can be calculated from its instances within a sample representative of a wider population); and *moderatum* generalizations (where aspects of a situation are exemplars of broader sets of features). Williams suggests that interpretive research does not aim to make total or statistical generalizations, but can (and should) make moderatum generalizations, within the limits of the inductive problem (that one cannot unproblematically generalize from a small number of cases to a large number of unknown cases), and the ontological problem of categorical equivalence (that generalizations within one category of experience of domain may not apply to other categories).

Interpretive discourse analysis is thus not content with merely identifying the subjective meanings attached to single texts; it considers multiple texts constituting bodies of discourse[3] and in doing so, it aims to identify discursive structures and patterns across these texts such as enthymemes, central themes or root metaphors, and to explore how these structures influence and shape agents' interpretations, actions, and social practices (e.g. Hardy and Phillips, 1999; Heracleous and Barrett, 2001).

The linguistic turn in the social sciences has drawn attention to the way language, as the building block of texts and discourses, shapes or constructs actors' first-order interpretations and actions and thus its role in shaping social practices and social reality. This orientation goes against earlier "correspondence" or "representational" views of language, as accurately representing (but not constructing) the world, and merely functioning as a conduit for the transfer of pre determined communicative messages. Wittgenstein's (1968) *Philosophical Investigations* was instrumental in advancing this constructive view of language, interestingly repudiating his earlier representational theory of language presented in his *Tractatus Logico-Philosophicus* (1955).

The next section addresses the theme of the discursive construction of social reality. Interpretive approaches assume that reality is socially constructed and that discourses have a central role in this process. Within this process, a useful way to view discourse is as situated symbolic action (originally proposed in the context of a

---

[3] As discussed in chapter 1, discourse and related terms, such as language, text or narrative, have been conceptualized and categorized in diverse ways in organization theory (e.g. Grant, Keenoy and Oswick, 1998; Mumby and Clair, 1997; Oswick, Keenoy and Grant, 1997). I take an interpretive approach, viewing discourses as collections of texts situated in social contexts, sharing certain structural features, and having both functional and constructive effects in their contexts. Texts are thus manifestations of discourses, and language, constituting texts, is the raw material of discourses.

structurational view of discourse by Heracleous and Hendry, 2000; and later theoretically expanded and illustrated empirically by Heracleous and Marshak, 2004). The generation and interpretation of discourses is context-dependent or *situated* in broader contexts; discourse is also *action* in the sense that its originators aim to achieve certain outcomes through communication; and finally discourse is *symbolic* not only in a textual, semantic sense, but in a more substantive sense indicating actors' assumptions, values and beliefs through their discursive choices (conscious or subconscious) that construct and evoke particular frames of reference for interpreting issues. The section on discourse and cognition adopts a cognitive perspective to suggest that discourse shapes social reality through its constructive effects on actors' cognitions.

The section on prominent interpretive approaches to organizational discourse discusses hermeneutics, rhetoric, metaphor, symbolic interactionism and storytelling. These theoretical fields all share a constructive ontology of social phenomena, ascribe a central role to discourse in this process, and offer complementary ways of understanding it. In other words these are not simply abstract theoretical approaches, but also offer more concrete analytical directions for conducting interpretively-oriented discourse analyses Table 2.1 summarizes the main conceptual orientations and potential analytical directions of these fields. Finally, the conclusion includes a brief outline of the main ideas in this chapter, and highlights the value of the interpretive discourse approaches discussed here.

The Discursive Construction of Social Reality

Social Constructionism and the Fluidity of Social Reality

How does discourse construct social reality? Underlying this question is the realization that social phenomena do not have the same solidity, stability, objectivity, and amenability to experimental manipulation and observation as natural phenomena. Rather, they are continuously (re)defined by actors themselves and can thus be better understood if we take into account the first-order meanings of the actors involved— a phenomenological view that has become a cornerstone of the interpretive paradigm (Burrell and Morgan, 1979). Social phenomena are characterized by high degrees of latitude in how they are portrayed

Table 2.1. *Conceptual Orientations and Analytical Directions*

Theoretical Approach	Main Conceptual Orientations	Potential Analytical Directions
Hermeneutics Giddens, 1979, 1987; Palmer, 1969; Ricoeur, 1991	• Focus on interpretation of texts and on nature of interpretation itself • Removal from subjectivist stance; some textual interpretations more valid than others, based on various aspects of textual context • Commitment to in-depth textual interpretation through researchers' longitudinal immersion in texts' social and organizational context	• Textual interpretations in context and over time, being sensitive to alternative interpretations • Search for central themes, thematic constructions and thematic interconnections • Triangulation of patterns in textual and ethnographic data, iteratively moving from part to whole and vice versa
Rhetoric Aristotle, 1991; Gill and Whedbee, 1997	• Rhetoric as the applied art of persuasion • Focus on study of rhetoric-in-use, and on its situational, temporal and social contexts • Rhetoric as both functional and constructive, employed in both grand oratory and everyday life	• Aim to identify agents' rhetorical strategies and their central themes • Identify how themes are constructed in positive/normative orders • Identification of enthymemes and their functions in context • What do the implicit, assumed premises of argumentations reveal?

Theoretical Approach	Main Conceptual Orientations	Potential Analytical Directions
Metaphor Black, 1979; Lakoff and Johnson, 1980; Lakoff, 1990	• Metaphors prevalent in social and organizational discourses • Epistemic and ontological correspondences between source and target domains are constructive of social reality and scientific inquiry • Metaphors encompass evaluative loadings that can influence social action	• Identification of root metaphors and aspects of metaphors highlighted by actors over time and in context • Mapping target and source domains and their implication complexes • Mapping inter metaphor systematicity and its implications • How do metaphors influence social reality construction and agents' actions?
Symbolic Interactionism Mead, 1912, 1913, 1922, 1925; Blumer, 1969	• Meanings arise, are modified, and become institutionalized, through symbolic interaction • Actors' interpretive schemes and even identity itself arise through (discursive) social interaction • Action arises out of subjective meanings that agents attach to situations	Focus on social interaction and on the meanings involved in interaction Study of discourse-in-use and its relation to subjective meanings How does discourse-in-use embody and construct subject identities, interpretive frames, and various organizational processes?

Table 2.1. (continued)

Theoretical Approach	Main Conceptual Orientations	Potential Analytical Directions
Storytelling Boje, 1991, 1995; Gabriel, 1991a,b, 1995, 2004	• Organizations seen as storytelling systems where story performance is a key aspect of shared sensemaking • Stories not seen as representations of facts or truth, but as symbolic reconstructions of events, as storytellers wish to represent them • Stories can provide access to the symbolic, ideational, sub conscious, un managed organizational domains	• Attention to multiple renditions and interpretations of stories, in context, ideally longitudinally • Focus on how agency subjectivity of story actors is constructed • What is accentuated or omitted in stories, and why? What does this say about the ideational world in which these stories circulate?

Source: Adapted from Heracleous (2004)

and interpreted by social actors. Consequently, actors can take control, shape or manipulate how they present issues, as well as employ selective perception (selective exposure, interpretation and retention) in order to protect and maintain their routinized or comfortable ways of perceiving issues. As Hardy and Phillips (2002: 2) have put it: "[T]he things that make up the social world—including our very identities— appear out of discourse . . . without discourse, there is no social reality, and without understanding discourse, we cannot understand social reality, our experiences, or ourselves".

Early social constructivisits provide some interesting insights into this process. Berger and Luckmann (1966) suggested that social reality is known to individuals in terms of symbolic universes constructed through social interaction. They viewed language as the "most important sign system of human society" (1966: 51), the primary means through which "objectivation" the manifestation of subjective meanings through actions, proceeds. Language makes subjective meanings "real" and at the same time typifies these meanings through creating "semantic fields or zones of meaning" (1966: 55) within which daily routines proceed. Language also creates mental frames that are "metacommunicative" (Bateson, 1972: 188), simultaneously highlighting certain meanings and excluding others, evoking particular typifications and associations through framing and connotation (Phillips and Brown, 1993: 1564). Discourses thus create, embody and sustain conditioned local rationalities (Gergen and Thatchenkery, 1996), as opposed to universal rationalities which would apply to closed systems such as mathematics or geometry. In other words, discourses are intimately and causally interrelated with the ways of thinking and acting of members of particular social systems or cultures (Sherzer, 1987).

Social reality, seen as shared mental schemes or, as Moscovici (1981) has termed it, social representations, is thus mainly based on *discursive* social interaction. Social representations are "largely acquired, used and changed, through text and talk" (van Dijk, 1990: 165). More generally, "all concepts, categories, complex representations, as well as the processes of their manipulation, are acquired and used mostly in social contexts of perception, interpretation and interaction" (van Dijk, 1988: 134).

Discourse As Situated Symbolic Action

As illustrated in detail in chapter 6, one useful way of understanding the nature of discourse and its effects on social reality is to view it as situated symbolic action. Speech act theory (Austin, 1962; Searle, 1975) offers a compelling statement of *discourse as action*. Austin (1962: 12) challenged the traditional assumption of the philosophy of language, that "to say something . . . is always and simply to *state* something" that is either true or false, and developed the influential thesis that "to *say* something is to *do* something". Austin went on to distinguish analytically between locutionary speech acts (the act of saying something) (1962: 94), illocutionary speech acts (what individuals intend to achieve in saying something) (1962: 98), and lastly perlocutionary speech acts (the actual effects of utterances on their audience) (1962: 101). In practice, of course, an utterance can perform all three simultaneously. The insights of speech act theory formed the theoretical foundation for discourse pragmatics, the study of language-in-use in the field of linguistics (Blum-Kulka, 1997).

Speech act theory, however, essentially remains at the micro level of single utterances without readily extending to the broader level of discourse as patterned collections of texts, so that it cannot analyze what van Dijk (1977) has termed "macro" speech acts, or Alvesson and Karreman (2000) "grand" or "mega" discourses. To achieve this, a more contextually sensitive and holistic approach would be needed, such as hermeneutic or rhetorical analysis. At the same time discourse is *symbolic* in that it conveys actors' values and beliefs, and constructs or evokes frames for interpreting the issues at hand, as social constructionism highlights (Berger and Luckmann, 1966). Discourse is also *situated* in that discursive interaction takes place within embedded contexts that condition intended and perceived meanings, and pose rules of discursive and behavioral appropriateness, as vividly shown by ethnographies of communication (Gumperz and Levinson, 1991; Hymes, 1964).

Discourses can operate at various levels: the trans national level (e.g. discourses of pro-globalization as well as anti globalization), the national level (e.g. discourses of race and gender equality, immigration policy, or national security); the industry level (e.g. discourses embodying the "industry recipes" to use Spender's 1989 term, the conventional wisdom of how business should be conducted in particular industries) or the organizational level, where researchers employ in-depth qualitative methodologies to identify specific discourses within particular social and organizational contexts.

Discourse and Cognition: Constructing First-Order Realities

Cognition has been posed as the "missing link" (van Dijk, 1993: 251) between discourse and action. The interaction of discourse and cognition can be elucidated through the key concept of schema (Condor and Antaki, 1997). Originally developed by Head and Bartlett, the concept of schema has since become a central construct of cognitive psychology (Rumelhart, 1984). A schema is "a cognitive structure that consists in part of the representation of some stimulus domain. The schema contains general knowledge about that domain, including a specification of the relationships among its attributes, as well as specific examples or instances of the stimulus domain" (Taylor and Crocker, 1981: 91). Interpretive schemes and discourse are mutually constituted in a process of continuous interaction, where "understanding is accomplished and communicated mainly by means of symbols (most notably in the form of metaphorical language) which are then retained in a structured or schematic form via scripts. The scripts subsequently serve as a basis for action that further facilitates the meaning construction and sensemaking processes" (Gioia, 1986: 50). In this perspective discourse is not merely informative but "transformative" (Phillips and Brown, 1993: 1548). Cognitive structures can be affirmed, elaborated or challenged when discourse is both interpreted and produced through them (Eoyang, 1983: 113).

Discourse influences not only the functioning of existing schemata but also the longer term delineation of their parameters. Linguistic labels learned through social interaction influence cognitive development, and during communication or even during actors reflections, linguistic labels evoke and utilize particular cognitive schemata. When schemata are developed, they are heuristically employed as interpretative tools in the long term and in a variety of situations (Bloom, 1981).

Interpretive schemes and agents' (discursive) actions are interrelated in a continuously dialectic fashion; action arises out of interpretive schemes, and new experiences or reflections influence interpretive schemes and thus subsequent action (Gioia, 1986). Discursive social interaction is thus central to the construction of social reality and to agents' actions based on this reality (Berger and Luckmann, 1966; Moscovici, 1981). This interactive view between cognition and discursive action emphasizes the relatively malleable nature of interpretive schemes, which can progressively be re defined through the addition or attrition of concepts, the transformation of perceived causal associations, or the altered salience of concepts (Eoyang, 1983).

Interpretive Approaches to Organizational Discourse

In this section five prominent interpretive approaches to the study of discourse are discussed: hermeneutics, rhetoric, metaphor, symbolic interactionism, and storytelling. These approaches are included here for four reasons. Firstly, they all assume a constructive ontology of social phenomena. Secondly, they ascribe a central role to discourse (or texts that constitute discourses, and on language as the raw material of texts) in the constructive process. Thirdly, they view, in their own particular ways, discourse as context-dependent or situated; as a form of action, where textual communications are intended to achieve things in their social context; and as symbolic, not only in a semantic sense but in a more substantive sense of indicating agents' assumptions, values and beliefs and invoking frames of reference for interpreting issues. Fourthly, all these fields do not remain at an abstract level but provide more specific directions for conducting discourse analyses, which can shed light on different angles of the discursive construction of social reality and its effects on agents' actions, social practices, organizations and societies.

Table 2.1 portrays the main conceptual orientations and potential analytical directions suggested by the five approaches discussed.

Hermeneutics[4]

The roots of the word hermeneutics lie in the Greek term *hermeneuein* to interpret. The earliest usage of the term referred to principles of

---

[4] For a more extensive discussion of hermeneutics see Heracleous (2007b).

biblical interpretation, but this was subsequently broadened to refer to general rules of philological exegesis. Hermeneutics involves both the task of textual interpretation and the reflexive concern with the nature of understanding and interpretation itself (Palmer, 1969). Hermeneutics has had a rich conceptual history. Key figures in its development include Schleiermacher, who sought to develop a general hermeneutics whose principles could serve as the foundation for all kinds of textual interpretation; Dilthey, who saw hermeneutics as the core discipline that could serve as the foundation for all humanistic studies; Heidegger, who developed a view of hermeneutics as the phenomenological explication of human existence, and finally Gadamer, who followed the lead of Heideggers work to develop philosophical hermeneutics the encounter with Being through language (see Ricoeur, 1991: 53–74 for an overview of these scholars' work).

Ricoeurs work returned the focus of hermeneutics to its initial concerns with textual interpretation. He has defined hermeneutics as the art of interpreting texts (Ricoeur, 1997: 66), posing as a fundamental concern that once discourse is inscribed as text it is severed from its author and its meaning as interpreted by new audiences may not necessarily coincide with the authors original intentions (Ricoeur, 1991: 105–124). Thus, one key aspect of the hermeneutical task, according to Ricoeur, becomes the interpretation of texts in contexts different from that of the author and the original audience, with the ideal intent of discovering new avenues to understanding.

Ricoeur notes that there may be several interpretations of texts depending on readers pre-understandings (interpretive schemes) and their particular interpretations of a text in relation to their own perceived situation. Acknowledging the possibility of various textual interpretations, however, does not necessitate a lapse to relativism, the resignation to the idea that there is no way to arrive at certain textual interpretations that are more valid than other potential interpretations. In contrast to post-structuralist approaches, for example, which the text is seen as having a plurality of indeterminate and irreducible meanings and which practices the infinite deferment of the signified (Barthes, 1977: 158), hermeneutic approaches assume that some meanings are more valid than others, given a texts particular social-historical context (Phillips and Brown, 1993). For Ricoeur (1991: 144–167), for example, a text displays a limited field of potential interpretations as opposed to being a repository of potentially unlimited meanings.

Giddens suggests that the interpretive validity of texts can be improved through ethnographic inquiry in the settings of production of the text, the intellectual resources the author has drawn on and the characteristics of the audience it is addressed to (Giddens, 1987: 106). He emphasizes the necessity of studying texts as "the concrete medium and outcome of a process of production, reflexively monitored by its author or reader" inquiry into this productive process comprises exploring the authors or speaker's intentions as well as the practical knowledge involved in writing or speaking with a certain style for a particular audience (1979: 43).

Key concepts in hermeneutics thus include the hermeneutic circle (the need to understand part in the context of whole and vice versa); understanding texts in their historical and cultural context; understanding the "fusion of horizons" between the interpreter and the text; the relevance of the intentions of the author; and the potential use of hermeneutics as emancipatory critique (Prasad, 2002). Researchers employing hermeneutical discourse analysis search for central themes in texts, for thematic unity (how central themes are interrelated in broader argumentations both within texts and inter-textually), and often relate these to patterns in ethnographic data over time. The analysis is treated as a process of discovery, going round the hermeneutic circle, from part to the whole and vice versa, each time further enriching the interpretations until a level of saturation is reached (Kets de Vries and Miller, 1987; Thachankary, 1992).

Rhetoric

Rhetorical discourse analysis is highly versatile (Van Graber, 1973), and has been extensively utilized in organizational analysis (e.g. Finstad, 1998; Hopkins and Reicher, 1997; Huff, 1983; Watson, 1995). Rhetoric can explore the situation, the audience, the rhetor, and textual features such as structure and temporality, enthymemes, metaphor and iconicity, not for their own sake, but in order to discover how rhetorical discourse can influence actors' understandings, values and beliefs by eloquently and persuasively espousing particular views of the world (Gill and Whedbee, 1997). Rhetorical principles have thus been fruitfully applied to wider, macro-level discourses to explore the discourses' constructive effects on actors' understanding of pressing social issues (e.g. Charland, 1987; Gronbeck, 1973). Analyses can also focus on how apparently plain speaking can actually be rhetorical (Gowler and Legge, 1983) through the use of certain ideas but not others, through the particular implications and connotations of the ideas used, through the construction of certain kinds of subjects, and through what the "frame" evoked by the ideas used highlights or excludes (Bateson, 1972; Harré, 1981).

Rhetorical principles and processes have often been perceived as morally questionable, a view initiated since Platos condemnation of rhetoric as inducing "belief without knowledge" and as "ignoble and bad" (Kinneavy, 1971: 221–22). One can see the Platonic view of rhetoric as a tool for making manipulative representations in work such as Keenoy (1990) or Alvesson (1993). Although views of rhetoric diverge in their evaluative standpoint, they do presuppose an understanding of rhetoric as a potent tool for constructing social reality. Rhetoric, for example, can be used to manage social representations (Moscovici, 1981) to initiate change (Bitzer, 1968), to sustain existing socio political arrangements in ways that advantage certain social groupings at the expense of others (Gowler and Legge, 1983), or to achieve "appropriate" self-presentation of actors to a community of peers (Harré, 1981).

Rhetorical strategies most often take the form of enthymemes, whose deeper features are not necessarily consciously evoked, located in actors practical consciousness rather than discursive consciousness (Giddens, 1984: 44–45; Heracleous, 2006). Rhetoric, in this perspective, is not necessarily some sort of grand oratory, but a mundane, everyday aspect of human competence (Watson, 1995). Enthymemes are rhetorical structures of argumentation. In contrast to syllogisms in logic, enthymemes are usually not fully expressed, one or more of their premises taken for granted or assumed by the audience (Eemeren et al., 1997). The premises in enthymemes are only generally or probably true in a particular social context; their truth or rationality is not universal, but is conditioned by and arises from the socio cultural features in that context (Gergen and Thatchenkery, 1996).

In terms of organizational discourse analysis, therefore, persistent patterns in argumentations that pervade and operate in diverse situational, organizational and temporal contexts can be seen as actors rhetorical strategies (Heracleous, 2006). Identification and analysis of enthymemes, and particularly their unstated and assumed premises, can enable researchers to uncover the taken for granted values and beliefs of actors in a particular social context (Gill and Whedbee, 1997; Heracleous and Barrett, 2001).

Metaphor

It has been recognized since Aristotle that metaphor is more than just a figure of speech. Seeing A in terms of B metaphor is not only the archetype of related tropes such as metonymy, synecdoche, simile and analogy but more importantly, it is constructive of both social reality (Lakoff and Johnson, 1980) and scientific inquiry (Heracleous, 2003; Morgan, 1980, 1983, 1986), inducing, in actors' minds, ontological and epistemic correspondences between otherwise distinct domains (Lakoff, 1990).

Literal views of metaphor see it as merely a statement of similarity or analogy that is potentially expendable, since what was stated metaphorically could also be stated literally (Black, 1979). This perspective is identified by Tsoukas (1993) as consistent with objectivist approaches in social science that view the use of metaphor as not only unnecessary but also distorting of the "facts" that should be expressed in literal language (e.g. Pinder and Bourgeois, 1982; see Morgan, 1983 for a reply).

Constructivist views of metaphor, on the other hand, such as the "interaction" view (Black, 1979) hold that metaphor is involved in fundamental thought processes through the projection of "associated implications" of a secondary subject on a primary subject, in which individuals both actively and sub consciously select, emphasize, suppress, and organize features of the primary subject by applying to it statements isomorphic with the secondary subjects implicative complex. Lakoff and Johnsons (1980) seminal study on the metaphorical structuring of experience emphasizes the status of metaphor as a constructive influence on social actors conceptual system, in terms of which thought and action occur. Lakoff provided a compelling statement of the constructivist view of metaphors through his "invariance hypothesis" in which he suggested that metaphors involve both ontological correspondences (in which entities in the target domain correspond systematically to entities in the source domain) and epistemic correspondences (where knowledge about the source domain is mapped onto knowledge about the target domain) (Lakoff, 1990: 48).

The creative potential of metaphors has formed the basis for metaphorical typologies. Schön, for example, distinguished generative metaphors from nongenerative ones by the formers ability to generate new perceptions, explanations and inventions (1979: 259); and Black distinguished strong from weak metaphors by the formers possessing a high degree of "implicative elaboration" (1979: 27). But are metaphorical statements creative by revealing aspects of the target domain that were already there, or by constituting such aspects by virtue of the two domains that they bring into interaction? Black argues that the latter is possible in the form of his "strong creativity thesis" (1979: 37–39). The creative potential of metaphorical statements depends upon there being sufficient differences between the two domains for a creative tension to exist (Morgan, 1983). As Aristotle put it, "metaphors should be transferred from things that are related but not obviously so" (3: 11: 5).

The potency of metaphor to re frame situations and move individuals to action in a particular direction has been illustrated by the significant amount of research in organization theory on the role of metaphors in facilitating organizational change (e.g. Marshak, 1993; Pondy, 1983; Sackmann, 1989). Metaphors can offer new ways of looking at existing situations (Crider and Cirillo, 1991; Lakoff, 1990; Morgan, 1980, 1983), while simultaneously acting as a bridge from a familiar to a new state (Pondy, 1983). The high latitude of interpretation afforded by metaphorical statements can help to accommodate the interpretations of organizational groups perceiving their interests to be mutually incompatible (Crider and Cirillo, 1991), and unstructured situations can be made more concrete and comprehensible through the use of metaphor (Sackmann, 1989).

Metaphorical discourse analysis can focus on the root metaphors underlying a certain discourse, on the nature of the target and source domains and their implication complexes, on the presence of inter metaphor systematicity (interrelations among metaphors underlying a discourse), or on the longitudinal shifts in root metaphors and the aspects of their implication complexes, as employed by actors in a social system.

Potential disagreements and ambiguities in metaphor use remain whether a single or several metaphors should be used to understand a given situation, to what extent politics are involved in metaphor use, to what extent literal language is needed (or is feasible) in analyzing organizations, and to what extent different metaphors are incommensurable or complementary (Palmer and Dunford, 1996). These ambiguities raise the importance and desirability of researcher reflexivity, particularly in empirical studies, a central issue in organizational discourse. Researcher reflexivity highlights the need to clarify one's assumptions and ideological biases and to consider how these shape various aspects of the research process (Heracleous, 2001).

Symbolic Interactionism

Symbolic interactionism as a term was first used by Herbert Blumer (1969), drawing primarily on the work of George H. Mead, to propose a new paradigm for the study of social issues. While symbolic interactionism originated as a reaction to the dominant positivist paradigm in sociology, many of its core premises have progressively been accepted in mainstream research (Fine, 1993). For symbolic interactionism, meanings do not reside in objects themselves, as distinct from social interaction. It assumes that individuals' action arises out of the meanings that situations have for them; that meanings arise from social interaction with others; and that individuals modify meanings in the process of thinking through issues and interacting further with other individuals (Blumer, 1969: 2; Thomas and Thomas, 1970). The main distinguishing factor of human from animal behavior, from a symbolic interactionist perspective, is the use of language and other forms of symbolic communication.

Methodologically, symbolic interactionism has a dual focus on social interaction and on the meanings involved in, and shaped through, interaction (Prasad, 1993). Its preferred methods involve participant observation and intensive in-depth interviewing. Even though it favors in-depth qualitative methods, symbolic interactionism also encourages generalizations derived inductively from qualitative data, consistent with the other fields discussed in this chapter.

Mead, the intellectual precursor of symbolic interactionism, was particularly concerned with the nature of the self, which he conceptualized as a social object arising out of a process of social interaction (Mead, 1912, 1913), and primarily through "vocal gesture" or talk, suggesting that "the 'me' is a man's reply to his own talk" (1912: 405). The self becomes a social object when it "assumes . . . the attitudes of generalized others" (1925: 275). For Mead, not only self but also mind was discursively constituted. When individuals talk to themselves as they talk to others, "in keeping up this conversation in the inner forum constitutes the field . . . of mind" (1922: 160).

Through discursive symbolic interaction, therefore, meanings become institutionalized or "objectified" (Berger and Luckmann, 1966), acquiring a longer-term solidity and reification. Institutionalized meanings have their discursive correlates in the form of discursive deep structures that are inter textual, persist in the long term, are constructive as opposed to merely communicative, transcend individual situations, and are implicit, residing in actors' practical consciousness (Heracleous and Hendry, 2000).

Storytelling

The storytelling approach was highlighted in organization studies primarily through the work of Boje (1991, 1995) and Gabriel (1991a,b, 1995, 2004). In this approach, stories are seen as symbolic artifacts, as reconstructions of events not as they "really" happened (if they did at all), but as storytellers themselves wish to reconstruct and represent them. Storytelling can fulfill a number of psychic needs, including providing an outlet for creativity, allowing a cathartic discharge of emotion and censored or repressed ideas and wishes, and humanizing impersonal and invisible organizational contexts (Gabriel, 1991a,b). From a storytelling perspective, organizations can be seen as story performance systems where stories are more prevalent, dynamic and constitutive of shared sensemaking than usually assumed (Boje, 1991).

Functionally oriented advocates of storytelling emphasize the organizational outcomes that managers can aim to achieve by effectively employing storytelling. It is suggested that various types of stories can be employed to achieve particular outcomes (Denning, 2004), such as engaging the emotional commitment of internal and external stake-holders (Kaufman, 2003; McKee, 2003), or developing high-potential managers into leaders (Ready, 2002).

From an interpretive research point of view, a key assumption is that stories can provide access to the symbolic, ideational, sub conscious, unmanaged, fantasy-oriented organizational domains (Gabriel, 1995). Daft (1983) even viewed research itself as storytelling, characterized by the need to tell a plausible story effectively and believably linking the data, their interpretation, and the outcomes. Employing literary metaphors, he advocated designing research as a poem, containing just a few (two to four) research variables that cohere together and provide depth of meaning, rather than a novel that has numerous variables without all having tight inter connections within a meaningful whole.

Ideally, organizational discourse researchers should endeavor to study stories in context, through longitudinal, ethnographic engagement with the organizations in which stories are developed, shared, altered, and interpreted (Boje, 1991; 1995). It is not the role of the analyst to judge whether stories are true or false, or have a factual basis, but rather to pay attention to the various interpretations, inter-relations, constructions, and renditions of stories by different actors and the organizational factors related to these (Gabriel, 1995). Researchers, for example, can pay attention to how the agency and subjectivity of story actors is constructed in the story, what is emphasized or downplayed and implicit in stories, and why (Gabriel, 1995), as well as the nature of dialogue or struggle among different stories, or different interpretations of the same story (Boje, 1995). The overall aim of these foci would be to gain insights to the ideational world of the organization through the symbolic medium of stories and story performance.

Conclusion

In the introduction to this chapter, the meaning of interpretivism was outlined as the commitment to in-depth understanding of actors' first-order interpretations. Interpretivism was distinguished from subjectivism in terms of interpretivism's acceptance of more general frameworks derived inductively from data that extend beyond individual, subjectivist viewpoints. Organizational discourse analysis, in this vein, focuses on bodies of texts that constitute discourses, and on the discursive structures and patterns that pervade these texts rather than on individual texts, seeking to relate such inter-textual structures to their cognitive correlates and to the social practices associated with specific discourses.

The chapter expanded on discourse as constructive of social reality, noting the constructive ontology of social phenomena and the potential for actors to manage social representations through discourse. Discourse was viewed as action that is situated in particular social contexts, and as symbolic in terms of portraying actors' values and beliefs and invoking frames for interpreting the issues it refers to. A cognitive perspective to address the constructive effects of discourse on interpretive schemes.

Finally, five interpretive approaches to organizational discourse were discussed: hermeneutics, rhetoric, metaphor, symbolic interactionism, and storytelling. Their conceptual orientations as well as potential analytical directions for conducting discourse analyses were outlined, and summarized in Table 2.1.

Discussion of the nature of discourse as constituted of numerous texts that share certain structural features, which engender conditioned rationalities and influence agents' interpretations, actions, and social practices, has shown that interpretive discourse research is far from subjectivist (in the sense of delivering only idiosyncratic findings that cannot support the discovery of broader understandings of social systems or suggest any types of generalizations).

Moreover, inductive research grounded in field data and, where possible supported by field observations of agents' actions and social practices would certainly not support uncontrolled generalizations that go beyond what can reasonably be supported by the data. As Eco, Ricoeur, Giddens, and others have suggested, there are criteria for textual validity that severely undermine the notion of unlimited interpretation as an avenue to useful understanding of social processes. Even though, in a narrow sense, a text can mean what its reader wants it to mean, at the same time the nature and context of the text itself (and of bodies of texts that constitute discourses) cannot be completely ignored, manipulated or violated. For example, words have a semantic meaning on which communication is based; and this pre supposed meaning, as it were, provides one key dimension for interpretations and re interpretations of texts in context. If researchers of organizational discourse keep in mind the criteria for interpretive validity that Eco, Ricoeur, Giddens and others have proposed, and view the issue of multiple interpretations in a reasoned and substantive way, then some interpretations will be found to be more valid, useful and insightful than others. The approaches discussed in this chapter offer a number of ways through which to explore and develop them productively.

References

Alvesson, M. 1993. Organizations as rhetoric: Knowledge intensive firms and the struggle with ambiguity. *Journal of Management Studies*, 30: 997–1015.

Alvesson, M. and Karreman, D. 2000. Varieties of discourse: On the study of organizations through discourse analysis. *Human Relations*, 53: 1125–1149.

Aristotle. 1991. *On rhetoric*. G. A. Kennedy (trans.). New York: Oxford University Press.

Austin, J. L. 1962. *How to do things with words*. Cambridge, MA: Harvard University Press.

Barthes, R. 1977. *Image, music, text*. London: Fontana.

Bateson, G. 1972. *Steps to an ecology of mind*. London: Intertext.

Berger, P. and Luckmann, T. 1966. *The social construction of reality*. London: Penguin.

Bitzer, L. F. 1968. The rhetorical situation. *Philosophy and Rhetoric*, 1 (1): 1–14.

Black, M. 1979. More about metaphor. In A. Ortony, (ed.). *Metaphor and thought*: 19–43. Cambridge, UK: Cambridge University Press.

Bloom, A. H. 1981. *The linguistic shaping of thought*. Hillsdale, NJ: Erlbaum.

Blum-Kulka, S. 1997. Discourse pragmatics. In T. A. van Dijk (ed.), *Discourse studies: A multidisciplinary introduction*, vol. 2: 38–63. Beverly Hills, CA: Sage.

Blumer, H. 1969. *Symbolic interactionism: Perspective and method*. Berkeley, CA: University of California Press.

Boje, D. M. 1991. The storytelling organization: A study of story performance in an office-supply firm. *Administrative Science Quarterly*, 36: 106–126.

   1995. Stories of the storytelling organization. A post-modern analysis of Disney as "Tamara-Land". *Academy of Management Journal*, 38: 997–1035.

Burrell, G. and Morgan, G. 1979. *Sociological paradigms and organizational analysis*. Hants: Gower.

Charland, M. 1987. Constitutive rhetoric: The case of the peuple Quebecois. *Quarterly Journal of Speech*, 73: 133–150.

Condor, S. and Antaki, C. 1997. Social cognition and discourse. In T. A. van Dijk (ed.), *Discourse studies: A multidisciplinary introduction*, vol. 1: 320–347. Beverly Hills, CA: Sage.

Crider, C. and Cirillo, L. 1991. Systems of interpretation and the function of metaphor. *Journal for the Theory of Social Behavior*, 21: 171–195.

Daft, R. L. 1983. Learning the craft of organizational research. *Academy of Management Review*, 8: 539–546.

Denning, S. 2004. Telling tales. *Harvard Business Review*, May: 122–129.

Denzin, N. 1983. Interpretive interactionism. In G. Morgan (ed.), *Beyond method: Strategies for social research*: 129–146. Beverly Hills, CA.

van Dijk, T. A. 1977. *Text and context: Explorations in the semantics and pragmatics of discourse*. London: Longman.

1988. Social cognition, social power and social discourse. *Text*, 8: 129–157.

1990. Social cognition and discourse. In H. Giles and W. P. Robinson (eds.), *Handbook of language and social psychology*: 163–183. Chichester: Wiley.

1993. Principles of critical discourse analysis. *Discourse and Society*, 4: 249–283.

Eco, U. 1990. *The limits of interpretation*. Bloomington: Indiana University Press.

Eemeren, F. H., Grootendorst, R., Jackson, S. and Jacobs, S. 1997. Argumentation. In T. A. van Dijk (ed.), *Discourse studies: A multidisciplinary introduction*, vol. 1: 208–229. Thousand Oaks, CA: Sage.

Eoyang, C. 1983. Symbolic transformation of belief systems. In L. R. Pondy, P. J. Frost, G. Morgan, and T. C. Dandridge (eds.), *Organizational symbolism*: 109–121. Greenwich: JAI Press.

Fine, G. A. 1993. The sad demise, mysterious disappearance, and glorious triumph of symbolic interactionism. *Annual Review of Sociology*, 19: 61–87.

Finstad, N. 1998. The rhetoric of organizational change. *Human Relations*, 51: 717–740.

Gabriel, Y. 1991a. On organizational stories and myths: Why it is easier to slay a dragon than to kill a myth. *International Sociology*, 6: 427–441.

1991b. Turning facts into stories and stories into facts. A hermeneutic exploration of organizational folklore. *Human Relations*, 44: 857–875.

1995. The unmanaged organization: Stories, fantasies and subjectivity. *Organization Studies*, 16: 477–501.

2004. Narratives, stories, and texts. In D. Grant, C. Hardy, C. Oswick and L. Putnam (eds.) *The sage handbook of organizational discourse*: 61–77. London: Sage.

Gergen, K. J. and Thatchenkery. 1996. Organization science as social construction: Postmodern potentials. *Journal of Applied Behavioral Science*, **32**: 356–377.

Giddens, A. 1979. *Central problems in social theory*. London: Macmillan.
1984. *The constitution of society*. Cambridge: Polity.
1987. *Social theory and modern sociology*. Cambridge: Polity.

Gill, A. M. and Whedbee, K. 1997. Rhetoric. In T. A. van Dijk (ed.), *Discourse studies: A multidisciplinary introduction*, vol. 1: 157–183. Thousand Oaks, CA: Sage.

Gioia, D. A. 1986. Symbols, scripts and sensemaking: Creating meaning in the organizational experience. In H. P. Sims, Jr. and D. A. Gioia (eds.), *The thinking organization*: 49–74. San Francisco: Josey-Bass.

Gowler, D. and Legge, K. 1983. The meaning of management and the management of meaning. In M. Earl (ed.). *Perspectives in management*: 197–233. Oxford: Oxford University Press.

van Graber, M. 1973. Functional criticism: A rhetoric of Black power. In G. P. Mohrmann, C. J. Stewart and D. J. Ochs (eds.), *Explorations in rhetorical criticism*: 207–222. Pennsylvania: Pennsylvania State University Press.

Grant, D., Keenoy, T. and Oswick, C. 1998. Organizational discourse: Of diversity, dichotomy and multi-disciplinarity. In D. Grant, T. Keenoy and C. Oswick (eds.), *Discourse and organization*: 1–13. London: Sage.

Gronbeck, B. E. 1973. The rhetoric of social-institutional change: Black action at Michigan. In G. P. Morhmann, C. J. Stewart, and D. J. Ochs (eds.), *Explorations in rhetorical criticism*: 96–123. Pennsylvania: Pennsylvania State University Press.

Gumperz, J. J. and Levinson, S. C. 1991. Rethinking linguistic relativity. *Current Anthropology*, **32**: 613–623.

Hardy, C. and Phillips, N. 1999. No joking matter: Discursive struggle in the Canadian refugee system. *Organization Studies*, **20**: 1–24.
2002. Interpretive Approaches to Organizational Discourse *Discourse analysis: Investigating processes of social construction. Qualitative Research Methods Series*, 50. Thousand Oaks: Sage.

Harré, R. 1981. Rituals, rhetoric and social cognitions. In J. P. Forgas (ed.). *Social cognition: Perspectives in everyday understanding*: 211–224. London: Academic Press.

Heracleous, L. 2001. An ethnographic study of culture in the context of organizational change. *Journal of Applied Behavioral Science*, 37: 426–446.

2003. A comment on the role of metaphor in knowledge generation. *Academy of Management Review*, 28: 190–191.

2004. Interpretivist approaches to organizational discourse. In D. Grant, N. Phillips, C. Hardy, L. Putnam and C. Oswick (eds.), *Handbook of organizational discourse*: 175–192. Beverly Hills: Sage.

2006. A tale of three discourses: The dominant, the strategic and the marginalized. *Journal of Management Studies*, 43: 1059–1087.

2007a. Interpretive Theory. In S. Clegg (ed.), *International encyclopedia of organization studies*, vol. 1. Beverly Hills: Sage, forthcoming.

2007b. Hermeneutics. In S. Clegg (ed.), *International encyclopedia of organization studies*, vol. 1. Beverly Hills: Sage, forthcoming.

Heracleous, L. and Barrett, M. 2001. Organizational change as discourse: Communicative actions and deep structures in the context of information technology implementation. *Academy of Management Journal*, 44: 755–778.

Heracleous, L. and Hendry, J. 2000. Discourse and the study of organization: Toward a structurational perspective. *Human Relations*, 53: 1251–1286.

Heracleous, L. and Marshak, R. 2004. Conceptualizing organizational discourse as situated symbolic action. *Human Relations*, 57 (10): 1285–1312.

Hopkins, N. and Reicher, S. 1997. Social movement rhetoric and the social psychology of collective action: A case study of anti-abortion mobilization. *Human Relations*, 50: 261–286.

Huff, A. S. 1983. A rhetorical examination of strategic change. In L. R. Pondy, P. J. Frost, G. Morgan and T. C. Dandridge, (eds.), *Organizational symbolism*: 167–183. Greenwich: JAI Press.

Hymes, D. 1964. Toward ethnographies of communication. *American Anthropologist*, 66 (6), part 2: 12–25.

Kaufman, B. 2003. Stories that sell, stories that tell. *Journal of Business Strategy*, March–April: 11–15.

Keenoy, T. 1990. Human resource management: Rhetoric, reality and contradiction. *International Journal of Human Resource Management*, 1: 363–384.

Kets de Vries, M. F. R. and Miller, D. 1987. Interpreting organizational texts. *Journal of Management Studies*, 24: 233–247.

Kinneavy, J. L. 1971. *A theory of discourse*. NJ: Prentice-Hall.

Lakoff, G. 1990. The invariance hypothesis: Is abstract reason based on image schemas? *Cognitive Linguistics*, 1: 39–74.

Lakoff, G. and Johnson, M. 1980. *Metaphors we live by*. Chicago: Chicago University Press.

Light, D. Jr. 1979. Surface data and deep structure: Observing the organization of professional training. *Administrative Science Quarterly*, 24: 551–561.

Marshak, R. J. 1993. Managing the metaphors of change. *Organizational Dynamics*, 22: 44–56.

McKee, R. 2003. Storytelling that moves people. *Harvard Business Review*, June: 51–55.

Mead, G. H. 1912. The mechanism of social consciousness. *Journal of Philosophy, Psychology and Scientific Methods*, 9 (15): 401–406.

    1913. The social self. *Journal of Philosophy, Psychology and Scientific Methods*, 10 (14): 374–380.

    1922. A behavioristic account of the significant symbol. *Journal of Philosophy*, 19 (6): 157–163.

    1925. The genesis of the self and social control. *International Journal of Ethics*, 35 (3): 251–277.

Morgan, G. 1980. Paradigms, metaphor and puzzle solving in organization theory. *Administrative Science Quarterly*, 25: 660–671.

    1983. More on metaphor: Why we cannot control tropes in administrative science. *Administrative Science Quarterly*, 28: 601–607.

    1986. *Images of organization*. Beverly Hills, CA: Sage.

Moscovici, S. 1981. On social representations. In J. P. Forgas (ed.), *Social cognition: Perspectives on everyday understanding*: 181–209. London: Academic Press.

Mumby, D. K. and Clair, R. P. 1997. Organizational discourse. In T. A. van Dijk (ed.), *Discourse as social interaction*: 181–205. Beverly Hills, CA: Sage.

Oswick, C., Keenoy, T. and Grant, D. 1997. Managerial discourses: Words speak louder than actions? *Journal of Applied Management Studies*, 6: 5–12.

Palmer, I. and Dunford, R. 1996. Conflicting uses of metaphors: Reconceptualizing their use in the field of organizational change. *Academy of Management Review*, 21: 691–717.

Palmer, R. E. 1969. *Hermeneutics*. Evanston: Northwestern University Press.

Phillips, N. and Brown, J. L. 1993. Analyzing communication in and around organizations: A critical hermeneutic approach. *Academy of Management Journal*, 36: 1547–1576.

Pinder, C. C., and Bourgeois, V. W. 1982. Controlling tropes in administrative science. *Administrative Science Quarterly*, 27: 641–652.

Pondy, L. R. 1983. The role of metaphors and myths in organization and the
facilitation of change. In L. R. Pondy, P. J. Frost, G. Morgan, and T. C.
Dandridge (eds.), *Organizational symbolism*: 157–166. Greenwich: JAI
Press.

Prasad, A. 2002. The contest over meaning: Hermeneutics as an interpretive
methodology for understanding texts. *Organizational Research Methods*, 5 (1): 12–33.

Prasad, P. 1993. Symbolic processes in the implementation of technological
change: A symbolic interactionist study of work computerization.
Academy of Management Journal, 36: 1400–1429.

Ready, D. A. 2002. How storytelling builds next-generation leaders. *MIT
Sloan Management Review*, Summer: 63–69.

Ricoeur, P. 1991. *From text to action*. Illinois: Northwestern University
Press.

1997. Rhetoric-Poetics-Hermeneutics. In W. Jost and M. J. Hyde (eds.),
Rhetoric and hermeneutics in our time: A reader: 60–72. New Haven:
Yale University Press.

Rumelhart, D. E. 1984. Schemata and the cognitive system. In R. S. Wyer Jr.
and T. K. Srull (eds.), *Handbook of social cognition*: 161–188. Hillsdale, NJ: Erlbaum.

Sackmann, S. 1989. The role of metaphors in organization transformation.
Human Relations, 42: 463–485.

Schon, D. A. 1979. Generative metaphor. A perspective on problem-setting
in social policy. In A. Ortony (ed.), *Metaphor and thought*: 254–283.
Cambridge: Cambridge University Press.

Sherzer, J. 1987. A discourse-centered approach to language and culture.
American Anthropologist, 89: 295–309.

Searle, J. 1975. Indirect speech acts. In P. Cole and J. Morgan (eds.), *Syntax
and semantics 3: Speech acts*: 59–82. New York: Academic Press.

Spender, J. C. 1989. *Industry recipes*. Oxford: Blackwell.

Taylor, S. E. and Crocker, J. 1981. Schematic bases of social information
processing. In E. T. Higgins, C. P. Herman, and M. P. Zanna (eds.),
Social cognition: 89–134. Hillsdale, NJ: Erlbaum.

Thachankary, T. 1992. Organizations as "texts": Hermeneutics as a model
for understanding organizational change. *Research in Organization
Change and Development*, 6: 197–233.

Thomas, W. I. and Thomas, D. S. 1970. Situations defined as real are real in
their consequences. In G. P. Stone and H. A. Faberman (eds.), *Social
psychology through symbolic interaction*: 154–156. Toronto: Xerox
College Publishing.

Tsoukas, H. 1993. Analogical reasoning and knowledge generation in organization theory. *Organization Studies*, **14**: 323–346.

Watson, T. J. 1995. Rhetoric, discourse and argument in organizational sense making: A reflexive tale. *Organization Studies*, **16**: 805–821.

Weber, M. 1922. *Economy and society: An outline of interpretive sociology* (Roth, G. and Wittich, G. transl.). NY: Bedminster.

Williams, M. 2000. Interpretivism and generalization. *Sociology*, **34**: 209–224.

Wittgenstein, L. 1955. *Tractatus logico-philosophicus*. London: Routledge and Kegal Paul.

1968. *Philosophical investigations*. Oxford: Blackwell.

3 | *Functional Approaches: Metaphor in Organization Change and Development*[1]

IN chapter 1 we suggested that functional approaches view discourse as language-based communication to be employed by managerial and social actors for achieving certain organizationally (and often personally) relevant ends. Discourse is seen as a tool at actors' disposal rather than as a constraining, dominating feature of social life (as in the critical approach); or as a shaping influence and a window to the ideational, symbolic world of organizations (as in the interpretive approach). In this chapter we illustrate functional approaches to organizational discourse through a discussion of how aspects of discourse, particularly metaphors, can be employed in efforts to accomplish more effective organization change and development.

One key underlying assumption of functionally oriented approaches, often left implicit, is the interpretive insight that organizational discourse can not only provide access to the conceptual world of organizations but can also be used as an avenue for influencing this world. Effective organizational change and development presents a set of perennial managerial problems. A discourse perspective highlights and illustrates that dealing with such problems is not just about the "hard" structural aspects of organizations, but requires an in-depth appreciation of the cultural, human aspects of organizations, and taking corresponding actions based on this appreciation.

Soft aspects of Effective Change Management and the Role of Discourse

The management of change poses a fundamental challenge to managers, which has prompted an immense amount of practitioner-oriented literature on how to effectively manage change (e.g. Champy and Nohria, 1996; Kotter, 1996). Common prescriptions include

---

[1] This chapter draws from Heracleous (2002) and Jacobs and Heracleous (2006).

encouraging participation from as many employees as possible, addressing their concerns in change programs, tapping the energy and commitment of change champions, demonstrating the conviction of senior management by allocating time and resources to change programs, and ensuring that leaders act as role models for the desired changes. Even with ample advice, however, the vast majority of change-related programs fail to meet their objectives (Nohria, 1993). Many, such as downsizing or reengineering, can even lead to undesirable long-term consequences such as a depletion of the organization's knowledge and competence base and low employee morale (Eliezer, 1996; Mabert and Schmenner, 1997).

One reason for the high rate of failure of change programs is that the soft cultural and social aspects of organizations often receive insufficient attention in such programs (Heracleous, 2001; Pascale, Milleman, and Gioia, 1997). Change-management approaches oriented to hard understandings of organizations, such as "business process reengineering" or "restructuring," are unlikely to encourage attention to relevant cultural, political, and social issues, understand their impact on proposed changes, and try to address them accordingly.

There is often an assumed dichotomy between "understanding," associated with the interpretive paradigm, and "managing," associated with the functional paradigm. Even though the theoretical constructs and motivations of researchers in these paradigms may indeed be different (Heracleous and Barrett, 2001), there is also a complementary dimension where effective *management* of change also requires deep understanding of the subtle issues involved. Therefore in order to be able to improve the effectiveness of change management, a more refined understanding of not only the content of change but also its context and process is needed (Pettigrew, 1987).

The organization change literature contains analytical distinctions, such as anticipatory/reactive change or incremental/radical change (Nadler and Tushman, 1989), and describes several change-management styles that can potentially be adopted based on contingency considerations (Kotter and Schlesinger, 1979). Even though such prescriptions may be useful, by themselves they would be insufficient and would still need to be complemented by rich data derived from in-depth, time-sensitive methodologies that can adequately shed light on some of the complex issues involved in organizational change (Pettigrew, 1987).

Tan and Heracleous (2001), for example, explored the implementation of organizational learning in an Asian National Police Force in the context of a longitudinal action research program. The aim was to get an interpretive, in-depth understanding of the related processes of transformational change, and the barriers to change, in a public sector machine bureaucracy with entrenched structure and culture not ordinarily conducive to learning and adaptation; and to explore the applicability of universalist change-management prescriptions in this context. The barriers identified included interunit rivalries and turf battles, barriers to information flows, low interunit coordination due to rivalry and culture of secrecy, top-down rather than participative decision-making processes, a vision defined and directed from the top, and an orientation of sweeping mistakes under the carpet rather than learning from them. These barriers to change were being contested through a participative change process, the existence of change champions, experiences that challenged the prevailing bureaucratic culture, and change actions that were congruent with the organization's authorizing environment.

This study also found that universalist change-management prescriptions may not always be fully applicable because the nature, task, and culture of the organization influence what change approaches are appropriate. For example, public sector organizations are much more constrained relative to commercially oriented organizations with respect to how much they can adjust their reward and evaluation system in support of desired changes. In addition, whereas participation and critical questioning of the current and desired situations may be conducive to the success of change programs, the extent to which such critical questioning can take place, may be pragmatically reduced when an organization charged with the critical tasks of national security, keeping public order and fighting crime is involved.

Diagnosing and dealing with organizational culture is one of the key factors for achieving effective organizational change (Heracleous and Langham, 1996; Pascale, Milleman, and Gioja, 1997). In this context, Heracleous (2001) employed an ethnographic research approach, combined with a clinical element, to explore the nature and role of culture in the context of organizational change at the UK operations of a global consulting firm focused on people issues. Using Schein's (1992) levels of culture model, Heracleous identified cultural assumptions and values in this organization, and explored how these related to employee behaviors, based on ethnographic research as well as using his clinical relationship with the organization as a rich data source.

This study illustrates how an organizational culture develops historically, has internally coherent elements, and has potent effects on behaviors that should be studied and understood by managers and clinicians undertaking organizational change programs. For example, in this organization there were deep cultural assumptions relating to the organization's relationship to its environment, the nature of reality and truth, the nature of human nature, the nature of human activity, and the nature of time. These assumptions were deeply ingrained in the culture, and were continually manifested and reinforced in specific types of behaviors and organizational processes, in areas such as reward and evaluation processes, induction of new consultants, and even how the organization approached its relationship with the author, as an action researcher. Understanding such deep cultural assumptions helps change agents assess the extent to which organization change is compatible with the culture, the expected levels of cultural resistance, and to identify specific cultural and behavioral areas where change efforts should be focused.

Turning now to the role of discourse, if we accept Pondy and Mitroff's (1979) suggestions to view the nature of organizations as going beyond the orthodoxy (at the time) of open systems theory, and view them as composed of "self-conscious language users" who possess "a sense of social order, a shared culture, a history and a future, a value system" (1979: 9), it becomes apparent that any significant organizational change will affect and be affected by these softer aspects of organizations. Organizational discourses (with their own vocabularies, root metaphors, or rhetorical strategies) are both a mirror of the conceptual world of the organization and a central avenue by which this world can be influenced.

There is a significant amount of research on how change agents can use communication[2] to achieve more effective organizational change.

---

[2] Communicative actions in this sense can be seen as building blocks of texts and discourses. They occur at specific points in time, are functionally oriented, situational and explicit. Discourses, on the other hand, can be seen as constituted by collections of communicative actions that make up texts; and as exhibiting structural features that are longitudinal, constructive, transcending situations, and implicit (Heracleous and Barrett, 2001, Heracleous and Hendry, 2000). This structurational view of discourse is discussed in more detail in chapter 5.

Armenakis, Harris, and Mossholder (1993), for example, have argued that the change message is the primary means of creating readiness for change in an organization. Lengel and Daft (1988) stressed the importance of employing rich media (e.g. face-to-face communication) if the issue addressed is nonroutine and complex such as organization change. Chesley and Wenger (1999) suggested that strategic conversations can foster organizational transformation by helping organizational members surface their assumptions through dialogue, create shared understandings, and learn how to learn. Conger (1991), in addition, argued that great leaders will not only need to be effective strategists but also effective rhetoricians who can inspire, persuade, and energize their audience. They must be able to articulate and communicate a compelling organizational mission, explain convincingly its rationale, sketch an image of the "enemy" that compels people to expend discretionary effort, and build up the organization's confidence that it can succeed in spite of all the obstacles. The use of stories, analogies, and metaphors is a key feature of effective rhetorical discourse. Proponents of storytelling, for example, have emphasized the impact of stories on such outcomes as emotional commitment of stakeholders and personal development of leaders (McKee, 2003; Ready, 2002).

Heracleous and Barrett (2001) illustrate the unique capability of organizational discourse to contribute to in-depth understanding of organizational change and to aid its effective management. This research was conducted from a hermeneutic perspective, and explored the role of discourse in shaping organizational change processes through its influence on actors' interpretations and actions, using a longitudinal field study of electronic trading implementation in the London Insurance Market. Through a focus on both discourse and its context, the researchers were able to make sense of the multiple perspectives of different stakeholder groups and their interrelations. They were able to explore actors' own argumentations, interpretations, and actions with regard to the proposed implementation of electronic trading in order to gain in-depth hermeneutic understanding of the change processes involved. Agents' interpretations and actions in this case shaped the trajectory and ultimate failure of the process of electronic trading implementation.

Heracleous and Barrett's study sought to address the research challenge of exploring multiple discourses, their interrelations, and their impact on practice (Boje, 1995; Grant, Keenoy, and Oswick, 1998). It found that the discourses of each stakeholder group were pervaded and patterned by relatively stable deep structures, which functioned as organizing mechanisms that guided myriads of surface communicative actions which might otherwise appear unconnected and disparate. There were discursive clashes among stakeholder groups over contested terrain, illustrating both conflict and discursive interpenetration and influence among their discourses. There was fragile agreement and cooperation at the surface communicative level, which was based on potentially conflicting deep structures that could assert themselves in different ways under different contextual conditions. There was discursive fragmentation, leading to conflicting actions, even within the same stakeholder group sharing the same deep structures, arising because one actor can deem that their key goals can be better served by actions that are in conflict with the actions of their own stakeholder group. Finally, stakeholder groups talked past each other, rather than to each other, because of their almost diametrically opposed discourses, at both the deep structure levels and communicative action levels, with little common ground on which to base a dialogue. This study has illustrated the complementary nature of understanding and "explanation" as discussed earlier.

Discourse in this perspective is far from "just talk." It is central to individuals' interpretation and action, and it can help change agents both understand the intricacies of the organizational setting and manage the change process more effectively. Discourse itself becomes situationally specific action[3] that can either aid or hinder change processes, and paying insufficient attention to organizational discourse also means foregoing the richness that this lens can provide.

The Pervasive Role of Metaphor in Organization Theory

The literal view of metaphors, aligned with objectivist approaches in social science (Tsoukas, 1993) suggests that metaphors are primarily ornamental, expendable linguistic devices that simply indicate similarities between a source and a target domain (Black, 1993); not only do they not lead to additional understanding, but can also distort

---

[3] Chapter 6 expands on a view of discourse as situated symbolic action.

"the facts" that should be expressed in literal language (Pinder and Bourgeois, 1982).

From a constructionist viewpoint, however, this literal view of metaphors as unnecessary linguistic ornaments is rejected, and their central role in human sensemaking and understanding is emphasized (Lakoff and Johnson, 1980). Metaphors are viewed as primarily conceptual constructions that play a central role in the development of thought and intersubjective meaning making, allowing actors to reframe their perceptions, or "see the world anew" (Barrett and Cooperrider, 1990: 222). According to Lakoff (1993: 203), for example, "the locus of metaphor is not language at all, but in the way we conceptualize one mental domain in terms of another." In this respect, these conceptual similarities involve both ontological (target entities' nature corresponds in certain ways to source entities' nature) and epistemic correspondences (knowledge of source domain is mapped on to knowledge about the target domain) (Lakoff, 1990). Social constructionists suggest that these correspondences are created rather than just revealed by metaphor, thereby emphasizing the inherently creative dimension of metaphor rather than viewing it as something that can merely reveal an antecedently existing similarity (e.g. Black, 1993; Johnson, 1987).

Metaphors and stories are viewed as more memorable and impactful than literal language because they appeal simultaneously "to the emotions, to the intellect, to imagination, and to values" (Conger, 1991: 39). In terms of research on persuasive communication, organizational actors are more likely to both understand the message, take it as having personal relevance, and spend more time thinking about it (Petty and Cacioppo, 1986).

Morgan's work (e.g. 1980, 1983, 1986) has been seminal in fostering challenges to the dominant mechanistic and organic metaphors in organization theory, through a conscious understanding of the impact of such taken for granted metaphors on organizational theorizing. Morgan (1983) has gone as far as to suggest that seeking to minimize the influence of metaphors is not only counterproductive but also infeasible, given their integral role to theorizing and sensemaking. According to Morgan, "the linguistic aspect is just a surface expression of a deeper process. This is why I like to describe metaphor as a primal, generative process that is fundamental to the creation of human understanding and meaning in all aspects of life" (1996: 228).

Morgan's approach (and the stream of research inspired by it) has been criticized as potentially exercising an overly conservative influence on theorizing because of the suggested focus of metaphor on searching for similarities between the interrelated domains rather than highlighting differences and engendering "cognitive discomfort" (Oswick, Keenoy, and Grant, 2002). The inherent ambiguity and imprecision of metaphors (Tsoukas, 1993), in addition, entails some persistent question marks and disagreements regarding their usefulness in organizational theorizing. Pinder and Bourgeois (1982), for example, have suggested that metaphorical statements do not fulfill a critical condition of social science, that is, falsifiability. Morgan (1983, 1996) responds by suggesting that the views of his critics in essence seek to substitute the trope of metonymy for the trope of metaphor in social science theorizing. Morgan accepts many other critiques of his approach to metaphor and suggests that rather than dwelling on the limitations of metaphorical thinking, we should make productive use of this avenue for understanding, bearing in mind its limitations in terms of producing "partial truths" (1996: 232) that may at times be ideologically biased, or lack "rigor" as this concept is conventionally understood.

In spite of the earlier issues, the sheer influence of metaphorical thinking in organization theory over the years (e.g. Jacobs and Heracleous, 2006; Morgan, 1980, 1983; Oswick and Grant, 1996) bears testament to the usefulness and potential of metaphors as sense-making devices that can engender or stimulate novel or at least interesting different understandings of particular target domains through creating or eliciting correspondences with selected source domains. As Grant and Oswick (1996: 2) have maintained, "there can be little dispute about the inevitability of metaphor. Nor about its having a generative quality."

Metaphor in Organizational Change and Development

It has long been recognized that as primarily cognitive and semantic devices, metaphors play a vital role in the discursive construction of meaning in organizational change and development processes (Cleary and Packard, 1992; Marshak, 1993: 766; Sackmann, 1989: 954). According to Burke, metaphors can be "windows into the soul, if not collective unconscious, of the social system" (Burke, 1992: 255).

Metaphors are crucial dimensions of organization members' cognitive schemata, providing lenses for interpreting the world, embodying implicit evaluations, and implying "appropriate" actions based on the prevailing metaphors (Armenakis and Bedeian, 1992; Hirsch, 1986). Metaphors can help to concretize vague and abstract ideas, can holistically convey a large amount of information, and can foster new ways of looking at things (Sackmann, 1989).

Metaphors can offer new ways of looking at existing situations (Crider and Cirillo, 1991; Lakoff, 1990; Morgan, 1980, 1983) while simultaneously acting as a bridge from a familiar to a new state (Pondy, 1983). Researchers have shown that the metaphors used by organizational actors are empirically related to such areas as the extent and speed of organizational change (Oswick and Montgomery, 1999) or to aspects of organizational and national culture (Gibson and Zellmer-Bruhn, 2001). Change agents can employ an organization's prevalent metaphors as a diagnostic tool that reflects actors' ways of thinking about their organization and the need for change, as well as a facilitating mechanism for change by introducing metaphors that can align organizational participant's interpretations and actions toward a desired direction (Marshak, 1993).

Constructionist views of metaphor suggest that metaphor shapes agents' thoughts by projecting "associated implications" of a secondary subject on a primary subject. Agents creatively select, emphasize, suppress, and organize features of the primary subject by applying to it statements isomorphic with the secondary subject's implicative complex (Lakoff and Johnson, 1980). If a change program is portrayed as a journey, for example, actors can see it as a long-term effort that has a desired destination and will involve interesting learning experiences along the way. If a competitor's actions are interpreted as "war," then employees may perceive the situation as one that demands immediate, coordinated response and full commitment to staving off the threat.[4]

---

[4] Constructionist views of metaphor are aligned to the interpretive stream of discourse research in their assumptions about the potency of metaphor to re-define social reality. Metaphors per se are paradigm neutral, however, transcending individual discourse streams. Metaphors, for example, can be functionally utilized in organization change programs, they can be employed as tools of critical analysis, or their deep features can be identified and analyzed in research programs following the structurational paradigm.

Metaphors can move agents to action because of their usually rich evaluative loading that points implicitly toward what "ought" to be done under situations framed metaphorically; the "normative leap" resulting from metaphors' naming and framing processes (Schön, 1979: 264–265). As Hirsch and Andrews (1983) have noted in the context of their analysis of the language of corporate takeovers, "once the roles and relations are assigned, proper procedures and/or proper outcomes can be readily deduced. Sleeping Beauty must be liberated and wed; the shark must be annihilated; the black-hat brought to justice; the honorable soldier must fight doggedly, and so on" (1983: 149).

While a deductive approach to metaphors attempts to apply a generic set of metaphors to organizational situations, an inductive approach operates on the assumption that organizational members already generate and use metaphors in view of their context and experience that can be tapped for the purposes of system diagnosis and change. Stated another way, deductive metaphorical approaches attempt to suggest universal, archetypical sets of metaphors that in turn would then guide corresponding interventions; in contrast, inductive approaches emphasize the emergent, local and contextual nature of metaphors (Palmer and Dunford, 1996).

Operating from an inductive angle, Cleary and Packard (1992) suggest a two-phase process of assessment of metaphors and other symbolic aspects of the organization, and then development of change goals and planning of action steps based on that assessment. Marshak (1993), in addition, proposes that change agents can listen carefully to the metaphors used by organizational members as a means of diagnosing the organization, help them understand the implications of employing different types of metaphors by conducting relevant workshops, and try to shape the way people think about change by diffusing appropriate metaphors that align their conceptual system with the type of changes aimed for.

Perhaps the potency of metaphor to effect change is related to its complexity and ambiguity that allows for multiple interpretations to coexist but at the same time can provide a shared direction. According to Pondy (1983), "because of its inherent ambivalence of meaning, metaphor can fulfill the dual function of enabling change and preserving continuity" (1983: 164). This complexity and ambiguity is often downplayed in accounts of the use of metaphor in organization development interventions (Inns, 2002). Despite the advantages of using metaphor for diagnostic and intervention purposes, often organization members may use mutually incompatible metaphors to describe the same organization, as Oswick and Montgomery (1999) found. In such cases, more extensive collaborative efforts need to be undertaken to explore the sources of contradiction and make further, improved diagnoses and interventions.

In sum, metaphors can thus facilitate organizational change by creatively redefining reality for organizational actors and enabling them to see familiar situations or actions in a new light; they can help to mediate political conflict by providing mutually acceptable visions of the future; they can make otherwise abstract organizational futures appear more clear and desirable; and finally they can spur agents to action through their evaluative loading and memorable images.

From Semantic to Spatial, and on to Embodied Metaphors

Metaphors are often based on characteristics found in the physical world, as illustrated by the three generic image schemata of up/down, container, and link or connection. This suggests that metaphorical sensemaking draws from the human capacity of perceiving and mentally resonating with these physical relationships of and between objects (Johnson, 1987; Lakoff and Johnson, 1980). Going beyond metaphors' verbal, semantic dimension, Weick (1990), for example, highlighted the relevance of spatial relatedness in terms of maps as two-dimensional devices of sensemaking employed in organizational practices. Cognitive mapping has operationalized maps as spatial metaphors that can facilitate organizational change and development (e.g. Bougon, 1992; Brown, 1992; Eden, 1992; Hodgkinson and Johnson, 1994). Cognitive mapping involves the creation of visual representations of a domain and its most relevant entities as cognitively perceived, and portrays these entities within systems of relationships (Huff, 1990). Maps can serve as triggers or focal points of reference and meaning negotiation in conversations, and it is primarily this communication around the mapping process that can trigger fruitful insights. Importantly, given the recursive nature of meaning generation (Weick, 1990), a map does not solely represent but can rather construct the territory in important and consequential ways.

Proceeding one step further from spatial metaphors, Jacobs and Heracleous (2006) discuss "embodied metaphors" in organization change and development. The term "embodied" in this context encompasses two related ideas. First, the literal construction of a physical object as an occasion for sensemaking introduces the body in processes of creating and exploring metaphors. More importantly, however, the physical constructions are themselves metaphors in the flesh, tangible metaphors representing organizational domains of importance to participants. In the construction process agents get immersed in "practicing and 'doing metaphor'," a promising avenue for innovation in the field or metaphor (Morgan, 1996: 240). Both the analogical creation process and the resulting physical constructions can be fruitful occasions for collective sensemaking and social reality construction, which can be immensely useful in processes of organization development and change.[5]

Several organization development approaches involving embodied metaphors have emerged over the last few years. For example, Barry (1994) draws on depth psychology and art therapy to introduce the concept of "analogically mediated inquiry" in which an object or model created by participants ("the analog") allows the process consultant and the participants to engage in a collaborative process of interpretation and sensemaking. The analog embodies conscious and subconscious cognitions of participants and serves as a "positive scapegoat" for them, enabling the surfacing of issues that may be politically contentious or up till then undiscussable. Doyle and Sims (2002), in addition, propose "cognitive sculpting," the construction of three-dimensional objects in the context of conversations for change in which participants are invited, using several objects on a table, to form a sculpture of particular organizational issues. This process involves verbal and nonverbal meaning negotiation that has both a mnemonic and a constructive effect; the construction process provides a collaborative setting of shared sensemaking, and the resulting structures provide the opportunity for "decoding" of the issues, assumptions, and feelings embodied in them through skilled facilitation.

Buergi and Roos (2003), finally, suggest a process of "serious play" in which participants are invited to configure and represent abstract

---

[5] Jacobs and Heracleous (2006) draw from phenomenology and cognitive psychology to theorize embodied metaphors more extensively.

organizational issues, such as organizational identity or the landscape of an organization, by means of three-dimensional construction toys. As Heracleous and Jacobs (2005) suggest, such play-oriented, nonrational approaches can enable creative strategic and organizational insights to emerge, and can complement more traditional, rational, and structured approaches to think about the organization and its strategic direction.

Thus, through the *spatial* dimension, operationalized in concepts such as cognitive or strategic mapping, the inherently spatial nature of metaphors (as image schemata) can be brought to bear literally. Further, through the *bodily* dimension, exemplified in concepts such as analogically mediated inquiry, cognitive sculpting, or serious play, embodied metaphors can be brought to bear on processes of shared meaning construction and sensemaking about issues of shared concern. Both the concept and the technology of embodied metaphors operate within an emergent, inductive approach to metaphorical reasoning since organizational metaphors are intimately related to context and experience (Lakoff and Johnson, 1980). Embodied metaphors gain their currency from the ultimately local, contextual, and situated nature of their construction, rather than being based on assumptions of metaphorical generality and universality — a more deductive approach to metaphorical engagement in organization change and development programs.

Embodied Metaphors in Organization Change and Development

From a traditional perspective of organization development as involving an analytical distinction of people and organizational processes on the one hand (the human-processual approach) versus technology and organizational structures on the other (the technostructural approach) (Friedlander and Brown, 1974), an embodied metaphors approach lies within the human-processual domain. Organization development has from early on recognized the importance of people and cognitively related interventions: "the cognitive work of clients has become a point of diagnosis and intervention" (Alderfer, 1977). In addition, the organization development field has continuously encouraged new approaches. According to Friedlander and Brown (1974), "broader applications of a theory of planned change will require expanded intervention technologies" (1974: 335); in addition, Porras and Silvers (1991) noted that "we encourage the use of new tools in OD, especially when those tools are derived from a sound theoretical base" (1991: 65). Interventions based on embodied metaphors aim to expand organizational members' ways of seeing through active, collaborative construction of metaphorical structures, thus potentially leading to reframing or change in perceptions of reality (Porras and Silvers, 1991).

The dominant approach to employing metaphors in organization development suggests that change agents should take a leading part in diagnosing the organization through an understanding of the language-based metaphors used by organizational actors, and can then foster change through diffusing appropriate metaphors given the context and type of change aimed for (Cleary and Packard, 1992; Marshak, 1993; Sackmann, 1989). Further, the emphasis is usually on naturally occurring metaphor use rather than induced metaphorical creations; and on a metaphorical intervention designed by the OD practitioner rather than a collaborative effort of jointly developing and interpreting metaphors with organizational members. Finally metaphorical diagnosis is usually employed with reference to the whole organization rather than a targeted issue that the organization is facing.

As Howe (1989) noted, "at present, practice seems to be guided largely by intuition and accumulated experience" (1989: 81). Several years after this statement was made, there is still a lot to be learned about relevant intervention technologies. As Table 3.1 shows, the concept of embodied metaphors complements existing approaches to employing metaphor in organization development processes (e.g. Marshak, 1993; Morgan, 1996; Oswick and Grant, 1996) by emphasizing the relevance of actively induced metaphors; highlighting the social dimension of such literal social construction processes; fostering a client-driven intervention; and eliciting metaphors to assist with a targeted issue rather than a diagnosis and change of the whole system.

In this context, Jacobs and Heracleous (2006) describe the case of SwissBankCo in which the CEO and the senior team had decided to introduce a change in their marketing strategy with broader strategic implications. Introduction of the concept of "I know my banker" was intended to enable a more customer focused business practice throughout the bank. As part of a senior management retreat in 2003, a total of 47 managers of SwissBankCo, including the CEO, 6

Table 3.1. Traditional Use of Metaphor Versus Embodied Metaphors in OD

Traditional Use of Metaphor in OD	Embodied Metaphors in OD
Emphasis on naturally occurring, language-based metaphors	Emphasis on induced, embodied metaphors
Relatively little available knowledge on diagnostic and intervention technologies, the *how*	Builds on a developed base of diagnostic and intervention technologies
OD practitioners select appropriate metaphors for changing task and setting	Metaphors selected arise from collaborative effort
OD practitioners lead metaphorical diagnosis	Metaphorical diagnosis through shared sensemaking
Emphasis on whole system	Can be employed for targeted issue diagnosis and intervention

Source: Adapted from Jacobs and Heracleous (2006).

heads of departments and their direct reports, participated in a 1-day strategy workshop in which toy construction materials were employed in the process of meaning generation and sensemaking. The participants were divided into six groups, each including members from different departments of the bank. Following some "warm-up" exercises, the groups were invited to build models of what the recently developed strategic concept "I know my banker" meant to them and to discuss the consequences for their respective daily practices. Table 3.2 given an outline of the application of embodied metaphors to the Swiss Bank case.

The process of sensemaking by means of induced, embodied metaphors involves three generic, iterative stages that take place at both individual and collective levels: individual construction, collective construction, and collective inquiry into the respective constructions. Participants created a variety of embodied metaphors, portraying the need to "raise customers up to the same level" as bankers improve mutual understanding by "getting on the same wavelength" or develop a much closer relationship by even "getting into the jacuzzi" with customers. Jacobs and Heracleous (2006) discuss in detail two of the

Table 3.2. Using Embodied Metaphors in OD: The Swiss Bank Case

Embodied Metaphors in OD	Application to Swiss Bank Case
Inducing embodied metaphors	Intervention process emphasized the construction of physical models of a strategic concept important to the client
Builds on a developed base of diagnostic and intervention technologies	Antecedents include analogically mediated inquiry, cognitive sculpting, and serious play technologies
Metaphors arise from collaborative efforts	Metaphors collaboratively developed by participants, rather than selected by the facilitator, formed the core of the intervention
Metaphorical diagnosis through shared sensemaking	This process helped to surface conceptual differences within groups in the construction process and across groups through differences in the resulting analogs
Emphasis on targeted issue diagnosis and intervention	Cognitive divergences embedded in analogs formed the basis for probing questions by facilitator and further interpretation and collective sensemaking by participants

Source: Adapted from Jacobs and Heracleous (2006).

constructions developed during this workshop. The first, more mechanistic construction, was composed of two intersecting circles. The small circle represented the clients and their needs, the large circle represented the bank and its machinelike organization, and the intersection between them showed the ground where client and banker could meet and interact. The second construction took a more developmental, relationship-oriented view, presenting growth in the relationship between banker and client as a five-stage progression moving from the first state of a huge gap between them to the final state of proximity and mutual understanding.

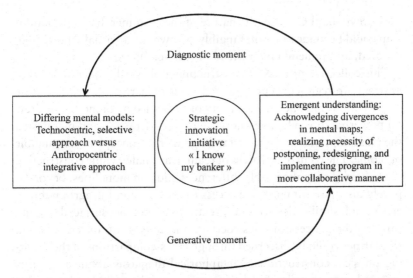

Figure 3.1. Diagnostic and Generative Moments in Dialogue Occasioned by Embodied Metaphors. Source: Jacobs and Heracleous (2005)

The constructions generated in this process illustrated the divergences of interpretations of the new strategic concept "I know my banker." For example, was the concept referring to ways through which customers can get to know us as bankers better? Or is the slogan just another twist to the ubiquitous "know your customer" rhetoric? Are we talking about all customers? Or do we focus on a yet-to-be-defined subset of premium customers? If yes, who are they and how do we identify them? How can we discuss the consequences of this change for our daily practices, if we do not even know what it means? As Jacobs and Heracleous (2005) have shown, the process of reflective dialogue engendered through the construction and decoding of embodied metaphors can assist participants to surfacing and diagnosing their existing mental models, and in doing so generating more sophisticated understandings of relevant issues. Figure 3.1 illustrates this process.

When faced with such variety of metaphors and interpretations, the facilitator helps participants explore these divergences constructively by surfacing and debating the differences, critically examining the implications of each alternative perspective, and inviting participants to explore how they can potentially integrate divergent perspectives. The physical differences in embodied metaphors make the conceptual differences literally tangible, facilitating such processes of inquiry.

In the SwissBankCo case, the nature of the customer–banker relationship could be made sense of; tangibly "shown"; and visually presented, debated, and remembered instead of just verbalized.

This collective process of constructing a physical model of a rather abstract strategic concept triggered a set of narratives around these constructions and induced a variety of embodied metaphors that drew on preverbal, pre-reflexive knowledge of participants, and manifested their assumptions and understandings of the concept in its tangible outcome. The recursive process of reading an analog while constructing it has helped to make visible differences and commonalities, beyond a purely discursive or cognitive access to the concept. Intragroup differences and similarities in interpretations could be surfaced in and through the process of construction, and intergroup differences and similarities could be discerned through cross-comparisons of the resulting physical constructions. Metaphorical diagnosis about a specific, targeted issue that the client was facing was therefore made possible in the context of a collaborative, discursive, and embodied effort.

The role of the organization development practitioner, as facilitator, is crucial to the effectiveness of such interventions. They can pose probing questions triggered by the model and its detailed features for example, why is there such a gap between customer and banker? Why does the banker sit much higher than the customer, even though they are supposed to be equals? Why is the circle of the "bank machine" much larger than the customer's needs circle? Within-model, intragroup interventions can help individuals or small groups in their local, collective construction processes, whereas cross-model, intergroup interventions can help to identify and explore differences and commonalities across models, and within the whole participant cohort.

The role of the OD consultant and process facilitator, moreover, is to encourage figurative rather than literal constructions; invite peer projections on individual as well as collective models; pose probing questions inviting critical inquiry into the constructions; and help in exploring similarities, differences, and blind spots. While the facilitator should be clear on the structure and constraints of the process, they should exercise a low level of directiveness in the construction and decoding activities since ownership of both constructions and interpretations lies with the participants. Being aware of group-specific play dynamics, a skilled facilitator can ensure, in addition, that the embodied metaphors created are genuinely interactive and group-based products.

Pondy (1983) suggested that metaphors could facilitate change by providing a bridge "from the familiar to the strange" (1983: 163). Embodied metaphors are particularly suited to serve as bridges between the old and the new since they represent, or embody, existing organizational elements as perceived by participants. From an intervention perspective, this can guide debate to precisely the things that matter to organizational actors (even if these were not the explicitly stated purpose of the workshop) and provide a nonintrusive and nonpersonalized way to address them.

Embodied metaphors are collective creations and therefore from a political perspective, they can make it easier for contentious issues to be placed on the agenda for discussion. Any individuals would not be likely to bring such issues up on their own, but as part of a group such concerns are easier to surface. In addition, embodied metaphors can bring to the agenda contentious issues because these issues are not overtly represented, but they have to be "decoded" with the help of the OD practitioner. Initially, participants may not be entirely clear why they built a certain structure in a certain way or what precisely it represents. Through the course of collaborative interpretation of the structure, new ideas and issues emerge.

From a creativity, generative perspective, embodied metaphors can help organizational members engage in both more conservative, experience-based "thought imagery" and unbounded, divergent "imagination imagery" (Howe, 1989). In doing so, they can reinterpret and debate existing issues that their organization is facing, as was done in the SwissBankCo case discussed here, or, more radically, imagine completely new possibilities, as can be done when participants are asked to construct analogs of how they see the future of their industry or organization. Such imagination imagery could thus fulfill the generative potential of metaphors not only in organizational theorizing but also in the applied domain. A fruitful area for further research, therefore, would be an exploration of the relative generative potential of embodied metaphors as compared to other types of metaphoricallybased organization development interventions, and whether different construction processes would be more suited to either thought imagery or imagination imagery.

From a change efficacy perspective in addition, metaphorical thinking is inherent in episodes of organization development and change. Embodied metaphors extend the traditional semantic and cognitive dimensions of metaphors by tapping into pre-reflexive knowledge contained in human bodily experience and interpretations embodied in the constructed analogs. Embodied metaphors are exceptionally vivid and memorable; photographs of structures (or actual structures) are often taken back to the organization where they serve as constant reminders of the issues that need to be addressed and the changes that need to be made. Embodied metaphors can thus contribute to developing and sustaining a shared set of metaphorical repertoires and shared understandings, vital to the success of organization change and development efforts. Further research can therefore explore the processes through which embodied metaphors can induce reframing of existing situations, and the potential differences of such processes from the way in which linguistic-based or map-based metaphors can induce reframing of perceptions or cognitive maps. Finally, further exploration into the political implications of embodied metaphors would be useful, especially as metaphorical theorization has been criticized as failing to pay due attention to political issues (Morgan, 1996).

This chapter has illustrated the functional approach to organizational discourse by discussing the role of semantic, spatial, and, particularly, embodied metaphors in organizational change and development. The functional approach to organizational discourse is underlied by the interpretive insight that meaning is constructed, sustained and potentially challenged through discursive social interaction and that discourse is not merely informational but constructive of social and organizational realities. Empirical research was drawn on to clarify the importance of understanding the soft aspects of organizations in the context of organizational change, and the role that discourse, particularly metaphor, can play in this process.

References

Alderfer, C. P. 1977. Organization development. *Annual Review of Psychology*, **28**: 197–223.

Armenakis, A. and Bedeian, A. 1992. The role of metaphors in organizational change. Change agent and change target perspectives. *Group & Organization Management*, **17**: 242–249.

Armenakis, A. A., Harris, S. G. and Mossholder, K. W. 1993. Creating readiness for organizational change. *Human Relations*, **46**: 681–703.

Barrett, F. J. and Cooperrider, D. L. 1990. Generative metaphor intervention: A new behavioral approach for working with systems divided by conflict and caught in defensive perception. *Journal of Applied Behavioral Science*, 26: 219–239.

Barry, D. 1994. Making the invisible visible: Using analogically-based methods to surface unconscious organizational processes. *Organization Development Journal*, 12 (4): 37–47.

Black, M. 1993. More about metaphor. In A. Ortony (ed.), *Metaphor and thought* (2nd edn.), pp. 19–4. Cambridge, MA: Cambridge University Press.

Boje, D. M. 1995. Stories of the storytelling organization: A postmodern analysis of Disney as "Tamara-Land." *Academy of Management Journal*, 38: 997–1035.

Bougon, M. G. 1992. Congregate cognitive maps. *Journal of Management Studies*, 29: 369–389.

Brown, S. M. 1992. Cognitive mapping and repertory grids for qualitative survey research. *Journal of Management Studies*, 29: 287–307.

Buergi, P. and Roos, J. 2003. Images of strategy. *European Management Journal*, 21 (1): 69–78.

Burke, W. W. 1992. Metaphors to consult by. *Group & Organization Management*, 17: 255–259.

Champy, J. and Nohria, N. 1996. *Fast forward: The best ideas on managing business change*. Boston, MA: Harvard Business School Press.

Chesley, J. A. and Wenger, M. S. 1999. Transforming an organization: Using models to foster a strategic conversation. *California Management Review*, 41 (3): 54–73.

Cleary, C. and Packard, T. 1992. The use of metaphors in organizational assessment and change. *Group & Organization Management*, 17: 229–241.

Conger, J. A. 1991. Inspiring others: The language of leadership. *Academy of Management Executive*, 5 (1): 31–45.

Crider, C. and Cirillo, L. 1991. Systems of interpretation and the function of metaphor. *Journal for the Theory of Social Behavior*, 21: 171–195.

Doyle, J. R. and Sims, D. 2002. Enabling strategic metaphor in conversation: A technique of cognitive sculpting for explicating knowledge. In A. S. Huff and M. Jenkins (eds.), *Mapping strategic knowledge*: 63–85. London: Sage.

Eden, C. 1992. On the nature of cognitive maps. *Journal of Management Studies*, 29: 261–265.

Eliezer, G. 1996. Cleaning up after reengineering. *Business Horizons*, 39 (5): 71–78.

Friedlander, F. and Brown, D. L. 1974. Organization development. *Annual Review of Psychology*, 25: 313–341.

Gibson, C. B. and Zellmer-Bruhn, M. E. 2001. Metaphor and meaning: An intercultural analysis of the concept of teamwork. *Administrative Science Quarterly*, **46**: 274–303.

Grant, D. and Oswick, C. (eds.) 1996. *Metaphor and organizations*. London: Sage.

Grant, D., Keenoy, T. and Oswick, C. 1998. Organizational discourse: Of diversity, dichotomy and multi-disciplinarity. In D. Grant, T. Keenoy, and C. Oswick (eds.), *Discourse and organization*: 1–13. London: Sage.

Heracleous, L. 2001. An ethnographic study of culture in the context of organizational change. *Journal of Applied Behavioral Science*, **37**: 426–446.

2002. The contribution of a discursive view to understanding and managing organizational change. *Strategic Change*, **11**: 253–261.

Heracleous, L. and Barrett, M. 2001. Organizational change as discourse: Communicative actions and deep structures in the context of IT Implementation. *Academy of Management Journal*, **44**: 755–778.

Heracleous, L. and Hendry, J. 2000. Discourse and the study of organization: Toward a structurational perspective. *Human Relations*, **53**: 1251–1286.

Heracleous, L. and Jacobs, C. 2005. The serious business of play. *MIT Sloan Management Review*, Fall: 19–20.

Heracleous, L. and Langham, B. 1996. Organizational change and organizational culture at Hay Management Consultants. *Long Range Planning*, **29**: 485–494.

Hirsch, P. M. 1986. From ambushes to golden parachutes: Corporate takeovers as an instance of cultural framing and institutional integration. *American Journal of Sociology*, **91**: 800–837.

Hirsch, P. M. and Andrews, J. A. 1983. Ambushes, shootouts and knights of the roundtable: The language of corporate takeovers. In L. R. Pondy, P. J. Frost, G. Morgan, and Dandridge, T. C. (eds.), *Organizational symbolism*: 145–155. Greenwich, CT: JAI Press.

Hodgkinson, G. P. and Johnson, G. 1994. Exploring the mental models of competitive strategists: The case for a processual approach. *Journal of Management Studies*, **31**: 525–551.

Howe, M. A. 1989. Using imagery to facilitate organizational development and change. *Group & Organization Studies*, **14**: 70–82.

Huff, A. S. 1990. *Mapping strategic thought*. Chichester, England: Wiley.

Inns, D. 2002. Metaphor in the literature of organizational analysis: A preliminary taxonomy and a glimpse at a humanities-based perspective. *Organization*, **9**: 305–330.

Jacobs, C. and Heracleous, L. 2005. Answers for questions to come: Reflective dialogue as an enabler of strategic innovation. *Journal of Organization Change Management*, **18** (4): 338–352.

2006. Constructing shared understandings. The role of embodied meta-phors in organization development. *Journal of Applied Behavioral Science*, **42**: 207–226.

Johnson, M. 1987. *The body in the mind: The bodily basis of meaning, imagination, and reason*. Chicago, IL: University of Chicago Press.

Kotter, J. P. 1996. *Leading change*. Boston, MA: Harvard Business School Press.

Kotter, J. P. and Schlesinger, L. A. 1979. Choosing strategies for change. *Harvard Business Review*, March–April: 4–11.

Lakoff, G. 1990. The invariance hypothesis: Is abstract reason based on image schemas? *Cognitive Linguistics*, **1**: 39–74.

1993. The contemporary theory of metaphor. In A. Ortonty (ed.), *Metaphor and thought*: 202–251. Cambridge, MA: Cambridge University Press.

Lakoff, G. and Johnson, M. 1980. *Metaphors we live by*. Chicago, IL: University of Chicago Press.

Lengel, R. H. and Daft, R. L. 1988. The selection of communication media as an executive skill. *Academy of Management Executive*, **2**: 225–232.

Mabert, V. A. and Schmenner, R. W. 1997. Assessing the roller coaster of downsizing. *Business Horizons*, **40** (4): 45–53.

Marshak, R. 1993. Managing the metaphors of change. *Organizational Dynamics*, **22** (1): 44–56.

McKee, R. 2003. Storytelling that moves people. *Harvard Business Review*, June: 51–55.

Morgan, G. 1980. Paradigms, metaphor and puzzle solving in organization theory. *Administrative Science Quarterly*, **25**: 660–671.

1983. More on metaphor: Why we cannot control tropes in administrative science. *Administrative Science Quarterly*, **28**: 601–607.

1986. *Images of organization*. Beverly Hills, CA: Sage.

1996. An afterword: Is there anything more to be said about metaphor? In C. Oswick and D. Grant (eds.), *Metaphor and organization*: 227–240. London: Pitman.

Nadler, D. A. and Tushman, M. L. 1989. Organizational frame bending: Principles for managing reorientation. *Academy of Management Executive*, **3** (3): 194–204.

Nohria, N. 1993. Managing change: Course overview. *Harvard Business School Teaching Note*, 9–494–042.

Oswick, C. and Grant, D. (eds.) 1996. *Organisation development: Metaphorical explorations*. London: Pitman.

Oswick, C. and Montogomery, J. 1999. Images of an organization: The use of metaphor in a multinational company. *Journal of Organizational Change Management*, **12**: 501–523.

Oswick, C., Keenoy, T. and Grant, D. 2002. Metaphorical and analogical reasoning in organization theory: Beyond orthodoxy. *Academy of Management Review*, **27**: 294–303.

Palmer, I. and Dunford, R. 1996. Understanding organisations through metaphor. In C. Oswick and D. Grant (eds.), *Organisation development: Metaphorical explorations*: 7–15. London: Pitman.

Pascale, R., Milleman, M. and Gioia, L. 1997. Changing the way we change. *Harvard Business Review*, November–December: 127–139.

Pettigrew, A. 1987. Context and action in the transformation of the firm. *Journal of Management Studies*, **24**: 649–670.

Petty, R. E. and Cacioppo, J. T. 1986. The elaboration likelihood model of persuasion. In L. Berkowitz (ed.), *Advances in experimental social psychology*, vol. 19: 123–205. Orlando, FL: Academic Press.

Pinder, C. C. and Bourgeois, V. W. 1982. Controlling tropes in administrative science. *Administrative Science Quarterly*, **27**: 641–652.

Pondy, L. R. 1983. The role of metaphors and myths in organization and in the facilitation of change. In L. R. Pondy, P. J. Frost, G. Morgan, and T. C. Dandridge (eds.), *Organizational symbolism*: 157–166. Greenwich, JAI Press.

Pondy, L. R. and Mitroff, I. I. 1979. Beyond open systems model of organization. *Research in Organizational Behavior*, **1**: 3–39.

Porras, J. and Silvers, R. 1991. Organizational development and transformation. *Annual Review of Psychology*, **42**: 51–78.

Ready, D. A. 2002. How storytelling builds next-generation leaders. *MIT Sloan Management Review*, Summer: 63–69.

Sackmann, S. 1989. The role of metaphors in organization transformation. *Human Relations*, **42**: 463–485.

Schein, E. 1992. *Organizational culture and leadership* (2nd edn.). San Francisco, CA: JoseyBass.

Schön, D. A. 1979. Generative metaphor: A perspective on problem-setting in social policy. In A. Ortony (ed.), *Metaphor and thought*: 254–283. Cambridge, MA: Cambridge University Press.

Tan, T. K. and Heracleous, L. 2001. Teaching old dogs new tricks: Implementing organizational learning in an Asian national police force. *Journal of Applied Behavioral Science*, **37**: 361–380.

Tsoukas, H. 1993. Analogical reasoning and knowledge generation in organization theory. *Organization Studies*, **14**: 323–46.

Weick, K. E. 1990. Introduction: Cartographic myths in organizations. In A. S. Huff and M. Jenkins (eds.), *Mapping strategic thought*: 1–10. Chichester: Wiley.

4 | Critical Approaches: Michel Foucault's Conceptions of Discourse[1]

As discussed in chapter 1, critical approaches view discursive social reality construction as imbued with power and interest considerations, where dominant groups attempt to shape reality, social practices, and even subjects' identities in ways that perpetuate these groups' own interests. Far from being neutral, language-based constructs, discourses are seen as the sites of polyphonic struggles as domains of power–knowledge relations that can dominate subjectivity in favor of the already powerful. The politically motivated task of critical discourse analysis is thus to demystify and expose the processes involved and ideally weaken their grip.

Michel Foucault has been a key figure providing inspiration, concepts, and analytical frameworks for critical discourse scholars. This chapter traces the development of Foucault's concept(s) of discourse from the Archaeological to the Genealogical periods, significantly drawing from Foucault's own texts. Second, it offers a critique of Archaeological conceptions of discourse, focusing on the discourse–subject relationship, and on Foucault's related conceptions of change, choice, and rules of discursive formations. Third, it traces Foucault's conceptual shifts and concerns in his Genealogical period, in particular his views on power, discourse as a manifestation of the will to power, and a tacit acceptance of the importance of agency. Finally, implications for organizational discourse analysis are discussed.

Critiques of Foucault's discussions of discourse have received much attention in philosophy (Frank, 1992; Habermas, 1987), literature (Kermode, 1973; Said, 1974), sociology (Brown and Cousins, 1994; Freundlieb, 1994), and organization studies (Newton, 1994, 1998; Reed, 1998). Despite trenchant criticisms, Foucault's work has endured as an insightful critical resource (e.g. Knights and Willmott, 1989;

---

[1] This chapter is based on Heracleous (2000), and Heracleous and Chan (2005).

McKinlay and Starkey, 1998; Townley, 1993a,b). It continues to be seen by many, however, as obscure, hard to understand, and difficult to operationalize in concrete analyses. This chapter aims to help in remedying this situation by providing an interpretation of the development of Foucault's concept(s) of discourse from the Archaeological to the Genealogical periods, significantly drawing from Foucault's own texts.

Five interrelated main conceptions of discourse identified in *The Archaeology of Knowledge* (1972) are outlined: First, discourses as groups of statements belonging to a discursive formation; second, discourses as rule-bound practices; third, discourses as practices specified in archives; fourth, discourses as practices constituting objects; and finally, discourses as totalities determining subject positions.

Then, a constructive critique of archaeological conceptions of discourse is offered, focusing on the discourse–subject relationship, and on Foucault's conceptions of change, choice, and rules of discursive formations. It is argued that Foucault attributes significant status to human agency at crucial junctures of his conceptual system while overall he denounces it. It is suggested that this is a manifest contradiction that ultimately derives from the fact that a foundational methodological choice in Foucault's project (to purposefully ignore human agency) implicitly promotes questionable ontological assumptions (that human agency is subordinated to and located in discourse); and that the lens of method should not be allowed by virtue of its employment to make assumptions on the ontology of entities under investigation. Further, a brief examination of Foucault's ideas on change and transformation reveals conceptual contradictions relating to the use of terms, such as "strategy" and particularly "choice," within a deterministic framework that is in conflict with the accepted assumptions connected to these terms (e.g. that choice implies an agent able to exercise it). In addition, beginning with the deterministic qualities that Foucault attributes to "rules" and "laws," it is suggested that his work confounds the logical necessity that subjects necessarily speak from within given structures, with the idea that the content of subjects' discourse (and even their reason) is unidirectionally determined by such structures.

Third, the chapter discusses how later Genealogical writings begin to address some of the earlier issues, particularly the issue of agency, by introducing a tacit acceptance of agency through Foucault's discussion of various facets of the "will" (will to power, will to truth, will to knowledge), and more explicit reference to the levels of action and meaning. In this period Foucault questioned traditional views of power by suggesting that power is a property of social relations woven into the social nexus rather than a top–down force, the exercise of power consists of insidiously guiding conduct and outcomes rather than the brute exercise of strength power could only be exercised over free subjects that power influences and shapes subjectivity and power is positive and productive rather than simply repressive and constraining. Discourse was now seen as a manifestation of the will to power, and far from being neutral or objective, was always imbued with biases in favor of dominant interests. However, it is suggested that even though Foucault accepted in his later work the notion of agency, it was only in a muted and implicit way. Often his writing portrays a notion of the will as a reified, outside force, rather than being intentionally derived from, and located in, individuals.

Finally, in undertaking the earlier analyses, this chapter aims to promote more fruitful appropriations of Foucault's work by discourse and organization scholars through raising awareness of how the concept of discourse developed over time in Foucault's writings, and exploring what this journey can offer to studies of discourse. It is suggested that the conceptual system and analytical approaches espoused by Foucault could contribute substantially to management and organizational discourse analyses, provided that their substantive assumptions and limits are kept in mind and treated critically.

Phillips and Hardy's (2002) framework of organizational discourse approaches is employed to suggest how Foucauldian concepts drawn from both the *Archaeological* and *Genealogical* periods could contribute to the various approaches. Even though Foucault's Genealogical writings still offer a reified conception of the will and lack an adequate conception of agency, coupled with earlier Archaeological concepts they do open up fruitful avenues for enquiry through offering a subtle and elaborate conception of the nature of power, a view of knowledge as an interest-laden force, and an explicit connection of discourse with power and social practices.

Foucault's Conceptions of Discourse in the Archaeological Period

Foucault's main theoretical development of the concept of discourse was set out in *The Archaeology of Knowledge* (1972) (hereafter

Archaeology), the culminating work of his Archaeological period. The *Archaeology* represented Foucault's attempts to challenge widely accepted conceptions and methods of history, and the assumed transcendental role of the subject in historical movements. This section draws extensively from Foucault's own writings as they usually defy reduction or paraphrase (all page references are to the *Archaeology* unless otherwise specified). According to Foucault, the *Archaeology* was

> an enterprise in which the methods, limits, and themes proper to the history of ideas are questioned; an enterprise by which one tries to throw off the last anthropological constraints; an enterprise that wishes, in return, to reveal how these constraints could come about. . . . (15)

In the *Archaeology*, Foucault developed his conceptions of discourse and proposed an elaborate methodological system for discourse analysis (see especially pp. 28–30, 70–72, 121–125, 138–140, 151–152, 158–162 and 170–177). Foucault's ideas on discourse in the *Archaeology*, however, are rarely drawn upon by organization theory and discourse scholars (for exceptions see Hopwood, 1987; Jacobs and Heracleous, 2001), who most often prefer to draw on later Genealogical writings linking discourse and power through the discursive production of truth effects and subjects' identity (e.g. Chan, 2000; Hoskin and Macve, 1986; Knights and Morgan, 1991, 1995; McKinlay and Starkey, 1998; Newton, 1994; Townley, 1993a). There are also other scholars, who, possibly discouraged by the obfuscated style of Foucault's writings, either do not draw on his ideas at all for their discussions of discourse (e.g. Rouleau and Seguin, 1995) or refer to them selectively and in passing (e.g. Mumby and Stohl, 1991).

In the *Archaeology*, Foucault realized that he gave several meanings to the concept of discourse:

> instead of gradually reducing the rather fluctuating meanings of the word "discourse," I believe that I have in fact added to its meanings: treating it sometimes as the general domain of all statements, sometimes as an individualizable group of statements, and sometimes as a regulated practice that accounts for a certain number of statements; and have I not allowed this same word "discourse," which should have served as a boundary around the term statement, to vary as I shifted my analysis or its point of application, as the statement itself faded from view? (80)

This section aims to clarify Foucault's treatment of discourse in his Archaeological period through a careful reading of the *Archaeology*. Five main conceptions of discourse are identified, which are inter-related and form part of Foucault's wider conceptual and methodological system. Foucault's "discourse" must therefore be understood in relation to, and as constituted by, other key concepts such as the statement, discursive formation, discursive practice, the archive, rules of formation, and the relation between discourses and subjects.

Discourses as Groups of Statements Belonging to a Discursive Formation

Foucault stated that:

We shall call discourse a group of statements in so far as they belong to the same discursive formation; it does not form a rhetorical or formal unity . . . it is made up of a limited number of statements for which a group of conditions of existence can be defined. Discourse in this sense is not an ideal, timeless form that also possesses a history . . . it is, from beginning to end, historical — a fragment of history, a unity and discontinuity in history itself . . . . (117)

In his attempts to arrive at a satisfactory definition of "the statement," Foucault dissociated it from identity with logical propositions, grammatical sentences, or speech acts (even though Foucault later admitted substantial similarity of his concept of statement with Austin's and Searle's concept of speech acts; see Dreyfus and Rabinow, 1983: 45–49). Foucault concluded that the statement

is not therefore a structure (that is, a group of relations between variable elements, thus authorizing a possibly infinite number of concrete models); it is a function of existence that properly belongs to signs and on the basis of which one may then decide, through analysis or intuition, whether or not they make sense. . . . (86)

The concept of "discursive formation" is arrived at with the realization that discursive unities could not be based on "a full, tightly packed, continuous, geographically well-defined field of objects," a "definite, normative type of statement," a "well-defined alphabet of notions," or the "permanence of a thematic." In each case Foucault found not unities but dispersions.

Hence the idea of describing these dispersions themselves. . . . Whenever one can describe, between a number of statements, such a system of dispersion, whenever, between objects, types of statement, concepts, or thematic choices, one can define a regularity (an order, correlations, positions and functionings, transformations), we will say, for the sake of convenience, that we are dealing with a *discursive formation*.
(38, emphasis in original)

(A discursive formation) is a space of multiple dislsensions; a set of different oppositions whose levels and roles must be described.   (155)

Toward the end of his Archaeological period, Foucault proposed that it was very important that *intradiscursive* dependencies (of elements within a discursive formation), *interdiscursive* dependencies (between different discursive formations), and *extradiscursive* dependencies (between discursive formations and external institutions) be analyzed (Foucault, 1991a: 58).

Discourses as Rule-bound Practices

Foucault's *Archaeology* treats discourses as "practices obeying certain rules" (p. 138) that are anonymous, historical, and deterministic, controlling what can be enunciated by subjects.

Discursive practice . . . is a body of anonymous, historical rules, always determined in the time and space that have defined a given period, and for a given social, economic geographical, or linguistic area, the conditions of operation of the enunciative function.   (117)

Discursive practices were important not simply because of what was said, or omitted, but because of their effects on the real. This was put succinctly in Foucault's summary of a course he taught at the *Collège de France* in 1970–1971:

Discursive practices are not purely and simply ways of producing discourse. They are embodied in technical processes, in institutions, in patterns for general behavior, in forms for transmission and diffusion, and in pedagogical forms which, at once, impose and maintain them.   (1977a: 200)

Discourses as Practices Specified in Archives

In concluding his discussion of the statement and the archive, Foucault maintained that "*Archaeology* describes discourses as practices specified in the element of the archive" (p. 131). Archives are systems that establish statements as events and things, and involve interstatement (intradiscursive) relations. Archives determine what can be said and how, and control the emergence and transformation of statements at the level of practice or enunciability (it is hard to ignore here the structuralist analogues between this conception of how what can be said is determined by the underlying archive, with Saussure's (1983) suggestion that *langue* or speech is determined by *parole* or the underlying linguistic rules):

We have in the density of discursive practices, systems that establish statements as events (with their own conditions and domain of appearance) and things (with their own possibility and field of use). They are all these systems of statements (whether events or things) that I propose to call *archive*. . . . The archive is first the law of what can be said, the system that governs the appearance of statements as unique events . . . it is that which, at the very root of the statement-event, and in that which embodies it, defines at the outset *the system of its enunciability* . . . it is that which defines the mode of occurrence of the statement-thing; it is *the system of its functioning.* . . . The *archive* defines a particular level: that of a practice that causes a multiplicity of statements to emerge. . . . It is *the general system of the formation and transformation of statements.*

(Foucault, 1972: 128–130, emphases in original)

Discourses as Totalities Determining Subject Positions

Foucault at several occasions made clear his opposition to forms of analysis that privileged the human subject as a driver of history, a causative agent of change, or as having any substantive freedom from subjugation to dominant discourses. This standpoint characterized his discussions of discourse in relation to speaking subjects, whose position was always said to be preset and determined by an anterior system of relations. Foucault even went as far as to assert that "our reason is the difference of discourses" (Foucault, 1972: 131).

In asserting the primacy of anterior systems of relations over sub-jectivity, for example, he bluntly argued that discourse should not be seen as the result of a thinking subject, but rather the anterior system in which subjects would be located and determined.

I shall abandon any attempt, therefore, to see discourse as a phenomenon of expression — the verbal translation of a previously established synthesis; instead, I shall look for a field of regularity for various positions of sub-jectivity. Thus conceived, discourse is not the majestically unfolding mani-festation of a thinking, knowing, speaking subject, but, on the contrary, a totality, in which the dispersion of the subject and his discontinuity with himself may be determined.   (55)

The enunciative domain, or the domain of things said, accordingly, was not the result of any authorial activity, or speaking subjects, but, "an anonymous field whose configuration defines the possible posi-tion of speaking subjects" (p. 122). Rather than the subject producing discourse, Foucault's archaeological position was in effect that discourse produces the subject:

. . . the position of the subject can be assigned. To describe a formulation *qua* statement does not consist in analyzing the relations between the author and what he says (or wanted to say, or said without wanting to); but in determining what position can and must be occupied by any individual if he is to be the subject of it.   (95–96, emphasis in original)

For a diametrically opposed view of the relation between discourse and subjectivity we can contrast Foucault's position with the herme-neutic position of Ricoeur (1991), who argues that "it is . . . necessary to situate discourse in the structures of being rather than situate the latter in discourse" (1991: 68).

Discourses as Practices Constituting Objects

When discussing the formation of objects, Foucault concluded that discourses should not be treated as groups of signs but "as practices that systematically form the objects of which they speak" (p. 49). Discourses as practices, in Foucault's scheme, are regulated by discur-sive relations, and discursive objects exist "under the positive condi-tions of a complex group of relations" (p. 45). He pointed out that these relations

are established between institutions, economic and social processes, behavioral patterns, systems of norms, techniques, forms of classification, modes
of characterization. . . . (45)

These relations are neither exterior nor internal to discourse, but at its
limit. These relations are said to (in a rather tautologous fashion)

determine the group of relations that discourse must establish in order to
speak of this or that object, in order to deal with them, name them, analyze
them, classify them, explain them, etc. (46)

He further distinguished "discursive relations" from "real or primary
relations," which can be described between institutions, techniques, or
social forms "independently of all discourse or all object of discourse,"
and "reflexive or secondary relations . . . formulated in the discourse
itself" (p. 45), and stated that "the problem is to reveal the specificity
of these discursive relations, and their interplay with the other two
kinds" (pp. 45–46). This theme of the interrelations between discursive and nondiscursive domains would be taken up extensively in
Foucault's later, genealogical writings, as will be discussed later.

In summary, in his archaeological writings, Foucault viewed discourses as groups of statements that do not form unities but dispersions, which should themselves be analyzed. Discourses are seen as
practices that obey certain rules, and are located in archives, or
systems that establish statements as events and things. Discourses are
constitutive of the objects they address, and especially subjectivity.
Subjects, rather than being intentional producers of discourse, are at
the mercy of anterior discursive structures.

A Critique of Foucault's Archaeological Conceptions of Discourse

Foucault's work has been criticized on several fronts, criticisms
deemed justifiable even by sympathetic reviewers of his work. One
issue that is seen as an important problem by many is Foucault's
"refusal to retain one position for longer than the period between his
last book and the next" (Burrell, 1988: 222). Although continuities in
Foucault's work can be discerned, the discontinuities and contradictions in methods and conceptualizations, especially between his
Archaeological and Genealogical periods are marked. Whereas, for

example, in the Archaeological period the analyst's aim was to act as an "excavator," seeking depth and interiority, with the aim of uncovering the rules regulating social practices and which were unknown to the actors involved, in the Genealogical period the aim became to "record the singularity of surface events looking at the meaning of small details, minor shifts and subtle contours" (Burrell, 1988: 229). The analyst should now oppose the search for depth and interiority since the world is as it appears.

Critics have engaged with foundational points of Foucault's conceptual system such as the concepts of statement, discursive formation, discourse, as well as his refusal to accept human agency within his theory (Brown and Cousins, 1994; Freundlieb, 1994). This chapter extends this critique by discussing Foucault's treatment of the discourse–subject relationship; the related issues of change and transformation in relation to discourse and the subject; and finally we examine his use of the concepts of rules and laws that are said to regulate discourse, and the role of the subject in this process. In the last section of this paper some key implications of the analysis for discourse scholars are discussed.

Discourse as Deterministic of the Subject

We employ the concept of agency to refer to the capability of agents to take action, and to potentially make choices to act differently, in an undetermined fashion. Drawing from Giddens's (1984) stratification model of the agent, actions take place in the context of unacknowledged conditions (including institutional structures) and have unintended consequences (partly in terms of reaffirming or challenging institutional structures). Agents are seen as having certain motivations for action, and to be engaged in both reflexive monitoring and rationalization of their actions.

Subjects in Foucault's *Archaeology* are not attributed to any degree of agency. What they can say and even their reason are *determined* by anterior discourses that are themselves determined by "rules of formation." Foucault's enunciative analysis is said to utilize a "great, uniform text, which has never before been articulated, and which reveals for the first time what men 'really meant'" (p. 118). Before the publication of the *Archaeology* Foucault had already proposed that discoursing subjects form a part of the discursive field—they have their place within it . . . and their function . . . . Discourse is not a place into which the subjectivity irrupts; it is a space of differentiated subject-positions and subject-functions. (Foucault, 1991a: 58)

This is a characteristically deterministic[2] view of human agency which is not entirely consistent with Foucault's own stated aim of finding out why one particular statement appeared rather than another (p. 27), implying that things could be different.

On the other hand, Foucault's method of analysis "purged of all anthropologism" (p. 16) and "cleansed of all transcendental narcissism" (p. 203), has, according to Foucault, an ultimate aim centerd on and justified by the condition of the subject. As Foucault concluded in the *Archaeology,*

On the contrary, my aim was to show . . . how it was possible for men, within the same discursive practice, to speak of different objects, to have contrary opinions, and to make contradictory choices . . . I wanted not to exclude the problem of the subject, but to define the positions that the subject could occupy in the diversity of discourse. (200)

Viewed in Ricoeurian terms, Foucault evokes interpretive "understanding," ideally deriving from structuralist "explanation" (Ricoeur, 1991: 121–122), said by Ricoeur to be the ultimate aim of structural analysis. Even though Foucault has repeatedly denied the structuralist or neostructuralist labels, several theorists (e.g. Frank, 1992; Freundlieb, 1994; Habermas, 1987) have insisted with them. Foucault's theoretical approach does echo that of Saussure (1983) in several respects, for example, the search for laws, rules, or structures (general for Saussure but local for Foucault); the accordance of methodological and substantive primacy to such structures; and the decentring of the subject.

However, Foucault's aim toward understanding is inconsistent with his overall theoretical scheme because the critical potential of such understanding, the capacity to make a difference, is curtailed in

---

[2] We employ the concept of determinism to imply the absence of agency as defined earlier. Determinism, identified with structural approaches in sociology, advances a view that events and actions do not derive from agency and choice, or the capacity to have acted differently; rather they are brought about by preexisting and all-embracing institutional structures that create constraining conditions within which events take place.

his archaeological conceptual system, by an overall deterministic view of human nature, which is at the mercy of discursive structures where human subjectivity *must* be located.

Foucault's approach could alternatively be seen as a form of institutional analysis, which can legitimately place in suspension the knowledgeability, skills, or awareness of social actors and study institutions as chronically reproduced rules and resources (Giddens, 1984), but only if such qualities of actors were accepted as relevant to the constitution of social life. The *Archaeology* does not lend itself to such a reading.

In concluding his discussion of the statement, Foucault defined the statement as

a function of existence that properly belongs to signs and on the basis of which *one may then decide, through analysis or intuition, whether or not they make sense.*   (86, our emphasis)

Considering this definition, a further issue arises by enquiring how can Foucault's method, whose author has carefully avoided all direct references to human agency and openly declared his dislike for interpretation (p. 202), appeal to agents' common sense for the identification of the cornerstone of the conceptual system developed, "the statement"? Why appeal to agents' reason, common sense, or intuition at crucial points of developing a conceptual system while denouncing "the speaking subject, or the author of the text, in short, all anthropological categories?" (p. 30) Why give the subject primacy at certain parts of the discourse and keep it into oblivion in the rest?

Foucault's archaeological project suffers from a methodological bias. Foucault placed into suspension all accepted unities including all anthropological categories such as the subject *"in the name of methodological rigour"* (p. 22, our emphasis). To attempt to understand the move in the history of ideas without reference whatsoever to human agents is a major demerit because of at least three reasons: first, it is agents who act and not discourses; second, human actions are influenced but not determined by anterior structures; and third, the effects of discourses on the world necessarily occur through the cognitive interface (van Dijk, 1993), which is no longer conceived as the black box of behaviorism, but as constituted of the active faculties of agents who interpret, sustain, or change social reality through interpretation and symbolic interaction (Blumer, 1969).

To suspend the relevance of human agency to the historical movements of systems of thought is to allow a methodological choice which should have been contingent on the ontology of the entities under investigation to imply debatable assumptions about this ontology (i.e. the human agency is subordinated or irrelevant to the historical movement of systems of thought and it is located in and determined by structures of discourse). Such a suspension of the relevance of agency might have been justifiable if the method allowed for the possibility of subsequent reintegration of agency, which is unfortunately not the case in Foucault's archaeological work. By placing into suspension the subject for the sake of methodological rigour, Foucault has in effect constructed a flawed methodology because substantive ontological assumptions are implicitly made under the guise of method.

A similar objection was made by Bourdieu (1992) to the structuralist separation of *langue* and *parole*. Bourdieu argued that this distinction, while at the surface methodological, has substantive implications in that it leads linguists to "take for granted an object domain which is in fact the product of a complex set of social, historical and political conditions of formation" (1992: 5).

Discursive Change, Strategic Choice, and the Role of the Subject

To understand discursive change, Foucault suggested that one has to analyze transformations in relationships between elements within discourses, between discourses, and outside discourses (Foucault, 1991a: 56–58). In the *Archaeology*, he further maintained that discourses can have various "degree[s] and form of permeability" (p. 167) and that the rules of formation can have various degrees of specificity and generality (p. 168). Accordingly, there may be changes at several levels within discursive formations:

the level of the statements themselves . . . the level of the appearance of objects, types of enunciation, concepts, strategic choices . . . the level of derivation of new rules of formation on the basis of rules that are already in operation . . . . Lastly, a fourth level, at which the substitution of one discursive formation for another takes place. (171)

However, these transformations are not seen as a consequence of, or influenced by, human agency, but instead as a determining factor of agency. Changes in discursive formations themselves provide a "new position and role occupied by the speaking subject in discourse" (Foucault, 1991a: 56).

The social construction of reality — and therefore transformations of such reality — is largely dependent on the discursive construction of objects (Berger and Luckmann, 1966). The construction of objects in Foucault's conceptual system, however, is *determined* by "a group of rules . . . [which] . . . define the dumb existence of a reality . . . the ordering of objects" (p. 49) and not by human agency. In the same way that speech in Saussure's (1983) structuralism is said to depend on a preexisting linguistic system, the positions of Foucault's subjects are said to depend on preexisting discursive formations. Although (or perhaps because) Saussure's ideas were not intended to explain social change, however, theoretical schemes employing structuralist assumptions about linguistic systems and applying them by analogy to social systems with the aim of attempting to account for social change are bound to run into conceptual difficulties.

A further issue arises by the employment by Foucault of terms such as "strategic choices." In the *Archaeology*, after the discussion of the formation of strategies Foucault concludes that

one must not relate the formation of theoretical choices either to a fundamental *project* or to the secondary play of *opinions*

(70, emphases in original)

thus emptying the idea of strategic choice of its proper meaning. This can be seen as self-contradictory, as the term choice logically implies an agent able to exercise it, and who has more than one option open to them as Foucault himself later argued in his genealogical writings, "power is exercised only over free subjects, and only insofar as they are free"; (Foucault, 1983: 221). Similarly, the term strategy implies a human agent or group of agents (the strategists) who make strategic choices. In Foucault's archaeological discourse, strategies exist without the subject-strategist (Foucault, 1980c: 202), governed by "a principle of determination" (p. 67), and choice is itself determined by anterior rules and laws of discursive formations.

When Foucault was later asked how he could talk about a strategy without the subject, he outlined his conception of strategies as already solidified, institutionalized social arrangements, supported by particular discourses, where it is no longer possible to identify specific individuals who conceived of them (Foucault, 1980c: 203). The continued existence of institutionalized arrangements, however, relies on their daily instantiation in social practices, by agents who are able, to varying degrees, to choose to act otherwise (Giddens, 1984). The notion of agency is thus not foreign or contradictory, but rather integral to an understanding of strategies as solidified institutional arrangements.

The overall deterministic character of Foucault's conceptual system in the *Archaeology* therefore compromises its critical potential, as demystification is not complemented with the capacity of human agents to make a difference and for such potential to be actualized.

Rules and Laws of Discursive Formations

At several points in the *Archaeology*, Foucault posits preexisting rules and laws which govern discourses. By rules he refers to rules of formation, being "conditions of existence . . . in a given discursive formation" (p. 38). These conditions of existence are said to bear on objects, enunciative modalities, concepts, and strategies. For example, referring to objects of discourse, Foucault asks: "What has *ruled their existence* as objects of discourse?" (p. 41, our emphasis). Referring to enunciative modalities: ". . . we must first discover the *laws operating behind all these diverse statements*, and the place from which they come" (p. 50, our emphasis). Referring to the formation of concepts: "Could a *law* not be found that can *account for* the successive or simultaneous emergence of disparate concepts?" (p. 56, our emphases). Foucault's search for deterministic, behind-the-scenes, and all-embracing rules is made apparent here. Human agency has no part to play in this conceptual scheme.

The conception of rules in other theoretical schemes, for example, structuration theory (Giddens, 1984), on the other hand, presupposes the existence of human agency. Giddens views rules as "techniques or generalizable procedures applied in the enactment/reproduction of social practices," which cannot be conceptualized apart from resources, the constitution of meaning, the sanctioning of modes of social conduct, or the acting agents themselves (1984: 18–21). In this sense social "practices" derive from "practical consciousness," what actors know or believe about social conditions and the conditions of their own actions, but cannot necessarily express discursively.

For Foucault, knowledge does not reside in human agents but is a "group of elements formed in a regular manner by a discursive practice" (p. 182). Foucault's "anonymous, historical" (p. 117) rules *are* the anterior system of discursive relations (p. 74) and do not reside in human conduct and human memory — but they are nevertheless seen as determining it. Discourse is "a practice with its own forms of sequence and succession" (p. 169). But as Habermas (1987) has observed, if Foucault's rules govern the conditions of possibility of a discourse as well as its actual functioning in practice, this is a conceptual contradiction since

there are no rules that could govern their own application. A rule-governed discourse cannot itself govern the context in which it is implicated.

(1987: 268)

Brown and Cousins (1994) emphasize the ambiguity of Foucault's use of rules and the implications of this ambiguity for the status of the concept of discursive formation:

. . .the question must remain. What are these rules and how do they function? . . . without the regularity of statements it would be impossible to cohere a discursive formation into a definite identity, even while stressing that this "identity" is composed of divisions and differentiations. But this loads the concept of rule with so many disqualifications that it is difficult to see how Foucault's tree of derivation can permit the specification of a regularity. It has not so many things that it is difficult to see what it is. This difficulty is compounded by the fact that the rule functions in three different ways.. . . . Possibility, regulation and regularity all tend to be run together in the service of protecting the discursive formation. It begins to seem that it is the very concept of discursive formation which is at risk . . . .

(1994: 198–199)

Foucault conceives of rules and laws that *determine* human conduct *unidirectionally*, human agents having no hand in influencing the development of the rules, and which are entirely distinct from human consciousness. Foucault's archaeological work has confounded the logical necessity that subjects necessarily speak from within given social and discursive structures, with the proposition that the content of their discourse (and their reason) is determined by such structures.

Foucault's emphasis on all - embracing rules and laws is a consequence of his concern with decentring the subject, an idea whose origins can be traced to Saussure's conception of language as a system of signs where the relation between the signifier and the signified is arbitrary, and where the meaning of signs derives from differences among them. Thus, according to Giddens, since the meaning of the sign "tree" is not the object tree, the "I" of the subject cannot refer to states of consciousness of that subject (Giddens, 1987: 87). This structuralist syllogism is not entirely valid, however, because it rests on an extreme interpretation of the supremacy of form over substance. However, difference logically presupposes substance, for if there was no substance there could be no difference — but the reverse is not true.

Discourse, Power, and the Subject in the Genealogical Period

. . . a whole number of interesting questions were provoked. These can all be summed up in two words: power and knowledge.   (Foucault, 1980b: 109)

In the Genealogical period, both Foucault's understanding of discourse and the analytical methods he espoused shifted markedly. Even though Foucault's concern with decentring the subject was common to both his Archaeological and Genealogical periods (Burrell, 1988: 229), there was a clear shift in later works to more pragmatic concerns with the effects of discourses on practices and how individuals construct their world, themes which largely found no place in the *Archaeology*. In this period, Foucault elaborated his views on power, politicized his views on knowledge and discourse by explicitly linking discourse to the "will to power," and saw knowledge not as a neutral force, but as one that was biased toward dominant interests.

Discourses as Manifestations of the Will to Power

Foucault signaled a move toward politicizing his views of discourse and knowledge when he argued that "selfish interest is radically posed as coming before knowledge, which it subordinates to its needs as a simple instrument" (1977a: 203). In this sense knowledge is not value neutral, but biased toward its producers and the interests it serves. In a conversation with Deleuze, Foucault then noted that "we continue to ignore the problem of power" (1977b: 212), so that "power remains a total enigma" that should nevertheless be further investigated (1977b: 213).

In his genealogical writings, Foucault challenged traditional views of power by suggesting that power is a property of social relations, woven into the fabric of society rather than simply a top–down force (Foucault, 1980b); the exercise of power consists of not simply forcing certain outcomes, but rather "guiding the possibility of conduct and putting in order the possible outcome" (Foucault, 1983: 221); power could only be exercised over free subjects, their freedom being a condition for the exercise of power as well as a limiting factor on its exercise; power influences and shapes subjectivity rather than being a force external to the subject; and power is positive and productive rather than simply repressive and constraining:

What makes power hold good, what makes it accepted, is simply the fact that it doesn't only weigh on us as a force that says no, but that it traverses and produces things, it induces pleasure, forms knowledge, produces discourse. It needs to be considered as a productive network which runs through the whole social body, much more than as a negative instance whose function is repression.   (Foucault, 1980b: 119)

Foucault suggested that power should be studied through examination of "forms of resistance against different forms of power" (Foucault, 1983: 211), through analysis of struggles. One can explore power in action by focusing on "power strategies," or "the totality of the means put into operation to implement power effectively or to maintain it" (Foucault, 1983: 225). Foucault clarified his view of how power is woven into the social nexus by making an analytical distinction between

power relations, relationships of communication, [and] objective capacities . . . it is a question of three types of relationships which in fact always overlap one another, support one another reciprocally, and use each other mutually as means to an end.   (Foucault, 1983: 218).

Foucault's genealogical thinking on discourse has thus sharply moved to concerns with power–knowledge links where discourses are manifestations of the "will to power":

We should admit rather that power produces knowledge . . . that power and knowledge directly imply one another, that there is no power relation without the correlative constitution of a field of knowledge, nor any knowledge that does not presuppose and constitute at the same time power relations.   (Foucault, 1977c: 27)

Foucault was emphatic on how discourses can serve the interests of power:

relations of power cannot themselves be established, consolidated nor implemented without the production, accumulation, circulation and functioning of a discourse . . . we are subjected to the production of truth through power and we cannot exercise power except through the production of truth. (Foucault, 1980a: 93).

Discourse was still constructive of the subjects it addressed, but in doing so it now had a surreptitious intent: to align itself with dominant interests through the production of loaded truths, to legitimize certain practices that promote these interests, and marginalize other practices and voices that can challenge established interests. In Foucault's own words:

If I have studied practices . . . it was in order to study this interplay between a code, which rules ways of doing things . . . and a production of true discourses which serve to found, justify and provide reasons and principles for these ways of doing things. To put the matter clearly: my problem is to see how men govern (themselves and others) by the production of truth . . . .
(Foucault, 1980a: 79)

The Subject Becomes Visible but Still Without an Explicit Theory of Agency

Our objective . . . was to initiate a series of individual analyses that will gradually form a "morphology of the will to knowledge." (. . .) We can indicate in a very general way the direction in which this study should proceed: establishing a distinction between knowledge and the rules necessary to its acquisition; the difference between the will to knowledge and the will to truth; [and] the position of the subject and subjects in relation to this will. (Foucault, 1977a: 199, 201)

This extract from a course description of Foucault's first year (1970–1971) at the *Collège de France* symbolized the dividing line between the Archaeological and Genealogical periods. A "morphology of the will," or genealogy, enabled Foucault to differentiate as well as make connections between the "will to knowledge" and the "will to truth." Foucault's shift of attention to the will in the Genealogical period enables a theorization of both the position of the subject (i.e. the experience of subjectivity and subjectivization) and a non-reduction of knowledge to the subjective "agent" since the will is both "anonymous, polymorphous, susceptible to regular transformations and determined by the play of identifiable dependencies" (Foucault, 1977a: 200–201).

In the Genealogical period, therefore, Foucault's views and methods became more subject-friendly in that they allowed for, and even encouraged, investigation at the level of meaning rather than at the level of impersonal and amorphous structures. In *Governmentality* (1991c), for example, where Foucault explored the historical conditions of emergence of government, he interpreted the debates on Machiavelli's *The Prince* as concerned with articulating a rationality intrinsic to the art of government. He pointed to changes in the meaning of words in different eras; selected specific words and remarks and discussed their intertextual connections and connections with practices; analyzed certain metaphors used in the debates in terms of their implication complexes; and examined definitions of terms, their implications for practice, and their connections with interrelated domains. This is undoubtedly closer to hermeneutic textual analysis (Palmer, 1969) than the discourse analysis of the archaeologist, who

is going to change talkative documents into mute *monuments*, objects that have to be freed from their own context in order to become accessible to a structuralist description.   (Habermas, 1987: 250, emphasis in original)

Foucault said that he wished to "contribute to changing certain things in people's ways of perceiving and doing things" and asserted, in an unprecedented manner, that "the problem, you see, is one for *the subject who acts*" (1991b: 83–84, our emphasis). He explicitly connected discourses with "the effects in the real to which they are linked" (1991b: 85). In this position, the cloak of determinism is lifted, and subjects, though still influenced by discourses, can also be seen as producers of such discourses.

Even here, however, Foucault advances a "theory of subjectivity which leaves out the subject" in the sense that explanation at the level of the subject is generally avoided (Newton, 1994), and an explicit theory of agency is not developed or proposed. There is no account of how, for example, individuals choose where to position themselves in relation to discourses, or how they can actively negotiate with, manipulate, or employ discursive practices for various ends (Newton, 1998).

Foucault, indeed, insisted that genealogy would still not need to make explicit reference to the subject:

this is what I would call genealogy, that is, a form of history which can account for the constitution of knowledges, discourses, domains of objects, etc., without having to make reference to a subject which is either transcendental in relation to the field of events or runs in its empty sameness throughout the course of history. (Foucault, 1977c: 117)

Analyzing Discourse: Implications for Discourse and Organization Scholars

In spite of all the critiques, both the conceptual system and the analytical directions espoused by Foucault in his Archaeological and Genealogical periods can contribute substantially to discourse analyses. Useful contributions from the Archaeological period include Foucault's view of discourses as groups of statements belonging to discursive formations that should be analyzed, particularly in terms of intradiscursive, interdiscursive, and extradiscursive dimensions; discourses as spaces of multiple dissensions; discourses as totalities determining subject positions and constituting objects; discourses as historical–institutional practices obeying certain rules; and finally discourses as practices specified in archives.

From the Genealogical period, useful contributions include Foucault's concept of discourses as manifestations of the will to power, linked to practices and institutions; discourses as producing regimes of truth that can be analyzed at the levels of meaning and subjectivity; and finally his emphasis on extensive analysis of specific textual fragments aimed at understanding their effects on social meanings and practices.

We employ Phillips and Hardy's (2002) analytical framework of organizational discourse approaches to discuss Foucault's potential contributions to organizational discourse. The horizontal axis in this framework relates to the extent to which the analysis emphasizes the processual, socially constructed nature of reality and the contribution of discourse to this process, or has a critical slant, focusing on exposing and demystifying the role of power and domination and its effects on social practices, as embodied in discourse systems. The vertical axis relates to whether the analysis focuses on the detailed study of linguistic microfeatures of the text, without much attention to context, or on the other hand pays significant attention to textual context (including proximate or distal contexts) and the effects of the text on the context. As the authors' note, these are relative and not absolute points of emphasis, since well-conducted studies of discourse will be sensitive to some degree to both text and context as well as to discursive social reality construction and the role of power. However, practical considerations of conducting empirical discourse analysis mean that researchers have to make choices along these and other dimensions.

If we locate these Foucauldian conceptual and analytical directions on Phillips and Hardy's (2002) framework, and bearing in mind that these axes represent relative rather than absolute points of emphasis, we can see that the four approaches could find potentially insightful conceptual resources in Foucault's ouvre, as Table 4.1 shows.

Critical discourse analyses have drawn heavily on Foucault, particularly the assumptions that discourses can have potent effects on the constitution of subjectivities and objects, originally advanced in the *Archaeology*, as well as the view of discourses as manifestations of the will to power linked to practices and institutions, emphasized in Genealogical writings.

Critical linguistic analyses, focusing on in-depth analysis of particular textual features and their potential links to power configurations could draw further from Foucault, in particular, on his Archaeological concepts of discourses as spaces of multiple dissensions, and the need to focus relations both within a text, across texts and between texts and extratextual formations. A focus on discourses as spaces of multiple dissensions would sensitize critical linguistic analyses further to the plurivocality and potential internal contradictions within discourses deemed on the surface to be unitary or uniform (a concern displayed in deconstruction, but drawing instead on Derrida's work—Kilduff, 1993). A conscious extension of focus from intradiscursive to inter- and extra discursive features, in addition, would extend the usual emphasis of such analyses from intratextual to intertextual and contextual concerns.

Social linguistic and interpretive structuralist analyses on the other hand have not yet drawn significantly on Foucauldian writings. We suggest that social linguistic analyses could benefit from Foucault's Archaeological conception of discourses as practices specified in

Table 4.1. Potential Focauldian Contributions to Organizational Discourse Analysis

Context	
Interpretive Structuralism	Critical Discourse Analysis
• Discourses as historical–institutional practices obeying certain rules (Archaeology)	• Discourses as totalities determing subject positions and constituting objects (Archaeology)
• Discourses as producing regimes of truth that can be analyzed at the levels of meaning and subjectivity (Genealogy)	• Discourses as manifestations of the will to power, linked to practices and institutions (Genealogy)
Constructivist	**Critical**
• Discourses as practices specified in archives (Archaeology)	• Discourses as spaces of multiple dissentions (Archaelogy)
• Extensive analysis of specific textual fragments aimed at understanding their effects on social meaning and practices (Genealogy)	• Discourses as groups of statements belonging to a discursive formation: intradiscursive, interdisccursive, and extradiscursive formations should be analyzed (Archaeology)
Social Liniguistic Analysis	Critical Liniguistic Analysis
Text	

archives, as well as the Genealogical injunction to focus on specific textual fragments with the aim of understanding their effects on social practices and subjectivity. These conceptual and analytical directions would further sensitize social linguistic analyses toward exploring the particular social meanings and practices linked to, and enabled by, discourses, thereby resulting in more holistic forms of analysis.

Finally, with regard to interpretive structuralist approaches, we suggest that such analyses could benefit from Foucault's Archaeological conception of discourses as historical–institutional practices obeying certain rules, and his Genealogical conception of discourses as producing regimes of truth, that can be analyzed at the levels of meaning and subjectivity. Interpretive structuralist approaches consciously drawing from such Foucauldian concepts would be further sensitized to the longer term, institutional effects of discourses; as well as to a deeper focus on the levels of meaning and subjectivity linked to discourses.

Perhaps paradoxically, the main effect of consciously drawing on Foucauldian concepts would be to lead to a more holistic analysis and to a difficulty in locating a study within an approach or paradigm; something that Foucault would welcome, given his refusal to accept any labels that others have attributed to his work. If we attempt, for example, to outline Foucault's multidimensional view of discourses as it has manifested in the Archaeological and Genealogical periods, we could perhaps say that discourses are groups of statements that constitute discursive formations, which are historical, contextually embedded in shifting socioeconomic contexts with which they have a dialectical relationship, are characterized by both internal coherence and inconsistencies and contradictions, can construct objects and subjectivities, and are linked to power relations and regimes of truth. These concepts can be seen as a treasure trove of conceptual resources on which to draw a testament of which is Foucault's significant influence in a variety of scholarly fields.

Some words of caution, however, are in order. In spite of the richness of Foucault's work, management and organizational discourse theorists drawing from it should be cautious of its assumptions and limits. As discussed earlier, these relate, in particular, to Foucault's view of discourse as deterministic of subjects rather than potentially as a resource that could be employed to meet their ends; his interpretation of concepts such as discursive change and strategic choice as predetermined outcomes or institutional–historical configurations rather as situations where outcomes could be different; and his view of discursive rules as independent and all-embracing laws of discursive formations rather than as structuring patterns intimately linked to the agents' actions.

For example, Foucault's view of discourses as rule-bound practices that construct objects and regimes of truth can be useful in sensitizing discourse theorists to the fact that discursive formations are structured or patterned by intertextual, longitudinal, constructive, transsituational, and implicit elements (such as root metaphors or enthymemes), whose identification is crucial in shedding light on the nature of the discursive formation itself, as well as its effects on social practices and social reality (Heracleous and Hendry, 2000). However, attention is warranted here, since in Foucault's *Archaeology* such rules are seen as laws that unidirectionally determine subject positions and subject functions, and importance of agency, as the capacity to act otherwise and make a difference, is denied. In this perspective, subjects are trapped in the webs of discourse. An interpretation of discourses as rule-bound practices would limit the analytical fruitfulness of the concept, unless such rules are viewed from a theoretical perspective that recognizes the importance of agency, and that rules are kept viable only insofar as they are instantiated and reaffirmed in daily practices of agents, as argued by structuration theory (Giddens, 1984).

Foucault's deterministic assumptions as explicated in the *Archaeology* can be seen as limiting his conceptions of discourse by locating them in the domain of explanation, where the theoretical scheme does not allow for the actualization of the critical potential of understanding which ideally follows from explanation (Ricoeur, 1991). Discourse analyses drawing from Foucault's work have to recognize the relevance of human agency (even if it is bracketed out for structural analysis) as well as avoid the reductionism of causation to anonymous rules and laws whose own ontological status is unclear and appear in the conceptual system as *causa sui*.

Foucault's Genealogical writings, even though they still lack an adequate conception of agency, do open up new avenues for enquiry through the explicit connection of discourse and power, a view of knowledge as an interest-laden force, and a subtle and elaborate conception of the nature of power. In particular, Foucault's suggestion of complexes created through intimate connections between power, discourse, and social practices, and his injunction to study their interrelationships (Foucault, 1983), opens up discourse analysis as a critical operation that can make a difference by delegitimizing and demystifying dominant discourses aligned with the centers of power. At the same time, his view of power, as not necessarily oppressive but also positive and productive, differentiates Foucault's position from the Marxist legacy and offers a perspective that is more free from evaluative loading, and able to engage more inductively with the particular features of the discursive formation and institutions under investigation. The two periods can be seen as complementary in the development of insightful and theoretically robust analyses that are more holistic, and contextually and temporally sensitive, in this way helping to address calls for analyses that go beyond the raw material of the text (Cicourel, 1981; Fairclough, 1992).

In spite of the significant departures in thinking in the Genealogical period, there are certainly certain continuities in Foucault's work. For example, Foucault's concern with decentring the subject continued throughout his Genealogical writings (Burrell, 1988) even though a tension is obvious. Foucault realizes that his methodological choice of decentring the subject compromises the potential application of Archaeological findings to the domains of social practices; in Genealogical writings he occasionally cannot resist advocating analysis at the levels of action and meaning, and even positing the acting subject as the *raison d'être* of his investigations (Foucault, 1991b). Foucault's focus on historicity (the embeddedness of discourses, practices, and institutions, in particular historical trajectories that pattern their nature), accompanied with a rejection of modernist notions of continuous progress toward a final state of enlightenment, are further points of continuity throughout his writings.

Both the Archaeological and the Genealogical periods, therefore, have fruitful insights to offer to discourse scholars, if employed critically, which is of course what Foucault would have wanted. Perhaps it is fitting to conclude with Foucault's own view of continuities in his work in terms of archaeology as a method, and genealogy as enlightened action:

"Archaeology" would be the appropriate methodology of this analysis of local discursivities, and "genealogy" would be the tactics whereby, on the basis of the description of these local discursivities, the subjected knowledges which were thus released would be brought into play.

(Foucault, 1980a: 85)

References

Berger, P. and Luckmann, T. 1966. *The social construction of reality.* London: Penguin.

Blumer, H. 1969. *Symbolic interactionism: Perspective and method.* Berkeley, CA: University of California Press.

Bourdieu, P. 1992. *Language and symbolic power.* Cambridge, MA: Polity.

Brown, B. and Cousins, M. 1994. The linguistic fault: The case of Foucault's Archaeology. In B. Smart (ed.), *Michel Foucault: Critical assessments*: 186–208. London: Routledge.

Burrell, G. 1988. Modernism, post modernism and organizational analysis 2: The contribution of Michel Foucault. *Organization Studies*, 9 (2): 221–235.

Chan, A. 2000. Redirecting critique in postmodern organization studies: The perspective of Foucault. *Organization Studies*, 21 (6): 1059–1075.

Cicourel, A. V. 1981. Three models of discourse analysis: The role of social structure. *Discourse Processes*, 3: 101–131.

van Dijk, T. A. 1993. Principles of critical discourse analysis. *Discourse and Society*, 4: 249–283.

Dreyfus, H. L. and Rabinow, P. 1983. *Michel Foucault: Beyond structuralism and hermeneutics*. Chicago, IL: University of Chicago Press.

Fairclough, N. 1992. Discourse and text: Linguistic and intertextual analysis within discourse analysis'. *Discourse & Society*, 3: 193–217.

Foucault, M. 1972. *The archaeology of knowledge*. London: Routledge.

1977a. History of systems of thought [1970]. In D. Bouchard (ed.), *Language, counter-memory, practice: Selected essays and interviews by Michel Foucault*: 199–204. Ithaca, NY: Cornell University Press.

1977b. Intellectuals and power [1972]. In D. Bouchard (ed.), *Language, counter-memory, practice: Selected essays and interviews by Michel Foucault*: 205–217. Ithaca, NY: Cornell University Press.

1977c. *Discipline and punish*. London: Penguin.

1980a. Two lectures [1977]. In C. Gordon (ed.), *Power/Knowledge: Selected interviews and other writings 1972–1977*: 78–108. New York, NY: Pantheon.

1980b. Truth and power [1977]. In C. Gordon (ed.), *Power/Knowledge: Selected interviews and other writings 1972–1977*: 109–133. New York, NY: Pantheon.

1980c. The confession of the flesh [1977]. In C. Gordon (ed.), *Power/Knowledge: Selected interviews and other writings 1972–1977*: 194–228. New York, NY: Pantheon.

1983. The subject and power [1982]. In H. L. Dreyfus and P. Rabinow (eds.), *Michel Foucault: Beyond structuralism and hermeneutics*: 208–226. Chicago, IL: University of Chicago Press.

1991a. Politics and the study of discourse [1968]. In G. Burchell, C. Gordon, and P. Miller (eds.), *The Foucault effect: Studies in governmentality*: 53–72. Hemel Hempstead: Harvester Wheatsheaf.

1991b. Questions of method [1980]. In G. Burchell, C. Gordon, and P. Miller (eds.), *The Foucault effect: Studies in governmentality*: 73–86. Hemel Hempstead: Harvester Wheatsheaf.

1991c. Governmentality [1978]. In G. Burchell, C. Gordon, and P. Miller (eds.), *The Foucault effect: Studies in governmentality*: 87–104. Hemel Hempstead: Harvester Wheatsheaf.

Frank, M. 1992. On Foucault's concept of discourse. *Michel Foucault: Philosopher*. T. Armstrong (trans.): 99–116. Hemel Hempstead: Harvester Wheatsheaf.

Freundlieb, D. 1994. Foucault's theory of discourse and human agency. In C. Jones and R. Porter (eds.), *Reassessing Foucault: Power, medicine and the body*: 152–180. London: Routledge.

Giddens, A. 1984. *The constitution of society*. Cambridge, MA: Polity.
1987. *Social theory and modern sociology*. Cambridge, MA: Polity.

Habermas, J. 1987. *The philosophical discourse of modernity*. Oxford: Oxford University Press.

Heracleous, L. 2000. *Reflections on Foucault's conceptions of discourse*. Paper presented at the 4th International Conference on Organizational Discourse, King's College London, July 26–28.

Heracleous, L. and Chan, A. 2005. Foucault's conceptions of discourse in the Archaeological and Genealogical periods. An interpretation, critique, and analytical implications. Working paper.

Heracleous, L. and Hendry, J. 2000. Discourse and the study of organization: Toward a structurational perspective. *Human Relations*, 53: 1251–1286.

Hopwood, A. 1987. The archaeology of accounting systems. *Accounting, Organizations and Society*, 12 (3): 207–234.

Hoskin, K. and Macve, R. 1986. Accounting and the examination: A genealogy of disciplinary power. *Accounting, Organizations and Society*, 11 (2): 105–136.

Jacobs, C. and Heracleous, L. 2001. Seeing without being seen: Towards an archaeology of controlling science. *International Studies of Management and Organization*, 31 (3): 113.

Kermode, F. 1973. Crisis critic: Review of the archaeology of knowledge and the discourse on language. *New York Review of Books*, 17 (May): 36–39.

Kilduff, M. 1993. Deconstructing organizations. *Academy of Management Review*, 18: 13–27.

Knights, D. and Morgan, G. 1991. Corporate strategy, organizations and subjectivity: A critique. *Organization Studies*, 12 (2): 251–273.
1995. Strategy under the microscope: Strategic management and IT in financial services. *Journal of Management Studies*, 32 (2): 191–214.

Knights, D. and Willmott, H. 1989. Power and subjectivity at work: From degradation to subjugation in social relations. *Sociology*, 23 (4): 535–558.

McKinlay, A. and Starkey, K. (eds.), 1998. *Foucault, management and organization theory: From panopticon to technologies of self*. London: Sage.

Mumby, D. and Stohl, C. 1991. Power and discourse in organization studies: Absence and the dialectic of control. *Discourse and Society*, 2 (3): 313–332.

Newton, T. 1994. Discourse and agency: The example of personnel psychology and assessment centres. *Organization Studies,* 15 (6): 879–902.

1998. Theorizing subjectivity in organizations: The failure of Foucauldian studies? *Organization Studies,* 19 (3): 415–447.

Palmer, R. 1969. *Hermeneutics.* Evanston, IL: Northwestern University Press.

Phillips, N. and Hardy, C. 1997. Managing multiple identities: Discourse, legitimacy and resources in the UK refugee system. *Organization,* 4: 159–186.

2002. *Discourse analysis: Investigating processes of social construction.* London: Sage.

Reed, M. 1998. Organizational analysis as discourse analysis: A critique. In D. Grant, T. Keenoy, and C. Oswick (eds.), *Discourse and organization:* 193–213. London: Sage.

Ricoeur, P. 1991. *From text to action.* Evanston, IL: Northwestern University Press.

Rouleau, L. and Seguin, F. 1995. Strategy and organization theories: Common forms of discourse. *Journal of Management Studies,* 32: 101–117.

Said, E. 1974. An ethics of language: Review of Michel Foucault's the archaeology of knowledge and the discourse on language. *Diacritics,* 4: 28–37.

de Saussure, F. 1983. *Course in general linguistics.* London: Duckworth.

Townley, B. 1993a. Foucault, power/knowledge, and its relevance for human resource management. *Academy of Management Review,* 18 (3): 518–545.

1993b. Performance appraisal and the emergence of management. *Journal of Management Studies,* 30 (2): 221–238.

5 | A Structurational Approach to Discourse[1]

As noted in chapter 1, interpretive and functional conceptions of discourse tend to privilege the action level of analysis, whereas critical approaches tend to privilege the structural level, each conception illuminating certain aspects of discourse but potentially downplaying other dimensions of the fundamental social processes involved. As a basis for a more encompassing understanding of organizational discourse, this chapter draws on the work of Anthony Giddens to propose a structurational conceptualization. In this approach, discourse is viewed as a duality of communicative actions and deep structures, recursively linked through the modality of actors' interpretive schemes. The chapter concludes by exploring some of the implications of this conceptualization for theory and for the methodology of organizational discourse analysis.

Giddens's Theoretical Project and its Use in Organizational Research

Giddens's structuration theory has had a significant and growing influence in organizational research (e.g. Barley and Tolbert, 1997; Heracleous, 2006; Weaver and Gioia, 1994; Whittington, 1992). Giddens's work aims to transcend persistent dualisms in social theory, especially that of structure and action, proposing among other influential concepts, the notion of "duality of structure," fostering a view of structure as inherent in agents' (recursive) actions rather than as a distant, external, determining factor. From the perspective of the duality of structure, daily practices (including communicative actions) are manifestations of deeper structures of signification, domination, and legitimation. These structures are not seen as separate from action

---

[1] This chaper is based on Heracleous and Hendry (2000).

but are instantiated, reproduced, and can thus potentially be changed through daily practices (Giddens, 1984: 36).

In this sense, social systems thus do not "have" structures as ontological entities in themselves, but rather exhibit structural properties through the recursiveness of action forming social practices (Giddens, 1984). Similarly, discourses do not have structures as separate ontological entities but exhibit structural properties that are largely implicit, intertextual, transtemporal, and transsituational (Heracleous and Hendry, 2000). In the same way that structural properties of social systems are manifested and instantiated as social practices, the structural properties of discourses are manifested and instantiated in daily communicative actions and texts.

Giddens's structuration theory has been criticized by numerous scholars from both structural and agency perspectives as reducing one perspective to the other or conflating rather than bridging or integrating the two (e.g. Byrne, 1991; Callinicos, 1985; Held and Thompson, 1989; Layder, 1987; Willmott, 1986). In spite of these critiques, the structurational approach is arguably one of the most promising avenues available in its ability to provide a useful metatheoretical framework for developing a view of discourse that addresses both the action and structure levels as well as the modality of interpretive schemes.[2]

Giddens's work can be located in the theoretical tradition that aims to transcend the structure/agency dualism and to reconcile interpretive and functionalist sociological views, in common with the work of such theorists as Bhaskar (1979), Bourdieu (1977), and Silverman (1970). Each of these approaches is different, but they all share the concern of bridging the gap between action and structure in social life, the recognition that in the study of social systems, understanding individual actors' meaning is of paramount importance, and the proposition that meaning, and therefore social reality, is constructed, sustained, and changed through social interaction.

---

[2] Giddens's own response to many of the critiques suggests that structuration theory can be useful as a metatheoretical framework sensitizing researchers to important dimensions of social life rather than forming a tight set of hypotheses to be tested or that are directly applicable to explaining specific fragments of empirical evidence (Giddens, 1984: 376; see also Weaver and Gioia, 1994).

A fundamental theme underlying Giddens's work is the rejection of a whole range of dualisms that have characterized social thought, especially the dualism of structure and agency, and the reformulation of such dualisms in terms of dualities. He sees interpretative sociologies as "strong on action but weak on structure," and functionalist and structuralist sociologies as "strong on structure but weak on action" (Giddens, 1993: 4). The concept of the duality of structure, central to Giddens's theoretical scheme, emphasizes that "social structure is both constituted *by* human agency and yet is at the same time the very *medium* of this constitution" (1993: 128–129, emphasis in original). Daily practices such as communicative actions are the main substantive form of the dimensions of the duality of structure, which is instantiated, reproduced, and potentially changed through such practices (Giddens, 1984: 36).[3] Daily practices are thus implicated in continuous processes of structuration, "the structuring of social relations across time and space" (1984: 376). From a methodological perspective, an adequate understanding of structurational processes entails in-depth involvement in the routinized, daily interactions of knowledgeable agents in order to discover the conditions influencing the continuity or change of social and organizational structures (1984: 25).

Structuration theory has been used both as a metatheory that can enable multiparadigmatic inquiry without resorting to paradigm incommensurability (Weaver and Gioia, 1994) and as a useful complement to institutional theory that can add a much-needed process perspective on the link between institutions and actions (Barley and Tolbert, 1997). It has also been applied to more specific areas, including the study of politics as an aspect of organizational culture (Riley, 1983), the development of a deeper understanding of the role of advanced information technologies in organizational change (DeSanctis and Poole, 1994), the expansion of the scope of management accounting research from a primarily technical focus to include sociopolitical issues (Macintosh and Scapens, 1990), and to the development of new perspectives in communication research such as the "genre" perspective (Orlikowski and Yates, 1994; Yates and Orlikowski, 1992).

---

[3] For useful outlines of the theory of structuration please see Bryant and Jary (1991), Thompson (1989), and Jones, (1999).

These applications of structuration theory have often generated lively responses and debates, from the initial response to Ranson, Hinings, and Greenwood (1980) by Willmott (1981), to the protracted exchange prompted by the Macintosh and Scapens (1990) work (Boland, 1993, 1996; Scapens and Macintosh, 1996). A consideration of the organizational literature that has utilized the theory of structuration for theory development and empirical analysis reveals considerable diversity in both interpretations and applications of the theory (Jones, 1999). At the risk of oversimplification of a complex set of concepts we can, however, say that a structurational view of organizations entails a focus on both observable action and the deeper structures that guide action; a recognition of their dynamic interrelation; a view of social structures as rules and resources drawn on in everyday interaction, shaping but not determining human agency; an understanding that structures can thus be reproduced or potentially changed through interaction and over time; and a treatment of people as active, knowledgeable agents who reflexively monitor their situation as opposed to being "structural dopes" determined by social structures.

Giddens on Discourse and Language

Giddens on Discourse

Although the concept of discourse has not played a central role in Giddens's work, it has arisen in at least three contexts. First, in the context of Giddens's distinction between "practical" and "discursive consciousness," discursive consciousness refers to what actors are able to say about social conditions and the conditions of their own actions. Discourse, accordingly, is "what actors are able to 'talk about' and in what manner or guise they are able to talk about it" (Giddens, 1979: 73). Second, in the context of Giddens's discussion of ideology and consciousness, discourse is seen as ideology in its most "conscious" and "superficial" form, involving the direct manipulation of communication by dominant classes to further their own interests (1979: 190–193). Finally, discourse plays a role in the social positioning of actors. According to Giddens, agents are positioned or situated in time-space as well as socially within a network of social relations. Their social position is constituted within structures of signification, domination, and legitimation, within which social interaction takes place. Giddens maintains that the knowledgeability incorporated in practical activities is a primary constitutive feature of the social world. Knowledge, in this context, is seen as accurate or valid awareness that exists at both the discursive and practical levels, and discourse is accordingly seen as a mode of articulation of such knowledge (Giddens, 1984: 83–92).

Giddens on Language

Giddens has outlined his views on language on several occasions. He holds a constructive view of language as not just a means of information exchange but as constitutive of social life (1984: xvi) through its nature as a medium of practical, recursive social activity (1993: 25). Language is thus a medium of not only communication but also characterization or typification (1993: 54). Giddens refers to language as an apt example of his concept of "duality of structure," which holds that social structures are both medium and outcome of human agency (1984). The rules of language are constantly evoked in the course of daily activities, and "enter into the structuring of the texture of everyday life" (1984: 22). But linguistic rules and language as a structure exist only insofar as they are manifested in daily communicative actions (1993: 129), and this use is enabled by the nature of language rules as interpretive schemes located in agents' practical consciousness (1984: 48).

Giddens's work stresses the context-dependence of practical activities, including the use of language: "context dependence . . . is aptly regarded as integral to the production or meaning in interaction, not as an embarrassment to formal analysis . . . . Interaction . . . is temporally and spatially situated" (1993: 111). As an example of context dependence in operation, Giddens suggests that we can only understand seeming contradictions in linguistic utterances, such as irony or sarcasm, through an awareness of their context (1993: 154–155).

Giddens's views on language also become apparent in his trenchant critique of the structuralist tradition,[4] as outlined in chapter 1.

---

[4] See particularly "Structuralism and the theory of the subject," in Giddens (1979: 9–48), and "Structuralism, post-structuralism and the production of culture" in Giddens (1987: 73–108). Even though there are important differences between the structuralist and poststructuralist traditions, Giddens's original critique has

Through this critique, Giddens emphasizes the need of considering the social–cultural context of texts in textual interpretation, that meaning arises not only from textual content but also from how the content relates to this context, a view of individuals as knowledgeable agents and competent users of language, and an emphasis on the importance of temporality in textual interpretation.[5]

Toward a Structurational View of Discourse

Although there are common threads in Giddens's views on discourse and language throughout his writings, he has not developed an integrated framework that addresses both the action and structure dimensions; this chapter proposes such a framework. In addition to structuration theory, we draw from hermeneutically oriented work within the fields of cultural anthropology (e.g. Bateson, 1972), ethnography (e.g. Frake, 1964, van Maanen, 1973), sociocognitive linguistics (e.g. van Dijk, 1988; McCann and Higgins, 1990; Saferstein, 1992), cognitive psychology (e.g. Moscovici, 1981; Rumelhart, 1984; Taylor and Crocker, 1981), organizational cognition (e.g. Gioia, 1986a,b; Weick, 1979), and interpretive sociology (e.g. Berger and Luckmann, 1966) as appropriate. In order to clarify certain theoretical aspects of the structurational view of discourse proposed, we also juxtapose some aspects of a structurational view of discourse with the views of structuralist and poststructuralist authors such as Barthes (1994) or Foucault (1972).

A Structurational View of Discourse

As noted earlier, in the same way that social systems do not have structures but exhibit structural properties (Giddens, 1984), discourses can also be seen as not having structures but as exhibiting structural properties that are implicit, intertextual, transtemporal, and

---

focused on issues that are arguably common in both traditions, for example, the privileging of written text to spoken discourse and the consequent neglect of textual context and human agency.

[5] Giddens has not given a systematic exposition of the relationship between the terms "language" and "discourse." As noted in chapter 1, the term language is used in this book to refer to the building blocks of texts, that are themselves the building blocks, and manifestations of discourses.

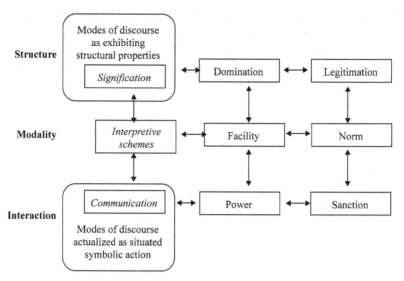

Figure 5.1. Discourse and structuration theory. Source: Adapted from Giddens (1984)

transsituational. As the structural properties of social systems are instantiated as social practices and memory traces orienting agents' conduct (1984: 17), so the structural properties of discourse are instantiated in social interaction at the communicative level through the modality of agents' interpretive schemes. The two levels of discursive structures and communicative action are thus analytically distinct but practically interrelated, as represented in Fig. 5.1, adapted from Giddens (1984: 29). For the purposes of this section, we bracket out structures of domination and legitimation and focus on the structures of signification, interpretive schemes, and communicative action, since these are the main elements of the structuration of social life most relevant to symbolic orders such as modes of discourse (1984: 33).

The communicative manifestations of structural features of discourse point to the simultaneously enabling and constraining nature of these features. Actors "know" in their "practical consciousness" (Giddens, 1984: 44) that specific modes of discourse must be employed in particular contexts in order for their opinions, ideas, or argumentations to be seen as legitimate and deserving of attention (Heracleous, 2006). Discursive structural features are thus used as a resource for effective argumentation which is characterized by a

Table 5.1. Features of the Communicative and Structural Levels of Discourse

Communicative Level		Structural Level
Intratextual		Intertextual
Specific point in time		Longitudinal
Functional		Constructive
Situational		Transcends the situation
Explicit		Implicit
	Common Features	
	Systematic	
	Contextually located	
	Linked to power relationships, ideologies, and institutions	

Source: Adapted from Heracleous and Hendry (2000).

"seeming" probability, what actors in a social context believe to be the case and not necessarily what is the case (cf. Aristotle, 1991).

The Communicative Level: Discourse as Situated Symbolic Action

From a structurational viewpoint, discourse at the communicative level is constituted of communicative acts, whose features are shown in Table 5.1. A communicative act is defined as an action "in which an actor's purpose, or one of an actor's purposes, is linked to the achievement of passing on information to others" (Giddens, 1993: 94; cf. Austin, 1961). From a structurational perspective, discourse, at this level, is communicative (inter)action which draws from structures of signification through actors' interpretive schemes (Giddens, 1984). In this sense, discourse as action arises out of the subjective meanings which individuals attach to situations and which orient their actions (Weber, 1991), as active agents pursuing their perceived interests in specific contexts (Blumer, 1970). The view of discourse as situated symbolic action assumes that utterances not only say things, but also do things; discourse is, thus, in a fundamental sense, action (Oswick, Keenoy, and Grant, 1997).

In structuralism meaning is said to derive from internal relations among signifiers (Saussure, 1983), and in poststructuralist approaches, such as the latter Barthes (1977: 155–164), it resides in intertextual networks and can be created and recreated by active experiencing of the text. From an interpretive viewpoint, however, which structuration theory adopts through its conceptualization of human agency as knowledgeable and reflective (Giddens, 1993), meaning derives from the interaction among signifiers within nested contexts, including social practices and agents' interpretations of signifiers: "The word is the *context* of the phoneme. But the word only exists as such—only has 'meaning'—in the larger context of the utterance, which again has meaning only in a relationship. This hierarchy of contexts within contexts is universal for the communicational (or 'emic') aspect of phenomena . . ." (Bateson, 1972, p. 408, emphasis in original). The contexts shaping the meaning of communicative actions include the semantic context (Eysenck, 1993; Rumelhart, 1984), the situational and organizational contexts (Donnellon, 1986; Goffman, 1972; Saferstein, 1992; Schultz, 1991), and the cultural/societal context (Hofstede, 1985).

Contrary to (post)structuralist thought, from a structurational viewpoint, signification is thus not the outcome of relations in the intra- or intertextual domains but arises from the interaction of these domains with settings of practical action (Giddens, 1987: 99). Giddens's approach to understanding human agency, accordingly, gives primary importance to such features as "practical consciousness" (what actors know or believe about social conditions and their own actions but cannot express discursively) and the contextuality of action (the situated character of interaction in time-space), features which are absent or downplayed in structuralist accounts (1987: 98).

This situated character of communication has been emphasized by ethnographic research that has emphasized the cultural and situational determinants of communicative legitimacy or appropriateness (Frake, 1964; van Maanen, 1973; Malinowski, 1970). The symbolic nature of communication, in addition, has been elucidated by studies from a psycholinguistic perspective. In this view, ordinary argumentations and explanations are seen as speech actions that have their sociocognitive correlates, occur on the basis of shared represen- tations, and are active discursive constructions of reality (McCann and Higgins, 1990; Xu, 1992). From a structurational viewpoint, such underlying sociocultural beliefs and ideologies, as well as perceptions of communicative appropriateness, are not only mirrored but also constituted, reproduced, and potentially changed through communi- cative actions. A view of discourse as situated symbolic action is illustrated empirically in chapter 6.

The Structural Level: Discursive and Social Structures

The concept of "deep structures" is key to a fuller understanding of social and natural systems at various levels of analysis (Gersick, 1991; Light, 1979). Deep structures are stable, largely implicit, and conti- nually recurring processes and patterns that underlay and guide sur- face, observable events and actions. The interpretation and use of the concept of deep structures varies in different theoretical domains. In the domain of discourse, we have approached deep structures as persistent features of discourse which transcend individual texts, speakers or authors, situational contexts and communicative actions, and pervade bodies of communicative action as a whole and in the long term. Such structural features include central themes (Kets de Vries and Miller, 1987; Thachankary, 1992), root or generative meta- phors (Pondy, 1983; Schon, 1979), and rhetorical strategies in parti- cular social contexts (Hopkins and Reicher, 1997; Kamoche, 1995). These are structural features of discourse because they pertain to bodies of communicative actions or texts as a whole, persist over time, in a variety of situational contexts, and in communicative actions or texts produced by different actors. In addition, they are most often implicit as opposed to explicitly stated in texts and communicative actions, and are constructive of the subjects they are about, in line with a constructive view of language.

Finally, both communicative actions and discursive structures are systematic, contextually located, and linked to power relationships, ideologies, and institutions, although in different ways. Communi- cative actions and texts, for example, are systematic in that they obey linguistic rules and belong to a commonly accepted system of gram- mar within a community; discursive structures, on the other hand, are systematic in the sense that within local contexts of use characterized by distinct cultures and practices, they may exhibit features such as systematic cross-metaphor coherence (Lakoff and Johnson, 1980: 87–105), or thematic unity of what may at the surface appear as diverse and disconnected themes (Kets de Vries and Miller, 1987, Thachankary, 1992). Similarly, communicative actions and texts are located within embedded semantic, situational, organizational, and societal contexts, and discursive structures are, from a cognitive viewpoint, located in interpretive schemes which are themselves located contextually within other interpretive schemes, given the hierarchical structuring of cognition (Eysenck, 1993). Finally, features of communicative texts and actions, which support, perpetuate, or potentially challenge established ideologies and power relations, are the instantiations of deeper discursive structures pertaining to dominant elites or marginal groups (van Dijk, 1988); and in this sense both communicative actions and discursive structures are linked with wider social structures.

The nature of the linkages of discourse with wider social structures is important. In structuralist approaches such as Foucault's (1972), subjects' actions and even their reason are seen to be determined by anterior discursive structures. Our use of "structures" here is, however, a structurational and not a structuralist one. For Giddens, structures are the rules and resources that actors draw on in their daily practices. In this sense, structures have no existence other than their instantiation in action and as memory traces (or interpretive schemes) orienting agents' conduct (Giddens, 1984). From a structurational perspective, therefore, as discussed earlier, social structures and the discursive structures they are linked to are not separate from and determinative of human actions but are both the medium and the outcome of such actions (Giddens, 1984).

On one hand, discursive structures cannot be seen simply as the tools of intentional agents, since agency itself is influenced (but not determined) by these structures and the power–knowledge relationships and institutional structures with which they are bound up. On the other hand, discursive and social structures cannot be seen as fully determinative of individuals, who remain agents and could choose to do otherwise (Giddens, 1993: 81), taking within perceived constraints imposed by structures a potentially active, self-reflective role in the construction of their social realities.

Discourse and Interpretation

We draw from the field of social cognition to elucidate the interrelationship between discourse and interpretation. The key concept in this field is that of schema. Originally developed by Head (1926) and Bartlett (1932), this has since become a central construct of cognitive psychology (Rumelhart, 1984; Taylor and Crocker, 1981) and can be defined as "a cognitive structure that consists in part of the representation of some stimulus domain. The schema contains general knowledge about that domain, including a specification of the relationships among its attributes, as well as specific examples or instances of the stimulus domain" (Taylor and Crocker, 1981: 91). A schema can thus be seen as a psychological frame (Bateson, 1972: 186), providing the cognitive structuring necessary for actors to construct workable cognitive representations of the world and for consistency among cognitive elements and between these cognitive elements and actions (Festinger, 1959). Schemata can operate at various levels of detail or abstraction, and can be both evaluative, as in the case of attitudes, and descriptive. Schemata, therefore, have basic and vital functions in the interpretation of experience and indication of appropriate action (Taylor and Crocker, 1981).

The concept of cognitive schemata at the organization level (Bougon, Weick, and Binkhorst, 1977; Weick, 1979) and the related concept of interpretive schemes (Bartunek, 1984; Bartunek and Moch, 1987; Dougherty, 1992) have long been incorporated in organization theory and various ways of conceptualizing and mapping cognitive maps have been developed (Eden, 1992; Huff, 1990).

We follow Giddens (1984: 29) in defining interpretive schemes as "the modes of typification incorporated within actors' stocks of knowledge, applied reflexively in the sustaining of communication." From a structurational view of discourse, interpretive schemes are the modality through which discursive structures are instantiated at the level of communicative interaction, and through which communicative interaction can reproduce or challenge such structures.

This interaction is central to the construction of social reality and thus to agents' actions based on this reality, as emphasized by interpretive approaches to the sociology of knowledge (Berger and Luckmann, 1966; Moscovici, 1981), which consider language as the most important sign system of human society, objectifying and typifying experiences and meanings in the "here and now." In this view language assumes symbolic significance, being capable of building up semantic fields or zones of meaning and thus social reality (Berger and Luckmann, 1966: 49–61).

Gioia (1986) elucidates the structurational process between interpretive schemes and language as follows: "Understanding is accomplished and communicated mainly by means of symbols (most notably in the form of metaphorical language) that are then retained in a structured or schematic form via scripts. The scripts subsequently serve as a basis for action that further facilitates the meaning construction and sensemaking processes" (Gioia, 1986: 50). In a fundamental sense, cognitive structures are symbolic in nature since they are mental representations of experience and knowledge stored in memory (Gioia, 1986). Symbols, including communicative action, are integrated into individuals' cognitive structures when they are interpreted through them and connected with existing ideas and beliefs (Eoyang, 1983: 113). A structurational view emphasizes the malleable nature of interpretive schemes, which can progressively be redefined through the addition and attrition of concepts, the transformation of perceived causal associations, and the altered salience of concepts (Eoyang, 1983), through individuals' learning from new experiences, actions, or introspection.

Language influences not only the functioning of existing schemata but also the development of their parameters. During cognitive development schemata are constructed and reconstructed to meet the requirements of linguistic labels, and during communication or even during actors' reflections, linguistic terms evoke these schemata that are essentially carriers of meaning. Once schemata are developed, they are used as tools of thought without exerting more cognitive energy than is required in making use of their simpler components (Bloom, 1981; Donnellon, 1986).

Indicating the vital influence of interpretive schemes on action, Weick (1977) has suggested that people "act out and real-ize their ideas," collectively creating their own realities. Individuals' actions are based on their definitions of the situation, whether or not these definitions correspond to the situation's less subjective (or more inter-subjective) features (Thomas and Thomas, 1970). Interpretive schemes and agents' (communicative) actions are thus interrelated in a continual dialectic fashion: action arises out of interpretive schemes, and new experiences or reflections influence interpretive schemes and thus subsequent action (Gioia, 1986). Chapter 7 presents an empirical illustration of a structurational view of discourse (for a further illustration see also Heracleous and Barrett, 2001).

Implications of a Structurational View of Discourse

Placing Alternative Approaches in Context

A structurational view of discourse can encourage more empirical studies of discourse that link the action and structure domains, contributing to a broader-based stream of such research in organization theory (e.g. Barley and Tolbert, 1997; Heracleous, 2006; Heracleous and Barrett, 2001; Ranson, Hinings, and Greenwood and 1980; Weaver and Gioia, 1994). Such studies would also respond to calls for further integration between organization theory and discourse-related perspectives (Zald, 1996). In this spirit, the structurational view of discourse developed here contributes to bridging the long-standing chasm in the social sciences between approaches privileging structure or action, by elucidating how a key process, communicative (inter) action, is dialectically related to discursive and social structures through the modality of actors' interpretive schemes.

A structurational view of discourse can also place alternative approaches to discourse in context. In light of the metaphorical nature of scientific inquiry (Morgan, 1980, 1983; van Maanen, 1979), alternative approaches to discourse highlight some aspects of the phenomenon and hide others (Lakoff and Johnson, 1980). Interpretive approaches to discourse highlight the role of discourse in the construction of social reality and the role of the acting agent in this process, and functional approaches emphasize the intentionality of the acting agent in using discourse to facilitate managerially relevant outcomes, but both tend to downplay or ignore the links of the structural features of discourse with broader organizational and societal structures of domination. Critical approaches emphasize these links but tend to downplay or ignore the role of the acting subject in employing discourse to achieve functional outcomes, or in developing shared meanings within local organizational contexts. In addition, these approaches have not as yet developed a more comprehensive understanding of the role of interpretive schemes as a modality between the action and structure levels. A structurational view of discourse offers a more integrative framework which can accommodate these diverse perspectives and place them in context of other, potentially complementary perspectives. This more encompassing view can facilitate theoretical cross-fertilization and reduce any tendencies of seeing issues such as the discourse–subject relation in unidimensional terms.

Extending Current Theoretical Perspectives

A structurational view of discourse can extend current theoretical perspectives through a combination of its insights with existing theory. The genre perspective of organizational communication (Orlikowski and Yates, 1994; Yates and Orlikowski, 1992), for example, is informed by the theory of structuration. A "genre" is defined as a "typified communicative action invoked in response to a recurrent situation" (Yates and Orlikowski, 1992: 301), examples being memos, proposals, or meetings. Genres are enacted through "genre rules," which "associate appropriate elements of form and substance with certain recurrent situations" (1992: 302). A structurational view of discourse can extend the genre perspective in at least two significant ways. First, it draws attention to discursive structures, such as central themes, root metaphors, or rhetorical strategies, which are instantiated in communicative actions that cut across genres of organizational communication, in this way providing linkages across apparently diverse genres. For example, a particular rhetorical strategy or central theme can be used in several different genres such as meetings, speeches, or memos. In this sense, discursive structures are enacted through and across genres, adding a useful lens for exploring the linkages and interrelationships across genres, and between genres and their social context.

Second, a structurational view of discourse draws attention to an additional type of rules to genre rules, involved in genre enactment. By highlighting the fact that particular communicative actions draw from discursive structures of communicational legitimacy or appropriateness in local organizational contexts, a structurational view suggests that genres are enacted not only through genre rules but also through discursive structures that cut across genres within a particular social or organizational context. Identifying such discursive structures and relating them to genre rules would enhance a researcher's understanding of the local context, as well as processes of communicative interaction in that context.

Further, approaches to discourse in social and organization theory involve diverse understandings of the relationship between discourse and the subject.[6] Critical approaches in organization theory see the subject's identity and rationality as constituted by discourses of social domination, thus having little or no place for knowledgeable and intentional human agency. Functional approaches emphasize the acting subject as a relatively unconstrained agent, employing communicative actions to achieve particular outcomes, largely ignoring the constraining effects of existing discursive and social structures. Interpretive approaches emphasize the social construction of reality through communicative action, but often downplay the potential of intentional and knowledgeable agency in influencing this construction of reality, seeking description rather than prescription.

A structurational view of discourse portrays the subject as both constrained and enabled by existing structures of signification, legitimation, and domination. Giddens's discussions of agency emphasize that an individual could have acted otherwise, that the world does not hold a predetermined future, and that agents' purposive conduct (such as communicative action) involves the application of knowledge to achieve certain outcomes (Giddens, 1993). Agents' choices may be constrained by existing structures but are not determined by them. From a structurational perspective, therefore, agents can, through purposive communicative action, achieve functional outcomes (functional view), within a socially constructed reality (interpretive view), and in so doing, potentially challenge and ultimately transform entrenched, constraining societal structures (critical view).

---

[6] The issue of subjectivity has been directly and extensively addressed mainly from a critical perspective (e.g. Knights and Willmott, 1989; Willmott, 1997); the discussion here does not aim to go in detail in issues of subjectivity but rather to indicate how a structurational perspective can help us view the discourse–subject relationship in nonsingular terms.

Methodological Implications of a Structurational View for Organizational Discourse Analysis

Given the importance of context and the concept of reversible time in structuration theory, a structurational discourse analysis approach would need to address both of these aspects in the analysis; and be able to go beyond explicit communicative actions to identify and track over time discursive structural features and link them theoretically to wider social structures. Even though the need to address context and temporality sounds relatively uncontentious, inadequate consideration of these aspects has been a persistent issue in discourse analysis (Cicourel, 1981: 102; Fairclough, 1992: 212–213).

Adequate consideration of textual *context* calls for a hermeneutic analytical orientation. Contrary to structuralist approaches, hermeneutically inspired analyses emphasize the interpretive need of grasping other forms of life through researchers' immersion into them, and interpreting texts in the light of ethnographic data gathered longitudinally (Giddens, 1987, 1993). In this view texts should be studied as "the concrete medium and outcome of a process of production, reflexively monitored by its author or reader." Inquiry into this productive process involves exploring the author's or speaker's intentions as well as the practical knowledge involved in writing or speaking with a certain style for a particular audience (1979: 43). Interpretive accuracy of texts can thus be improved by inquiring in the settings of production of the text, the intellectual resources the author has drawn on, and the characteristics of the audience it is addressed to (1987: 106). What is required of researchers at the methodological plane, therefore, is to immerse themselves in other forms of life, acquire the mutual knowledge required to sustain encounters, and converse meaningfully with the "natives" (Geertz, 1973, Giddens, 1993: 156–157).

Adequate attention to *temporality* calls first for a clear definition of what exactly it means. The concept of temporality has been variously understood by theorists. In Barthes' structuralism, for example, "temporality is only a structural class of narrative (of discourse) . . . from the point of view of the narrative, what we call time does not exist . . ." (Barthes, 1994: 112). In conversation analysis, the concept of "temporal organization" of utterances refers to the timing or sequencing of particular utterances within conversations, how this influences the meaning of what is said and what it indicates about the speakers and their interrelationships (Pomerantz and Fehr, 1997). In rhetoric, attention to temporality refers not only to the location of particular statements in the context of other statements, but also to the treatment of the concept of time itself (e.g. past, present, future) in persuasive discourse (Gill and Whedbee, 1997). In Gadamer's hermeneutics "temporal distance" refers to the time that elapsed between the original production of the text and the time of hermeneutic interpretation (Palmer, 1969: 184–185).

From a structurational perspective[7] temporality is seen as a key aspect of textual context that influences the intended and received meaning of texts. A key idea is "reversible time" that refers to the repetitive character of social life; "time here is constituted only in repetition" (Giddens, 1984: 35). This conception of time is important in structurational processes because structures only exist as repeated manifestations in daily actions and as memory traces or interpretive schemes. This orientation can afford a way of first identifying structural features of texts (whose structural nature is substantiated by virtue of their persistent manifestation in communicative actions by different agents in different contexts), and second linking texts to wider social structures, since repeated central themes in texts have both cognitive and social–structural correlates.

Paying attention to temporality in methodological terms, therefore, would necessitate that the analysis of communicative actions (seen as textual "fragments" or as constituents of texts that intertextually constitute discourses) should first take account of the timing of communicative actions as an aspect of textual context and second track texts and their contexts longitudinally, noting shifts over time in both and uncovering and theorizing their interconnections. As Giddens (1984: 142) has observed, "no strip of interaction—even if it is plainly bracketed, temporally and spatially—can be understood on its own. Most aspects of interaction are sedimented in time, and sense can be made of them only by considering their routinized, repetitive character." (Discursive) structures are thus reproduced, replicated, or

---

[7] Giddens referred to time as "perhaps the most enigmatic feature of human experience" (1984: 34). He developed concepts such as time–space distantiation, time–space edges, and world-time, which he integrated in his theory of structuration. Here we address one aspect of Giddens's theorizing on time, the concept of reversible time, which is in our view more relevant to the analysis of discourse.

plausibly challenged by (communicative) actions that are temporally recursive. An understanding of how communicative actions interact dialectically with discursive structures thus requires longitudinal monitoring of communicative actions and an exploration of their deep structures. A study of how temporally recursive communicative actions within an earlier period, for example, diffuse central themes, premises, or assumptions in a social context that become aspects of deep structures at a later period (a structurational process between actions and structures), and how structures may resurface in communicative actions cross-situationally requires longitudinal tracking of texts and social practices at these different levels of analysis.

With regard to the first analytical direction, the need to consider the temporal context of communicative actions, the meaning of the same communicative action can vary in different contexts (especially since different temporal contexts most often imply different situational contexts). Taking into account the timing of a communicative action can thus improve researchers' interpretations of what agents' first-order meanings are. With regard to the second analytical direction, the need for longitudinal textual analyses is highlighted by the concept of "reversible time." A longitudinal analysis from a structurational perspective would focus on the extent to which discourses (as constituted by texts in turn constituted by communicative actions) exhibit shifting surface communicative actions and deep structures over time (these being key analytical levels in the theory of structuration), and how these relate to textual context. In addition, it would focus on uncovering and theorizing the cognitive correlates of such discursive structures, the interpretive schemes in which such structures are enshrined, through which they manifest in communicative actions and acquire social significance by influencing agents' views of the world.

Finally, a structurational view of discourse, in uncovering the mostly unconscious structural features of discourse (and their cognitive correlates in the form of interpretive schemes), can provide a way to access parts of agents' practical consciousness; what actors "know" but cannot express explicitly except through patterns in their (communicative) actions that are manifestations of these aspects of practical consciousness. This conception does not resort to deterministic concepts of structure but acknowledges that such structures not only constrain but also enable agents by providing resources for social interaction and private reflection that agents draw on; the concept of duality of structure in structuration theory. More importantly, it provides the conceptual basis and the liberating potential for social change by emphasizing the dynamic process thought which structures are formed and also potentially altered and re-formed through social interaction.

In this chapter we suggested that existing approaches to discourse in organization theory tend to privilege either the action or structure dimensions, mirroring long-standing divisions in social science. We then proposed a structurational view of discourse, where discourse is seen as a duality of communicative actions and structural properties, recursively linked through the modality of actors' interpretive schemes. This was offered as a more encompassing approach that can address a plurality of aspects of the nature and operations of discourse, place in context alternative views, aid cross-fertilization between domains, extend current theoretical perspectives, and indicate useful methodological directions for discourse analyses.

References

Aristotle. 1991. *On rhetoric*. G. A. Kennedy (tran.). Oxford: Oxford University Press.

Austin, J. L. 1961. *How to do things with words*. Oxford: Oxford University Press.

Barley, S. R. and Tolbert, P. S. 1997. Institutionalization and structuration: Studying the links between action and institution. *Organization Studies*, 18: 93–117.

Barthes, R. 1977. *Image, music, text*. London: Fontana.

1994. *The semiotic challenge*. Berkeley, CA: University of California Press.

Bartlett, F. C. 1932. *Remembering*. Cambridge, MA: Cambridge University Press.

Bartunek, J. M. 1984. Changing interpretive schemes and organizational restructuring: The example of a religious order. *Administrative Science Quarterly*, 29: 355–372.

Bartunek, J. M. and Moch, M. K. 1987. First-order, second-order, and third-order change and organizational development interventions: A cognitive approach. *Journal of Applied Behavioral Science*, 3: 483–500.

Bateson, G. 1972. *Steps to an ecology of mind*. London: Intertext.

Berger, P. and Luckmann, T. 1966. *The social construction of reality*. London: Penguin.

Bhaskar, R. 1979. *The possibility of naturalism: A philosophical critique of the contemporary human sciences*. Brighton, Sussex: Harvester.

Bloom, A. H. 1981. *The linguistic shaping of thought. A study on the Impact of thinking in China and the West*. Hillsdale, NJ: Erlbaum.

Blumer, H. 1970. Society as symbolic interaction. In J. G. Manis and B. N. Meltzer (eds.), *Symbolic interaction: A reader in social psychology*: 139–148. Boston, MA: Allyn and Bacon.

Boland, R. J., Jr. 1993. Accounting and the interpretive act. *Accounting, Organizations and Society*, **18** (2/3): 125–146.

1996. Why shared meanings have no place in structuration theory: A reply to Scapens and Macintosh. *Accounting, Organizations and Society*, **21** (7/8): 691–697.

Bougon, M., Weick, K. and Binkhorst, D. 1977. Cognition in organizations: An analysis of the Utrecht jazz orchestra. *Administrative Science Quarterly*, **22**: 607–639.

Bourdieu, P. 1977. *Outline of a theory of practice*. R. Nice (trans.). Cambridge: Cambridge University Press.

Bryant, C. G. A. and Jary, D. 1991. *Giddens' theory of structuration: A critical appraisal*. London: Routledge.

Byrne, R. 1991. Power-knowledge and social theory in the systematic misrepresentation of contemporary French social theory in the work of Anthony Giddens. In C. G. A. Bryant and D. Jary (eds.), *Giddens' theory of structuration: A critical appraisal*. London: Routledge.

Callinicos, A. and Giddens, A. 1985. A contemporary critique. *Theory and Society*, **14**: 133–166.

Cicourel, A. V. 1981. Three models of discourse analysis: The role of social structure. *Discourse Processes*, **3**: 101–131.

DeSanctis, G. and Poole, M. S. 1994. Capturing the complexity in advanced technology use: Adaptive structuration theory. *Organization Science*, **5**: 121–147.

van Dijk, T. A. 1988. Social cognition, social power and social discourse. *Text*, **8**: 129–157.

Donnellon, A. 1986. Language and communication in organizations: bridging cognition and behavior. In H. P. Sims, Jr. and D. A. Gioia (eds.), *The thinking organization*: 137–164. San Francisco, CA: Josey-Bass.

Dougherty, D. 1992. Interpretive barriers to successful product innovation in large firms. *Organization Science*, **3**: 179–202.

Eden. C. 1992. On the nature of cognitive maps. *Journal of Management Studies*, **29**: 261–265.

Eoyang, C. 1983. Symbolic transformation of belief systems. In L. R. Pondy, P. J. Frost, G. Morgan, and T. C. Dandridge (eds.), *Organizational symbolism*: 109–121. Greenwich, CT: JAI Press.

Eysenck. M. W. 1993. *Principles of cognitive psychology.* Hove: Erlbaum.

Fairclough, N. 1992. Discourse and text: Linguistic and intertextual analysis within discourse analysis. *Discourse and Society,* 3: 193–217.

Festinger, L. 1959. *A theory of cognitive dissonance.* London: Tavistock.

Foucault, M. 1972. *The archaeology of knowledge.* London: Routledge.

Frake, C. O. 1964. How to ask for a drink in Subanun. *American Anthropologist* 66 (6): 127–32.

Geertz, C. 1973. *The interpretation of cultures.* New York, NY: Basic Books.

1991. Revolutionary change theories: Multilevel exploration of the punctuated equilibrium paradigm. *Academy of Management Review,* 16: 10–36.

Giddens, A. 1979. *Central problems in social theory.* London: Macmillan.

1984. *The constitution of society.* Cambridge, MA: Polity.

1987. *Social theory and modern sociology.* Cambridge, MA: Polity.

1993. *New rules of sociological method* (2nd edn.). Stanford: Stanford University Press.

Gill, A. M. and Whedbee, K. 1997. Rhetoric. In T. A. van Dijk (ed.), *Discourse studies: A multidisciplinary introduction,* vol. 1: 157–183. Thousand Oaks, CA: Sage.

Gioia, D. A. 1986. Symbols, scripts and sensemaking: Creating meaning in the organizational experience. In H. P. Sims, Jr. and D. A. Gioia (eds.), *The thinking organization:* 49–74. San Francisco, CA: Josey-Bass.

Goffman, E. 1972. The neglected situation. In P. P. Giglioli (ed.), *Language and social context:* 61–66. London: Penguin.

Head, H. 1926. *Aphasia and kindred disorders of speech.* Cambridge, MA: Cambridge University Press.

Held, D. and Thompson, J. B. (eds.) 1989. *Social theory of modern societies: Anthony Giddens and his critics.* Cambridge, MA: Cambridge University Press.

Heracleous, L. 2006. A tale of three discourses: The dominant, the strategic and the marginalized. *Journal of Management Studies,* 43: 1059–1087.

Heracleous, L. and Barrett, M. 2001. Organizational change as discourse: Communicative actions and deep structures in the context of IT implementation. *Academy of Management Journal,* 44 (4): 755–778.

Heracleous, L. and Hendry, J. 2000. Discourse and the study of organization: Toward a structurational perspective. *Human Relations,* 53: 1251–1286.

Hofstede, G. 1985. The interaction between national and organizational value systems. *Journal of Management Studies,* 22: 347–57.

Hopkins, N. and Reicher, S. 1997. Social movement rhetoric and the social psychology of collective action: A case study of anti-abortion mobilization. *Human Relations,* 50: 261–286.

Huff, A. S. 1990. *Mapping strategic thought*. Chichester, England: Wiley.

Jones, M. Structuration theory. 1999. In W. Currie and R. Galliers (eds.), *Rethinking management information systems*. Oxford: Oxford University Press.

Kamoche, K. 1995. Rhetoric, ritualism and totemism in human resource management. *Human Relations*, 48: 367–385.

Kets de Vries, M. and Miller, D. 1987. Interpreting organizational texts. *Journal of Management Studies*, 24: 233–247.

Knights, D. and Willmott, H. 1989. Power and subjectivity at work: From degradation to subjugation in social relations. *Sociology*, 23: 535–558.

Lakoff, G. and Johnson, M. 1980. *Metaphors we live by*. Chicago, IL: Chicago University Press.

Layder, D. 1987. Key issues in structuration theory: Some critical remarks. *Current Perspectives in Social Theory*, 8: 25–46.

Light, D., Jr. 1979. Surface data and deep structure: Observing the organization of professional training. *Administrative Science Quarterly*, 24: 551–561.

van Maanen, J. 1973. Observations on the making of policemen. *Human Organization*, 32: 407–18.

1979. The fact of fiction in organizational ethnography. *Administrative Science Quarterly*, 24: 539–550.

Macintosh, N. B. and Scapens, R. W. 1990. Structuration theory in management accounting. *Accounting, Organizations and Society*, 15: 455–477.

Malinowski, B. 1970. The context of situation. In G. P. Stone and H. A. Faberman (eds.), *Social psychology through symbolic interaction*: 158–160. Toronto: Xerox College Publishing.

McCann, C. D. and Higgins, E. T. 1990. Social Cognition and Communication. In H. Giles and W. P. Robinson (eds.), *Handbook of language and social psychology*: 13–32. Chichester, England: Wiley.

Morgan, G. 1980. Paradigms, metaphor and puzzle solving in organization theory. *Administrative Science Quarterly*, 25: 660–671.

1983. More on metaphor: Why we cannot control tropes in administrative science. *Administrative Science Quarterly*, 28: 601–607.

Moscovici, S. 1981. On social representations. In J. P. Forgas (ed.), *Social cognition: Perspectives on everyday understanding*: 181–209. London: Academic Press.

Orlikowski, W. J. and Yates, J. 1994. Genre repertoire: The structuring of communicative practices in organizations. *Administrative Science Quarterly*, 39: 541–574.

Oswick, C., Keenoy, T. and Grant, D. 1997. Managerial discourses: Words speak louder than actions? *Journal of Applied Management Studies*, 6: 5–12.

Palmer, R. E. 1969. *Hermeneutics*. Evanston: Northwestern University Press.

Pomerantz, A. and Fehr, B. J. 1997. Conversation analysis: An approach to the study of social action as sense making practices. In T. A. van Dijk (ed.), *Discourse as social interaction*: 64–91. London: Sage.

Pondy, L. R. 1983. The role of metaphors and myths in organization and the facilitation of change. In L. R. Pondy, P. J. Frost, G. Morgan, and T. C. Dandridge (eds.), *Organizational symbolism*: 157–166. Greenwich, CT: JAI Press.

Ranson, S., Hinings, B. and Greenwood, R. 1980. The structuring of organizational structures. *Administrative Science Quarterly*, 25: 1–17.

Riley, P. 1983. A structurationist account of political culture. *Administrative Science Quarterly*, 28: 314–37.

Rumelhart, D. E. 1984. Schemata and the cognitive system. In R. S. Wyer, Jr. and T. K. Srull (eds.), *Handbook of social cognition*: 161–188. Hillsdale, NJ: Erlbaum.

Saferstein, B. 1992. Collective cognition and collaborative work: The effects of cognitive and communicative processes on the organization of television production. *Discourse and Society*, 3: 61–86.

de Saussure, F. 1983. *Course in general linguistics*. London: Duckworth.

Scapens, R. W. and Macintosh, N. B. 1996. Structure and agency in management accounting research: A response to Boland's interpretive act. *Accounting, Organizations and Society*, 21: 675–690.

Schon, D. A. 1979. Generative metaphor. A perspective on problem-setting in social policy. In A. Ortony (ed.), *Metaphor and thought*: 254–283. Cambridge, MA: Cambridge University Press.

Schultz, M. 1991. Transitions betweem symbolic domains in organisations. *Organization Studies*, 12: 489–506.

Silverman, D. 1970. *The theory of organizations*. London: Heinemann.

Taylor, S. E. and Crocker, J. 1981. Schematic bases of social information processing. In E. T. Higgins, C. P. Herman, and M. P. Zanna (eds.), *Social cognition*: 89–134. Hillsdale, NJ: Erlbaum.

Thachankary, T. 1992. Organizations as 'texts': Hermeneutics as a model for understanding organizational change. *Research in Organization Change and Development*, 6: 197–233.

Thomas, W. I. and Thomas, D. S. 1970. Situations defined as real are real in their consequences. In G. P. Stone and H. A. Faberman (eds.), *Social psychology through symbolic interaction*: 154–156. Toronto: Xerox College Publishing.

Thompson, J. B. 1989. The theory of structuration. In D. Held and J. B. Thompson (eds.), *Social theory of modern societies: Anthony Giddens and his critics*: 56–76. Cambridge, MA: Cambridge University Press.

Weaver, G. R. and Gioia, D. A. 1994. Paradigms lost: Incommensurability vs structurationist inquiry. *Organization Studies*, 15: 565–590.

Weber, M. 1991. The nature of social action. In W. G. Runciman (ed.), *Weber: Selections in translation*: 7–32. Cambridge, MA: Cambridge University Press.

Weick, K. 1977. Enactment processes in organizations. In B. M. Staw and G. R. Salancik (eds.), *New directions in organizational behavior*: 267–300. Chicago, IL: St. Clair Press.

1979. Cognitive processes in organizations. *Research in Organizational Behavior*, 1: 41–74.

Whittington, R. 1992. Putting Giddens into action: Social systems and managerial agency. *Journal of Management Studies*, 29: 693–712.

Willmott, H. 1981. The structuring of organizational structure: A note. *Administrative Science Quarterly*, 26: 470–474.

1986. Unconscious sources of motivation in the theory of the subject; an exploration and critique of Giddens' dualistic models of action and personality. *Journal for the Theory of Social Behavior*, 16: 105–121.

1997. Rethinking management and managerial work: Capitalism, control and subjectivity. *Human Relations*, 50: 1329–1359.

Yates, J. and Orlikowski, W. J. 1992. Genres of organizational communication: A structurational approach to studying communication and media. *Academy of Management Review*, 17: 299–326.

Zald, M. N. 1996. More fragmentation? Unfinished business in linking the social sciences and the humanities. *Administrative Science Quarterly*, 41: 251–261.

Xu, S. 1992. Argumentation, explanation, and social cognition. *Text*, 12: 263–291.

6 | Analyzing Discourse I: Discourse as Situated Symbolic Action[1]

THIS chapter presents a conceptualization of organizational discourse as situated symbolic action, drawing from the fields of speech act theory, rhetoric, ethnography of communication, and social constructionism. It is suggested that speech act theory presents a theory of discourse as *action*, but essentially remains at the microlevel of interaction, without sufficient attention to context and intertextual analysis. Rhetoric is introduced as an approach that can address both text and context, viewing discourse as a *situated* social practice. Further support for discourse as a situated practice comes from ethnographies of communication. Finally, social constructionism is discussed as a perspective that emphasizes the *symbolic* nature of discourse, both at the level of discursive action and bodies of discourse and their "metacommunicative" effects of framing issues in particular ways.

The conceptualization of organizational discourse as situated symbolic action is illustrated through analysis of an episode of negotiated order, a meeting of senior managers of Systech, a major information technology (IT) organization where a new business model for its advanced consulting division was being debated. The business model favored by the recently hired Group President entailed a move from the more traditional, functionally based, distributed model of client engagement employed at the division to a "principal-centered" consulting model involving principals who "owned" clients and were responsible for all aspects of the client engagement. This move would entail substantial reallocation of power, status, and influence within the division and was hotly contested. At a pivotal moment in the meeting, the chief advocate of the principal-centered model acknowledged that things were different in Systech and, therefore, some

---

[1] This chapter is based on Heracleous and Marshak (2004) and Marshak and Heracleous (2005).

responsibilities could be shared rather than fully led by the relevant principal. This led to a more cooperative, productive discussion in which an entirely new integrative model was developed, labeled by the participants as "The Advanced Services Division (ASD) Business Model." When the output was given to the Group President, who had not attended the meeting, he added "Principal-Led" in the name, re-affirming his desire for a business model with most of the power and status given to principals.

We proceed by analyzing this episode through the lens of discourse as situated symbolic action as witnessed and experienced by the facilitator of the meeting. There are three levels of analysis involved that are complementary and additive. We first adopt the view of discourse as action, examining what the participants said and what they may have intended to achieve through their communicative actions in the meeting. We then proceed to viewing discourse as situated action, examining the added value that arises from a knowledge of the different levels of context (interactional, organizational, and industrial) in discursive analysis. Finally, we proceed to the level of discourse as situated symbolic action. In addition to the examination of discourse from the perspective of what was said and what the participants intended to achieve (discourse as action), and to the contribution of contextual knowledge (discourse as situated action), viewing discourse as situated symbolic action adds a sensitivity to deeper considerations of how discourse frames, constructs, and represents issues in particular ways. For example, how discursive interactions that on the surface appear simply as an exchange of information can mirror considerations of power, and archetypal struggles for control and dominance.

We conclude by drawing some implications of conceptualizing and analyzing discourse as situated symbolic action. We suggest that this perspective helps to respond to some of the key challenges facing the organizational discourse field in terms of developing more structured and clearly specified conceptualizations of discourse that are appropriate to the organizational level of analysis; achieving a more holistic and discourse-sensitive understanding of empirical contexts by organizational researchers; and finally illustrating that organizational discourse analysis is not simply an intellectual luxury but can have pragmatic, relevant implications.

Conceptualizing Discourse as Situated Symbolic Action

Several theorists have called for the development of discourse analysis approaches that not only consider the text as a data source, but are more contextually sensitive and holistic, paying attention to how nested levels of context, such as the interactional, organizational, and societal contexts, interrelate and interpenetrate with the text (Cicourel, 1981; Hardy, 2001; Fairclough, 1992; Keenoy, Oswick, and Grant, 1997). In this spirit, and with the organizational level of analysis in mind, we propose an approach for addressing the integration of text, context, and symbolic meaning through conceptualizing organizational discourse[2] as *situated symbolic action*. This conceptualization draws primarily on speech act theory, rhetoric, ethnography of communication, and social constructionism.

Discourse as Action

Austin's (1962) speech act theory offers an influential statement of discourse as *action*. Austin's work challenged the traditional assumption of the philosophy of language that "to say something . . . is always and simply to *state* something," which is either true or false, and developed the influential thesis that "to *say* something is to *do* something" (1962: 12, emphases in original). Austin distinguished analytically between locutionary speech acts, the act of saying something (1962: 94); illocutionary speech acts, what individuals intend to achieve in saying something (1962: 98); and finally perlocutionary speech acts, the actual effects of utterances on their audience (1962: 101). Of course, it should be noted that an utterance could perform all three speech acts simultaneously.

---

[2] As discussed in chapter 1, by the term "discourse" we mean collections of texts, whether oral or written, located within social and organizational contexts, that share certain structural features and have both functional and constructive effects on their contexts. We view language as the raw material of discourse, and individual texts as constitutive, and as manifestations of broader discourses (Heracleous, 2004 Heracleous and Hendry, 2000;). This is a broad-level perspective amenable to various interpretations, and one such interpretation of discourse as situated symbolic action is employed in this chapter.

Extending Austin's speech act theory, Searle (1975) developed more elaborate typologies of illocutionary acts, specified further contextual conditions relevant to their functioning, and introduced the notion of indirect speech acts where the connection between the intended meaning and the utterance is not clear and direct. In addition to being highly influential in the philosophy of language, the insights of speech act theory formed the theoretical foundation for discourse pragmatics, the study of language-in-use (Blum-Kulka, 1997).

Even though speech act theory has laid the groundwork for understanding discourse as action, it essentially remains at the microlevel of single utterances without extending to the broader level of discourses as bodies of texts pervaded or patterned by structural features (Heracleous and Barrett, 2001). So, for example, speech act theory does not readily apply to what van Dijk (1977) has termed "macro" speech acts, or Alvesson and Karreman (2000) termed "grand" or "mega" discourses. It also tends to focus on the text itself without explicitly considering context as a crucial resource for interpreting texts as socially and contextually located entities.

Discourse as Situated Action

Several fields, including semiotics, rhetoric, and ethnographies of communication, have acknowledged and theorized a contextualized view of discourse, and are drawn on to develop a view of discourse as *situated* action.

In semiotics, for example, Jakobson's (1960) framework has been influential in grounding language use in an interactional setting, suggesting that the constitutive events of any speech event include addresser, addressee, message, context, code, and contact:

the addresser sends a message to the addressee. To be operative the message requires a context referred to . . . seizable by the addressee, and either verbal or capable of being verbalized; a code fully, or at least partially, common to the addresser and addressee . . . and, finally, a contact, a physical channel and psychological connection between the addresser and the addressee, enabling both of them to enter and stay in communication.

(Jakobson, 1960: 353).

However, Jakobson has posited the function of context as "referential" or "denotative" (an indexical perspective on context as the referent of the message; a view that became influential in structuralism and related fields), and in this sense his conception of context was relatively circumscribed, in comparison with other fields such as rhetoric and ethnographies of communication.[3]

Rhetoric encompasses a holistic conception of context that includes various aspects of the situation, the audience, the rhetor, as well as textual features such as structure and temporality, enthymemes, metaphor, and iconicity. These are researched not for their own sake, but to discover how rhetorical discourse can influence actors' perceptions and interpretations by eloquently and persuasively espousing particular views of the world (Aristotle, 1991; Gill and Whedbee, 1997). Rhetorical principles have been fruitfully applied to wider, macrolevel discourses to explore the discourses' constructive effects on peoples' interpretations and opinions of pressing social issues (e.g. Charland, 1987; Gronbeck, 1973).

Rhetoric also aims to explore the "dynamic interaction of a rhetorical text with its context" (Gill and Whedbee, 1997: 159). The important influence of the context or situation on what should and could be said was highlighted by Aristotle's definition of rhetoric as "an ability, in each particular case, to see the available means of persuasion" (Aristotle, 1991: 36). Bitzer (1968) furthermore suggested that a situation is not simply a necessary condition of rhetorical discourse, but more importantly that rhetorical discourse is constructed both with a view to addressing particular situational exigencies, as well as imbued with significance by those exigencies.

Ethnographies of communication (Hymes, 1964) offer further support for a view of discourse as situated action, emphasizing that discourse cannot be adequately understood or appropriately produced in separation from its context of use. Frake (1964), for example, has shown how in one tribe, "drinking talk" is simultaneously social interaction, entertainment, and the de facto governance institution, where leaders are determined based on their skill at "talking from the straw," both in terms of rational and aesthetic discourse (1964: 132). In an organizational context, Samra-Fredericks (2003) has employed

---

[3] Having said that, semiotics as a field has moved beyond a circumscribed, linguistically oriented view of context to encompass such aspects as shared knowledge, interrelationships among actors, or broader ideologies that shape textual meanings (see, e.g. Hodge and Kress, 1988, chapter 3 on "Context as Meaning: The Semiosic Dimension").

an ethnographic approach combined with conversation analysis to study the process and accomplishment of everyday strategizing, presenting a fine-grained analysis of talk in context, and how everyday talk links to the accomplishment of strategy.

Finally, Hymes (1964) has proposed several useful contextual elements for understanding communicative events: the participants, channels, shared codes, setting, messages, and topics. These elements were later extended and synthesized in terms of the influential SPEAKING[4] framework (Hymes, 1972). The embeddedness of discourse in its context, in addition, is not limited to the immediate situation, but is nested in wider social and cultural systems: "aspects of meaning and interpretation are determined by culture-specific activities and practices . . . [which] are interconnected in turn with the larger socio-political systems that govern and are in part constituted by them" (Gumperz and Levinson, 1991: 614).

Discourse as Symbolic Action

Constructionist approaches present discourse as *symbolic* action, viewing reality as a social construction and individuals as symbol creators and consumers (Morgan and Smircich, 1980). As Phillips and Hardy (2002) assert, "without discourse, there is no social reality, and without understanding discourse we cannot understand our reality, our experiences or ourselves" (2002: 2). The main aim of constructionist approaches is to understand this constructive process through hermeneutic exploration of the discourses involved. Berger and Luckmann (1966), in their influential statement of social constructionism, suggested that social reality is known to individuals in terms of symbolic universes constructed through social interaction. They viewed language as the "most important sign system of human society" (1966: 51), the primary means through which "objectivation," the manifestation of subjective meanings through actions, proceeds. Language makes subjective meanings "real" and at the same time typifies these meanings through creating "semantic fields or zones of meaning" (1966: 55) within which daily routines proceed.

---

[4] S (setting, scene); P (participants); E (ends); A (act sequence); K (key); I (instrumentalities); N (norms of interaction and interpretation); G (genre).

Searle (1995) more recently provided a further landmark rendition of social constructionism, in his view of institutional facts as language dependent, in the sense that such facts could not exist if it was not for the human faculty of language. Searle views language as epistemically indispensable for representing as well as constituting knowledge on complex social facts, knowledge that cannot be communicated save for the use of language, and that persists over time by virtue of the human ability to couch such knowledge in linguistic terms.

Discourse, in addition, creates mental frames that are metacommunicative (Bateson, 1972: 188), simultaneously highlighting certain meanings and excluding others. Discourse is thus not simply symbolic at the semantic level, by virtue of being composed of signs, but at a broader level of framing, evoking particular typifications and associations through connotation (Phillips and Brown, 1993: 1564) and inviting others to view the world in these terms. This is what Fairclough (2003) means when he refers to *discourses* (in the plural) as "positioned representations" that give rise to corresponding conceptualizations of social relations and social practices (2003: 23).

Discursive construction takes place through social interaction; in the organizational context it occurs when managers "author" their experiences in the process of interacting with others, simultaneously constructing a shared sense of their identities, organization, and of appropriate ways to talk and act (Cunliffe, 2001). Language, in this perspective, does not simply mirror social reality but constitutes it, creating conditioned rationalities as widespread ways of thinking within particular social systems (Gergen and Thatchenkery, 1996). Table 6.1 provides an outline of the earlier discussion and also suggests foci for organizational discourse analysis at each level of discourse.

Brief Background and Methodological Approach

Establishing Contact and Preliminary Data Gathering

In the Spring of 2002, the President and Vice President (VP) of Human Resources (HR) of one of the major divisions of Systech,[5] a large,

---

[5] The names of the company and all individuals have been disguised.

Table 6.1. *Discourse as Situated Symbolic Action*

Discourse as	Main Proposition	Theoretical Domains	Potential Foci for Discourse Analysis
Action	Discourse does not just *say* things, but *does* things	Speech act theory (Austin, 1962, Searle, 1975)	What is said, and what does the communicative action intend to accomplish?
Situated action	Discourse is fully meaningful only if viewed in context	Rhetoric (Aristotle, 1991; Gill and Whedbee, 1997); ethnography of communication (Hymes, 1964, 1972)	How can contextual knowledge inform discourse analysis? What does discourse reveal about its context?
Symbolic action	Discourse is symbolic and constructive at multiple levels including the semantic, metacommunicative, and interpersonal levels	Social constructionism (Berger and Luckmann, 1966; Searle, 1995)	What constructions and evaluations does discourse implicitly promote? How do these discursive constructions relate to context? What is happening at a deeper level?

Source: Adapted from Heracleous and Marshak, (2004).

global computer systems and IT corporation, met with an organization development practitioner[6] to discuss a potential OD intervention that was intended to address several pressing issues. These included pressure from the President's boss (the Group President) to change the organization's operating structure and culture, effectively integrate a recent acquisition, and create alignment on business strategy within the top team of executives. At that time, detailed information was provided about the situation and the actors involved, recorded in notes taken during and immediately after the interview discussion. This information was further augmented and documented during two subsequent telephone discussions with the VP, HR about how best to pursue the situation. Shortly thereafter, however, the budding project was "indefinitely delayed," according to the VP, HR "because the President was too consumed with the operational issues of a new work program."

No further contact occurred until almost 6 months later when the VP, HR called and desperately requested help for a critical meeting that would take place in 2 days. The VP explained that "the President had decided at the last minute that they needed a good facilitator otherwise the meeting could be a real disaster and that you knew the background and seemed to have the skills." After the organization development, practitioner agreed to help out on this extremely short notice, additional information was provided by the VP, HR, an assistant to the President, and the President himself in a further telephone conversation. The main objective of the meeting according to the President was to "get everyone aligned around a new business model being advanced by my boss." The President went on to say that "the meeting could be very difficult because most of the top team will be opposed to the proposed new arrangement and I'm not so sure about it myself."

Facilitating the Meeting and Conducting Action Research

For the meeting, the requested form of organization development was to facilitate and make interventions so as to help the group of executives reach the stated objective of achieving alignment around a new

---

[6] The organizational development intervention outlined in this chapter was conducted by my coauthor, Robert Marshak.

business model. Running notes as to the events, impressions, quotes of participants, and "hunches" were kept during the meeting by the facilitator as a way of tracking developments as they emerged. More detailed notes and reflections as to emergent themes and patterns were recorded after the session in preparation for further interventions; and as a means of reflecting on and interpreting what took place in the meeting.

The organization development process reflected in this episode at Systech is consistent with the dominant definition of *action research* as a process of both helping organizations and gathering data for further scholarly reflection and potential contribution to knowledge, wherein the researcher is an active, reflective participant in whatever effort is underway (e.g. Checkland and Holwell, 1998; Dickens and Watkins, 1999). Action research aims to describe holistically what happens in naturally occurring settings, and to derive from these observations more broadly applicable principles, or actionable knowledge (Argyris, 1996; Perry and Zuber-Skerritt, 1994).

Concerns about the action research approach (some of which arise from a positivist conception of science) include the low reproducibility of setting and findings, limitations on the means of collection and documentation of data, and the manner in which the personal interests, knowledge, and competencies of the researcher influence the research (Huxham and Vangen, 2003). These apply to some extent in any research effort. Within the context of the action research approach, it would be impossible to replicate the setting given that it is a live, actual organizational situation with all its inherent complexity. What matters therefore is to document as much relevant data as possible, and as accurately as possible given the circumstances, be reflective on what the data means drawing on knowledge of context, apply a thoughtful analytical framework to the data, and arrive at some valid insights that contribute to knowledge in some significant way. In this case, a perspective of discourse as situated symbolic action was applied to arrive at a nested, additive interpretation of the episode reflecting successively increasing complexity, and which was partially validated through real-time decisions and choices in the episode.

Some of the important advantages of action research that were applicable in this case, include being taken "behind the scenes," being afforded access to sensitive information and to participants' real experience as it is happening, as well as access to contextualized and live organizational settings rather than isolated and segmentalized laboratory experiments or surveys (Huxham and Vangen, 2003; Schein, 1987).

Exploring a Process of Negotiated Order Through Discourse

The Systech case can be seen as an episode of negotiated order, in which this negotiation took place in and through discourse. The negotiated order perspective was developed by Strauss et al. (1963, 1964) through their fieldwork in two psychiatric hospitals, although earlier renditions and aspects of the concept had already been introduced by theorists such as Mead (1934) in his discussion of the nature of society and Goffman (1961) in his analysis of total institutions. The negotiated order perspective suggests that all social order is continually negotiated through communicative actions and this process is influenced by existing structural arrangements that are themselves the result of earlier negotiations (Fine, 1984). This perspective highlights the first-order meanings of participants in the negotiation process and emphasizes, much like Giddens's (1984) structuration theory, that the social and organizational structures often taken for granted are in fact the outcome of patterns of actions at the micro, interaction level.

The Systech episode of negotiated order presents a vivid illustration of discourse as situated symbolic action. This episode describes how a team of senior managers implicitly negotiated a new organizational arrangement whose outcome would involve substantial power implications, in this sense also illustrating the political nature of organizations (March, 1962; Mintzberg, 1983). A key discursive element in this story is the specific label that was to be attached to this arrangement; the debate in some ways hinging on whether it should be, or contain, the words "Principal-Led."

The effects of labels on action have been vividly illustrated by Whorf (1941) who discussed several cases in which industrial accidents occurred because the labels used for machinery and other objects mistakenly implied certain qualities (such as noncombustibility) which allowed careless behavior around them. Weick (1995), in addition, described the pivotal role of words and labels in the sensemaking process: "sense is generated by words that are combined into the sentences of conversation to convey something about our ongoing experience . . . . Words constrain the saying of what is produced, the categories imposed to see the saying, and the labels with which the conclusions of this process are retained. Thus words matter" (Weick, 1995: 106). Labels are thus not simply denotation devices for transferring information, but also emotionally loaded "containers" that implicitly embody the communicator's evaluations and typifications regarding the issues they refer to (Hirsch, 1986; Strauss, 1967).

In this case the prospect of adopting and labeling this new organizational arrangement "Principal-Led" created significant political tensions within Systech, since it symbolized the triumph of a consulting business model alien to the organization where a single principal would dominate and control the process of service provision to clients, within an organization that had traditionally followed a more distributed, decentralized operating model of service provision. "Principal-Led" was therefore not simply a rational description of a prospective organizational arrangement, but a label filled with connotation and emotion that would radically alter a traditional way of doing business. "Principal-Led" was set to become the new order of business, structuring agents' actions in the context of service provision, and foreshadowing other contesting organizing possibilities.

Negotiating the New Order: The Systech New Business Model Meeting

Context

Historically, Systech was a primary provider of computer hardware and support services. In more recent years it has expanded its system engineering, IT, and systems consulting services to become a major provider of information systems hardware, software, and consulting services. In 2002, with the demise of Consultco, a large management services company, the ASD of Systech saw an opportunity to expand its consulting capabilities by acquiring *en masse* one of Consultco's consulting units, consisting of some 180 people. These people were added to the existing ASD workforce of some 1500 people. The acquisition was spearheaded by Group President John Duke, a former partner of one of the "Big 5" accounting/consulting companies (now, the "Big 4" after the demise of Arthur Andersen) who was hired in 2001 to head up the global services area for Systech. Duke's vision was to transform the more hardware and systems engineering "products" strategy of ASD into a high-end "consulting services" business model.

Following the traditional "Big 5/4" model, he envisioned a business-operating model wherein highly compensated principals "owned" different government agencies and were responsible for profit and loss and all products, services, and ASD employees associated with that organization. In this model most of the actual client work is done by lower paid and more junior consultants, thereby achieving significant leverage and profitability for the services provided under the auspices of the senior principal. This also creates a steep hierarchy where the incentives are to become a senior partner as quickly as possible. This was different from the traditional Systech operating model wherein business development (BD) and sales managers were responsible for bidding on and "selling" contracts which were then fulfilled through different functionally organized, operational business units (BU). There were also customer relationship executives (CRE) who were, in essence, account managers to help coordinate different interfaces, while ensuring service and delivery to the client agency. Duke's "Principal-Led" business model would dramatically alter the relatively balanced power of the BD, CRE, and BU managers in favor of "principals" (most of whom would come from the ranks of the newly acquired Consultco employees), change the delivery operations of ASD, and impact the traditional culture(s) of ASD and Systech by placing greater emphasis on leveraging and profitability over technical depth and product/service development. It would also tend to alter the traditional distribution of power, status, and respect within ASD that was based on technical expertise and distributed across multiple functional areas, toward a much steeper and narrower distribution of status, respect, and rewards in favor of principals.

The Actors Involved

To initiate the new principal-led business model, a 5-hour meeting of the top executives of ASD was set up so that "issues could be worked through and agreements reached." The meeting would be chaired by Sam Klein, the president of ASD, who reported to Group President Duke. Attending the meeting would be President Klein's direct reports, Lance Collins, Steve Grant, John Marshall, Ron Hogan, Cal Ramsey, and Mark Flowers. All the participants, except Steve Grant who was the former managing partner of the newly acquired Consultco unit, had between 12 and 30 years' tenure with Systech.

Two days before the meeting, an experienced external consultant, Bill Marsh, was asked to facilitate the meeting to help ensure it was as productive as possible since the general expectation of everyone was that it would be a highly contentious and unproductive session. In preparation for the session, Mark Flowers provided further background information about the situation and the participants and also commented that "It had been decided that John Duke would not attend the meeting for two reasons. First, because of his domineering personal style and second, to ensure that President Klein and his team would accept and implement the new model on their own." In addition, it was thought that a new member of the ASD team, Steve Grant, who had headed up the recently acquired Consultco consulting unit, would be able to fully describe the "Principal-Led" business model.

Outline of the Situation

In essence, then, the recently hired Group President John Duke was seeking to impose a new structure and culture on the ASD of Systech based on a management consulting business model. The ASD's leadership team, however, consisted mostly of Systech veterans who were used to a product/services and technical expertise business model and associated organizational culture. The only exception was Steve Grant who had joined the team only a few months earlier after John Duke acquired one of the consulting units of the failed Consultco company. ASD President Klein was under orders from Duke to implement the new "Principal-Led" business model even though he and the other members of the team were openly skeptical about it. As one member of the team commented privately, "Didn't we just buy Consultco? If the consulting model is so good and our model so bad, how come we bought them? We should be calling the shots."

The Showdown and Implicit Negotiation

President Klein opened the meeting by introducing the facilitator and stating that "the purpose of the meeting was to discuss how to take ASD forward" and "first and foremost we have to remember that the customer's first!" There was no mention of the new principal-led business model. Different participants then offered comments about what had to be addressed with most agreeing that "motivation and morale was so low we could start losing people." After about 30 min the facilitator interjected that he thought morale was an important topic, "but wasn't the purpose of the meeting to address the new business model?" President Klein said nothing, but Steve Grant began to explain the proposed principal-led business model. Almost simultaneously, Lance Collins said that Systech "couldn't have a principal-led model because it was a publicly held company not a partnership." Both Grant and Collins continued to give virtually simultaneous "speeches" for a few minutes before the facilitator stopped the interaction and summarized the points each was making as a way to document the different considerations as well as to invite more listening and understanding.

The pattern of virtually simultaneous speeches, for and against aspects of the principal-led model, given by Grant and Collins and then summarized by the facilitator, continued for another 30 min or so with the other participants, including President Klein, mostly quiet or asking a few clarifying questions. It was clear both men were used to being the center of attention and having their own way. The breakthrough in the meeting came when Steve Grant in a conciliatory voice acknowledged to Lance Collins that "Yes, things were different in Systech than in Consultco and maybe some responsibilities needed to be shared." Lance Collins quickly remarked "You're right" and began to discuss how things could be shared. The others now joined in with a burst of team productivity and relatively quickly developed an entirely new option in which a matrixed "integrated strategy team" for a client agency would be convened by a principal and include the relevant BD, customer relations, and BU managers, who would continue to report within their own organizational units. This integrative business model, as several of the team members remarked, "seemed to capture the best of both the new and the old ways of operating."

Naming the New Business Model: Should it be "Principal-Led"?

The participants were pleased and surprised at their agreement and ability to work together on developing the integrated strategy team model. At this point Mark Flowers wondered if the model could just be called "the Business Model" and to drop the term "Principal-Led" entirely "because it would be unnecessarily provocative." This sparked some discussion that came to a halt when President Klein said, "John Duke expects it to be called 'Principal-Led' and he would not be happy if it was called something else." This generated considerable push-back from all the other participants, including Steve Grant, who said, "the model we just agreed on was one of shared responsibility and that saying it was principal-led would be misleading." The meeting adjourned with general agreement that the new way of working should be called the ASD Business Model. It was proposed by Lance Collins and agreed to by all that Steve Grant should be the one responsible for writing up a summary of the ideas, concepts, and agreements from the meeting, coordinating with Lance Collins as needed.

A week later when President Klein's office distributed the summary report after clearing it with John Duke the title read "The ASD Business Model (Principal-Led)." Naturally, this caused uncertainty whether or not Duke had indeed accepted the substance of the integrative model proposed. A summary of the flow of events is provided in Table 6.2.

Analyzing Discourse as Situated Symbolic Action

If we examine the Systech episode from the prism of organizational discourse as situated symbolic action we can consider the three key frames of analysis: discourse as action, discourse as situated action, and discourse as symbolic action. Each of these frames adds a further layer to a more holistic understanding of what went on in the meeting, beyond the simple denotational or semantic level of discourse. They are analytically distinct but inseparable in practice. Although these layers are presented sequentially, they provide a nested, complementary, and additive analysis of successively increasing complexity, where each subsequent level assumes and encompasses the previous one.

The raw material for this analysis is based on the detailed field notes taken before, during, and after the episode; and is also informed by the knowledge of the interactional and organizational context acquired through the intervention experience. The analysis can be described as a mesodiscourse approach (Alvesson and Karreman, 2000: 1133), where the researcher is sensitive to both language use and its context,

Table 6.2. Sequence of Events: From Contest to Collaboration to Possible Confrontation

Contest	Transition Point	Collaboration	Confrontation/Coda
Group President Duke, a newcomer from a Big 5/4 consulting company orders ASD President Klein to implement a new "Principal-Led" business model	Grant acknowledges to Collins that "Yes, things were different in Systech than in Consultco and maybe some responsibilities needed to be shared"	Total team develops an integrative business model combining features from the current and proposed "Principal-Led" business models	Group President Duke via ASD President Klein reintroduces "Principal-Led" in name of ASD business model
Debate between Grant, a newcomer from Consultco, and Collins a 30-year Systech veteran over existing and new models	Collins quickly agrees, providing a bridge between the two groups and leading to a burst of productive energy by the participants	Grant, the newcomer, asked to summarize the meeting	Reintroduction of "Principal-Led" leads to uncertainty as to whether Duke indeed accepts the substance of the integrative model
Other meeting participants quiet		The name "Principal-Led" is intentionally dropped as too controversial and no longer accurately representing the adopted model	

Source: Adapted from Heracleous and Marshak, (2004).

149

interested in exploring linkages between the microlevel of interaction in distinct episodes, with features of the organizational context.

Discourse as Action

At the level of locutionary speech acts we might note the indirect introduction of the meeting by President Klein, not mentioning its purpose, and posing "customer's first" as a superordinate goal. In terms of illocutionary intent, President Klein in this case may have been intending to start off the meeting smoothly and to seek and encourage unity, bearing in mind the divergent positions and political stakes at the meeting. The relative silence by President Klein for the remainder of the meeting is also open to a range of interpretations, ranging from pre-existing intentions to give others a chance to own the issues, a desire to avoid conflict or confrontation, or even passive resistance to the new business model initiated by Group President Duke.

At the locutionary level, the group started off the meeting by engaging in a discussion of declining motivation and morale for around half an hour, which had to be redirected by the facilitator toward the stated purpose of the meeting, to discuss the potential implementation of a "Principal-Led" business model. At the illocutionary level, the engagement by all participants in this discussion of declining motivation and morale could again be seen as an attempt at group unity and/ or avoidance of the underlying conflict in the group.

Both the style (full "broadcast" mode) and substance of Grant and Collins remarks, in addition, could be seen as argumentative rhetorical ploys to advance or achieve their positions. Their illocutionary intents could have been to demonstrate to each other and their audience their severe conviction that their positions were the right thing for the organization. A contextual analysis as we will see later, however, raises the likelihood that this interpretation may be at best partly valid, given the high political stakes of the meeting.

Grant's comment that things were different in Systech and perhaps some responsibilities needed to be shared (locutionary level), indicated at the illocutionary level a desire for conciliation, which was enthusiastically responded to by all participants (perlocutionary level), who grasped the opportunity and indicated their willingness to actively participate in the discussion once again.

This level of analysis of discourse as action thus focuses primarily on who said what (locutionary speech act), what they intended to achieve (illocutionary speech act), and what effects these actions had on the audience (perlocutionary level). However, a fuller understanding of the illocutionary and perlocutionary dimensions of speech acts in particular needs to be informed by a contextual analysis (discourse as *situated* action) as well as by a symbolic analysis (discourse as *symbolic* action), as will be illustrated later.

Discourse as Situated Action (Action and Context)

In viewing discourse as situated action we must add several frames of context to more fully understand the actors' discourse, its intentions, and effects. In addition to the interactional context (what took place in the meeting and in what sequence), we have to add the organizational context and the broader industry context. The meeting was mandated by Group President Duke to initiate a partner-led business model. Duke came from one of the Big 5/4 accounting companies and had joined Systech less than 2 years ago. Duke had initiated the acquisition of the Consultco unit. Steve Grant had been the senior partner of the Consultco unit before it was acquired by Systech. Duke intended to change the Systech Advanced Services Division's operating model and culture in line with his previous experience in a major accounting firm.

Understanding this context helps to shed light on Duke's absence from the meeting. On the one hand he wanted the group to arrive at the "Principal-Led" business model "voluntarily," and on the other he knew that if he was at the meeting, there could be no real debate of the issues because everyone knew where he stood. His reputation of inflexibility would not have helped. Grant was therefore Duke's champion or implicit representative at the meeting. Lance Collins had 30 years experience at Systech and as head of BD and Sales had the most to lose in political terms with a change to a principal-led model, which may be why he assumed the role of champion in contesting the new business model.

President Klein was a 23-year Systech employee charged with implementing this new business model once it had been "accepted" by the relevant actors. Klein faced incompatible and conflicting pressures; his boss wanted him to implement an operating model that neither he nor most of his subordinates supported. However he had no choice, given his boss's determination and conviction that this was the right way to go. Understanding the organizational context of Klein's position can shed light on the nature of his discursive actions at the meeting, in particular his indirect introduction to the meeting and his subsequent silence, or discursive inaction, which given the context, becomes more understandable.

It was hard to ignore in this context the irony that the relatively small, newly acquired, "failed" Consultco unit (represented at the meeting by Grant) was now positioned by Group President Duke to tell the much larger acquiring Systech ASD how to do business. This was an irony not lost on participants, as private comments to the facilitator confirmed. Perhaps Grant was aware of the irony himself, as well as the strong likelihood that unless buy-in was achieved by the rest of the participants, the implementation of a "Principal-Led" model superficially accepted but deeply opposed would be in peril. Understanding this context sheds light on Grant's motivations for the pivotal discursive moment in the meeting, his conciliatory remark. The conflicting pressures within which other participants found themselves, shed light on their own motivations for grasping the conciliatory opportunity and working toward a commonly acceptable organizational model.

Discourse as Situated Symbolic Action (Action, Context, and Symbolism)

Finally, in viewing discourse as situated symbolic action, we must go beyond the meanings of words in context, and search for deeper symbolic meanings and discursive constructions that can shed light on what is observed and its context. In this case, the meeting ultimately involved issues of power, change, and adaptation; that is, a power struggle between oldtimers and newcomers over the appropriate operating structure and culture, of Systech. The discursive exchanges at the meeting can be viewed as a dramatic "showdown" between the proposed new operating model, culture, and power arrangements against the established ones at Systech ASD. The label "Principal-Led," in addition, was not simply a way to describe a certain operational model; it represented both a radical change in the existing order of things and the contest between oldtimers and newcomers, with the newcomers seeming poised to win given their support from the very top of the organization.

The initial discussion in the ASD team about low motivation and morale could be interpreted as an unconscious projection or an indirect means of expressing their own skeptical feelings and low morale about Group President Duke's intentions. Grant and Collins can be seen as symbolic champions of each camp engaged in combat over power, prestige, respect, and validation, in addition to the business future of ASD. After initial tests of strength, Grant's concession that "Yes, things were different in Systech than in Consultco and maybe some responsibilities needed to be shared," was a pivotal moment. That comment may have simultaneously signaled a willingness to compromise and an acknowledgment of the legitimacy of the established ASD culture and its managers. In the context it is important to note that it was the newly acquired Grant representing the new business model who made the initial conciliatory remark. This was quickly reciprocated by Collins and an understanding of how to share power in an integrated model containing aspects of both the old and the new models was reached.

Thus, at a symbolic level, the participants worked out their relative power positions in ASD and the framework for how to integrate or blend the old and the new. Group President Duke, however, who was not part of the symbolic negotiation, would not necessarily agree with the negotiated outcome. Duke's absence may have allowed the agreement to be reached, but not necessarily carried out, at least in name.

At the level of the symbolism of words, the label "Principal-Led" was a focus of debate, not only because it would influence existing power arrangements by symbolizing who would have the power to control the sales and delivery process, but also because it summed up and evoked in a single word the entire contest between oldtimers and newcomers over the future business model and culture of ASD, including all the associated thoughts and feelings of the involved participants. This illustrates the power of discursive labels to influence interpretation, action, and thus social reality. The latter reintroduction of "Principal-Led" into the title of the meeting report suggests that further negotiations with Duke may be needed to see if the substance of the new integrated model is, indeed, acceptable. Because Duke is characterized as insistent and not flexible, it might be likely that further attempts at "negotiating" relative power and change in ASD will be done symbolically and indirectly, or perhaps, not at all. Table 6.3 presents an outline of the earlier discussion.

Conclusions and Implications

In terms of organizational discourse, this analysis confirms the well-accepted insights that discourse cannot be adequately understood and interpreted in the absence of contextual knowledge; and that linguistic labels are more than just names, having the power, through their symbolic connotations to influence individuals' interpretations and actions and, thus, social reality. Beyond that, however, conceptualizing and analyzing discourse as situated symbolic action has a number of significant, interrelated implications. Specifically, it can help to respond to some of the key challenges facing the field of organizational discourse analysis in terms of providing a contextually sensitive approach to understanding organizational discourse, which is neither too narrow as to be unsuited to the organizational level of analysis nor too broad as to entail lax conceptualizations and debatable reasoning; supplying a framework by which discourse cannot only be empirically analyzed in a structured but also holistic and additive manner, involving progressive levels of complexity and appreciation; and finally demonstrating that organizational discourse analysis can have relevant, pragmatic implications that can help to narrow the gap between scholarly research and the concerns of organizational actors.

One key criticism of organizational discourse has been its lack of clarity with regard to the parameters of the field and in the specification or definition of the concept of discourse itself; in consequence leading to challenges to the theoretical value of discourse analysis (Grant, Keenoy, and Oswick, 2001; Keenoy, Oswick, and Grant, 1997). As van Dijk (1997: 1) notes, "the notion of discourse is essentially fuzzy" and can involve various dimensions, including language use, communication of beliefs, or social interaction. This fuzziness and difficulty of specifying the discourse concept relates to the rich antecedents of the field and to the variety of influences that bear upon it. This richness and diversity is a potential strength in terms of providing a treasury of ideas and frameworks from which organizational discourse researchers can draw. On the other hand, Alvesson and Karreman (2000: 1128) note the problem of lax conceptualization of the discourse concept: "we cannot help sometimes feeling that the word

Table 6.3. Outline of Discourse as Situated Symbolic Action in Systech Episode

Context	Discursive Actions	Symbolism
New group president hired from a Big 5/4 consulting firm	ASD president introduces meeting without mention of business model and posing customers as superordinate goal	Attempt by ASD president to encourage group unity and avoid conflict
Group President seeks to impose new, "Principal-Led" business model based on professional services consulting model	Participants initially talk about low motivation and morale	Struggle between oldtimers and newcomers over future of Systech-ASD
Group President buys part of failed firm Consultco	Debate between two individuals over "Principal-Led" versus existing business model	Fight between two leading representatives of each "side" to see who will win
Meeting of ASD without group president to discuss new business model	Acknowledgment by newcomer that current model has value and new model may need to be modified	Newcomer representative "yields" by acknowledging the legitimacy of the oldtimers and their ways of doing business

Table 6.3. (continued)

Context	Discursive Actions	Symbolism
Existing ASD president and top team sceptical about new model and new group president	Total team creates new, integrated model to be called "The ASD Business Model"	With the contest over status, legitimacy and future directions settled, the total team is free to "integrate" the old and the new in a new collaborative model
	Newcomer asked to summarize meeting	Newcomer is asked to write up summary as a sign of trust and acceptance
President of ASD under pressure from Group President to change and from his team to resist	Announcement a week later by President's office of "The ASD Business Model (Principal-Led)"	Despite team agreements within ASD, the new Group President is still calling the shots and cannot be ignored. His power is acknowledged by the ASD president who unilaterally inserts "Principal-Led" in the name of the new business model

Source: Adapted from Heracleous and Marshak, (2004).

discourse is used to cover up muddled thinking . . . . Discourse sometimes comes close to standing for everything, and thus nothing." The dilemma then becomes, how can researchers make the most of organizational discourse's rich conceptual antecedents, without falling into the trap of insufficient specification and lax conceptualization?

Paradoxically, a related issue is the existence of approaches that have a narrow, often exclusive focus on the text itself, and are thus unsuited or unwilling to more fully address and encompass contextual aspects within which texts circulate. Examples include ethnomethodological conversation analysis (Atkinson, 1988) or linguistic approaches focusing on such issues as intonation or grammatical cohesion (see, e.g. Couper-Kuhlen, 2003; Martin, 2003) and whose concerns tend to stop at the sentence rather than the level of whole texts or collections of texts within broader discourses. Such perspectives are perfectly legitimate given their specified tasks, but (at least in their conventional forms) are unsuited to organizational discourse analysis where an adequate understanding of text must be informed by an understanding of various levels of context. The postmodernist idea of unlimited interpretations and indeterminacy of meaning is indeed questioned by the potential of employing an understanding of context as a means to develop more grounded interpretations of textual materials (Eco, 1990; Giddens, 1987).

A conceptualization of discourse as situated symbolic action can potentially contribute to addressing the challenge of avoiding both the Scylla of lax conceptualization and insufficient specification on the one hand, as well as the Charybdis of too narrow conceptions on the other. Conceptualizing discourse as situated symbolic action provides a perspective that takes advantage of the rich theoretical antecedents of the concept of discourse, but at the same time is sufficiently structured and empirically applicable to organizational contexts. This perspective can potentially supply researchers in organizational discourse with a further framework with which to theoretically ground the concept of discourse and with a contextually sensitive approach to conducting empirical discourse analyses. Viewing discourse as situated symbolic action can thus help to address a further key challenge to organizational discourse, the development of discursive methodologies that are applicable to the organizational level, and that go beyond the text to address the linkages between text and context

(Hardy, 2001; Keenoy, Oswick, and Grant, 1997), as well as the symbolic and constructive aspects of discourse.

In this connection, the view of discourse advanced in this chapter proposes three interrelated analytical levels relating to discursive action, situation, and symbolism. Although these layers are presented sequentially, they provide a nested, complementary, and additive analysis of successively increasing complexity. Each subsequent level assumes and encompasses the previous one, both logically and empirically. For example, viewing discourse as situated symbolic action logically assumes that specific communicative actions are taking place, that a knowledge of several frames of context is employed by actors, and can be explored by organizational discourse researchers to interpret these discursive actions and to further validate their own understanding of context; and deeper symbolic meanings that relate to the very substance of language as integral to the social construction of reality are inherent in this process.

If speech act theory had solely been used to analyze the Systech episode, for example, a good idea of *what* was said and of the different types of speech acts used by the actors could be developed, as well as some idea of their intentions. However, it would not have been possible to more fully appreciate *why* they said what they did, why they at times kept silent, or how pivotal moments in the episode evolved such as when all participants grasped the opportunity to jointly construct a more broadly acceptable organizational model. In order to more fully appreciate such issues, a deeper understanding of relevant aspects of the group, organizational and industrial contexts, and how these nested levels of context related to communicative interactions at the meeting would be needed. For example, President Klein's discursive action of indirectly presenting the meeting without mentioning its purpose and posing client satisfaction as a superordinate goal could be illuminated through a knowledge of organizational context; in particular a knowledge of the high-political stakes in the meeting, the latent conflict relating to the proposed principal-led model, and the Group President's desire to have this model implemented against the wishes of most employees of that division.

Further, even by understanding communicative interactions and their context, we still would not have been able to more fully appreciate agents' intentions and interpretations and the constructive role of discourse unless we employ a symbolic lens. In the Systech episode, for example, why was the label "Principal-Led" such an emotionally loaded as well as fervently resisted term? This label can be understood symbolically, not simply as a way to "rationally" describe a potential operating model widely used in the industry and supported by the Group President, but as encompassing a radically new organizational order for this Systech division, involving significant shifts in power arrangements and fostering a tenacious contest between opposing camps. Each subsequent analytical level of discourse thus contributes an additive lens to the analysis with a view to reaching more in-depth understandings of the discourse and social context under investigation.

A further criticism of organizational discourse is that it is too abstract, an "intellectual self-indulgence with no practical payoff" (Grant, Keenoy, and Oswick, 2001: 10). This criticism is related to a broader issue of relevance in organization theory, the often discussed disconnect between what we study as academics and the concerns of organizational actors (Kerr, 2004). The perspective on discourse advanced in this chapter, and the analysis based on it, help to illustrate that organizational discourse can be compatible and complementary with more applied approaches to social science (such as action research in this case), and can produce actionable knowledge (Argyris, 1996). In this case, employing this perspective has enabled the facilitator to help the group move beyond internal, divisive conflict over a proposed organizational arrangement and to facilitate the joint crafting of a more broadly acceptable one.

Adopting a situated symbolic action perspective thus supports an integrative, as well as practically oriented, approach to research consistent with applied methodologies such as action research. Lewin (1947) intended action research to help address the inherent limitations of studying complex social events in a laboratory as well as the artificiality of separating out single-behavioral elements from an integrated system (Foster, 1972). He advocated the study of social dynamics "not by transforming them into quantifiable units of physical actions and reactions, but by studying the intersubjectively valid sets of meanings, norms and values that are the immediate determinates of behaviour" (Peters and Robinson, 1984: 115). In postulating that discursive events have integrated and contextualized literal and symbolic components, a discourse as situated symbolic action perspective is supportive of the action research orientation by inviting a more holistic consideration of social phenomena. Taking the constructive tenets of the organizational discourse field seriously, that talk is itself action and it is also the raw material of the social construction of reality (Berger and Luckmann, 1966; Oswick, Keenoy, and Grant, 1997; Searle, 1995), entails and calls for a more discourse-sensitive, holistic approach to organizational research (Marshak et al., 2000). This perspective on discourse can provide a dual applied and theoretical orientation to help both managers and organization development practitioners support a more reflexive stance as to the context and meaning of unfolding events, go beyond the literal aspects of talk and interaction, more fully appreciate the symbolic aspects in particular organizational contexts, and develop more in-depth understandings of the situation and more appropriate interventions. A view of discourse as situated symbolic action is offered as a potential contribution to this endeavor, thus helping to address a further lacuna in the field of organizational discourse, the "challenge to incorporate the insights of discourse analysis into diagnostic and intervention strategies" (Marshak et al., 2000: 246).

In conclusion, the view of discourse as situated symbolic action is offered as an additional perspective or lens in the emerging field of organizational discourse. This perspective could help organizational actors and organization development practitioners, who have to make decisions in real time and complex, shifting settings, "read" organizational talk and action in a manner that goes beyond what is literally said, in a contextually sensitive, symbolic way, and thus improve their ability to take responsive actions. It is also hoped that this approach will contribute to sustaining the discourse field's vibrancy and promise and at the same time help it address some of its fundamental challenges. Finally, it is hoped that this perspective will encourage more research that combines a scholarly orientation with applied concerns, as well as more holistic discursive studies of organizational phenomena.

References

Alvesson, M. and Karreman, D. 2000. Varieties of discourse: On the study of organizations through discourse analysis. *Human Relations*, 53: 1125–1149.

Argyris, C. 1996. Actionable knowledge: Design causality in the service of consequential theory. *Journal of Applied Behavioral Science*, 32: 390–408.

Aristotle. 1991. *On rhetoric*. Kennedy G. A. (trans.). Oxford: Oxford University Press.

Atkinson, P. 1988. Ethnomethodology: A critical review. *Annual Review of Sociology*, 14: 441–465.

Austin, J. L. 1962. *How to do things with words*. Cambridge, MA: Harvard University Press.

Bateson, G. 1972. *Steps to an ecology of mind*. London: Intertext.

Berger, P. and Luckmann, T. 1966. *The social construction of reality*. London: Penguin.

Bitzer, L. F. 1968. The rhetorical situation. *Philosophy & Rhetoric*, 1 (1): 1–14.

Blum-Kulka, S. 1997. Discourse pragmatics. In T. A. van Dijk (ed.), *Discourse studies: A multidisciplinary introduction*, vol. 2: 38–63. Beverly Hills, CA: Sage.

Charland, M. 1987. Constitutive rhetoric: The case of the peuple Quebecois. *Quarterly Journal of Speech*, 73: 133–150.

Checkland, P. and Holwell, S. 1998. Action research: Its nature and validity. *Systemic practice and action research*, 1: 9–21.

Cicourel, A. V. 1981. Three models of discourse analysis: The role of social structure. *Discourse Processes*, 3: 101–131.

Couper-Kuhlen, E. 2003. Intonation and discourse: Current views from within. In D. Schiffrin, D. Tannen, and H. Hamilton (eds.), *Handbook of discourse analysis*: 13–34. Oxford: Blackwell.

Cunliffe, A. L. 2001. Managers as practical authors: Reconstructing our understanding of management practice. *Journal of Management Studies*, 38: 351–371.

Dickens, L. and Watkins, K. 1999. Action research: Rethinking Lewin. *Management Learning*, 30: 127–140.

van Dijk, T. A. 1977. *Text and context: Explorations in the semantics and pragmatics of discourse*. London: Longman.

1997. The study of discourse. In T. A. van Dijk (ed.), *Discourse studies: A multidisciplinary introduction*, vol. 1: 1–34. Beverly Hills, CA: Sage.

Eco, U. 1990. *The limits of interpretation*. Bloomington, IN: Indiana University Press.

Fairclough, N. 1992. Discourse and text: Linguistic and intertextual analysis within discourse analysis. *Discourse & Society*, 3: 193–217.

2003. "Political correctness": The politics of culture and language. *Discourse & Society*, 14: 17–28.

Fine, G. A. 1984. Negotiated orders and organizational cultures. *Annual Review of Sociology*, 10: 239–262.

Foster, M. 1972. An introduction to the theory and practice of action research in work organizations. *Human Relations*, 25: 529–556.

Frake, C. O. 1964. How to ask for a drink in Subanun. *American Anthropologist*, **66**: 127–132.

Gergen, K. J. and Thatchenkery, T. J. 1996. Organization science as social construction: Postmodern potentials. *Journal of Applied Behavioral Science*, **32**: 356–377.

Giddens, A. 1984. *The Constitution of Society*. Cambridge, MA: Polity.
    1987. *Social Theory and Modern Sociology*. Cambridge, MA: Polity.

Gill, A. M. and Whedbee, K. 1997. Rhetoric. In T. A. van Dijk (ed.), *Discourse studies: A multidisciplinary introduction*, vol. 1: 157–183. Beverly Hills, CA: Sage.

Goffman, E. 1961. *Asylums*. New York: Anchor.

Grant, D., Keenoy, T. and Oswick, C. 2001. Organizational discourse: Key contributions and challenges. *International Studies of Management and Organization*, **31** (3): 5–24.

Gronbeck, B. E. 1973. The rhetoric of social-institutional change: Black action at Michigan. In G. P. Morhmann, C. J. Stewart, and D. J. Ochs (eds.), *Explorations in rhetorical criticism*: 96–123. Pennsylvania: Pennsylvania State University Press.

Gumperz, J. J. and Levinson, S. C. 1991. Rethinking linguistic relativity. *Current Anthropology*, **32**: 613–623.

Hardy, C. 2001. Researching organizational discourse. *International Studies of Management and Organization*, **31** (3): 25–47.

Heracleous, L. 2004. Interpretivist approaches to organizational discourse. In D. Grant, C. Hardy, C. Oswick, and L. L. Putnam (eds.), *Handbook of organizational discourse*: 175–192. Beverly Hills, CA: Sage.

Heracleous, L. and Barrett, M. 2001. Organizational change as discourse: Communicative actions and deep structures in the context of information technology implementation. *Academy of Management Journal*, **44**: 755–778.

Heracleous, L. and Hendry, J. 2000. Discourse and the study of organization: Toward a structurational perspective. *Human Relations*, **53**: 1251–1286.

Heracleous, L. and Marshak, R. 2004. Conceptualizing organizational discourse as situated symbolic action. *Human Relations*, **57**: 1285–1312.

Hodge, R. and Kress, G. 1988. *Social semiotics*. Cambridge, MA: Polity.

Hirsch, P. M. 1986. From ambushes to golden parachutes: Corporate takeovers as an instance of cultural framing and institutional integration. *American Journal of Sociology*, **91**: 800–837.

Huxham, C. and Vangen, S. 2003. Researching organizational practice through action research: Case studies and design choices. *Organizational Research Methods*, **6**: 383–403.

Hymes, D. 1964. Toward ethnographies of communication. *American Anthropologist,* 66 (6), part 2: 12–25.

1972. Models of the interaction of language and social life. In J. Gumperz and D. Hymes (eds.), *Directions in sociolinguistics: The ethnography of communication:* 35–71. New York, NY: Holt, Rinehart and Winston.

Jakobson, R. 1960. Closing statement: Linguistics and poetics. In T. Sebeok (ed.), *Style in language:* 350–77. Cambridge, MA: MIT Press.

Keenoy, T., Oswick, C. and Grant, D. 1997. Organizational discourses: Text and context. *Organization,* 42: 147–157.

Kerr, S. 2004. Introduction: Bringing practitioners and academics together. *Academy of Management Executive,* 18, 1: 94–96.

Lewin, K. 1947. Frontiers in group dynamics: Channels of group life: Social planning and action research. *Human Relations,* 1: 143–153.

March, J. G. 1962. The business firm as a political coalition. *Journal of Politics,* 24: 662–678.

Marshak, R. J. and Heracleous, L. 2005. A discursive approach to organization development. *Action Research,* 3: 69–88.

Marshak, R. J., Keenoy, T., Oswick, C. and Grant, D. 2000. From outer words to inner worlds. *Journal of Applied Behavioral Science,* 36: 245–258.

Martin, J. R. 2003. Cohesion and texture. In D. Schiffrin, D. Tannen, and H. Hamilton (eds.), *Handbook of discourse analysis:* 35–53. Oxford: Blackwell.

Mead, G. H. 1934. *Mind, self and society.* Chicago, IL: University of Chicago Press.

Mintzberg, H. 1983. *Power in and around organizations.* Englewood Cliffs, NJ: Prentice Hall.

Morgan, G. and Smircich, L. 1980. The case for qualitative research. *Academy of Management Review,* 5: 491–500.

Oswick, C., Keenoy, T. and Grant, D. 1997. Managerial discourses: words speak louder than actions? *Journal of Applied Management Studies,* 6: 5–12.

Perry, C. and Zuber-Skerritt, O. 1994. Doctorates by action research for senior practicing managers. *Management Learning,* 25: 341–365.

Peters, M. and Robinson, V. 1984. The origins and status of action research. *Journal of Applied Behavioral Science,* 20: 113–124.

Phillips, N. and Brown, J. L. 1993. Analyzing communication in and around organizations: A critical hermeneutic approach. *Academy of Management Journal,* 36: 1547–1576.

Phillips, N. and Hardy, C. 2002. *Discourse analysis: Investigating processes of social construction.* London: Sage.

Samra-Fredericks, D. 2003. Strategizing as lived experience and strategists' everyday efforts to shape strategic direction. *Journal of Management Studies*, 40: 141–174.

Schein, E. 1987. *The clinical perspective in fieldwork*. Qualitative Research Methods, CA: Sage.

Searle, J. 1975. Indirect speech acts. In P. Cole and J. Morgan (eds.), *Syntax and semantics 3: Speech acts*: 59–82. New York, NY: Academic Press. 1995. *The construction of social reality*. New York: Free Press.

Strauss, A. 1967. Language and identity. In J. G. Manis and B. N. Meltzer (eds.), *Symbolic interaction: A reader in social psychology*: 322–328. Boston, MA: Allyn and Bacon.

Strauss, A., Schatzman, L., Ehrlich, D., Bucher, R. and Sabshin, M. 1963. The hospital and its negotiated order. In E. Freidson (ed.), *The hospital in modern society*: 147–169. New York, NY: Free Press.

Strauss, A., Schatzman, L., Bucher, R., Ehrlich, D. and Sabshin, M. 1964. *Psychiatric ideologies and institutions*. Glencoe, IL: Free Press.

Weick, K. 1995. *Sensemaking in organizations*. Thousand Oaks, CA: Sage.

Whorf, B. 1941. The relation of habitual thought and behaviour to language. In L. Spier (ed.), *Language, culture and personality: Essays in memory of edward sapir*: 75–93. Menasha, WI: Sapir Memorial Publication Fund.

7 | Analyzing Discourse II: A Tale of Three Discourses[1]

T
HIS chapter provides an empirical illustration of a structurational view of discourse, outlined in chapter 5, where discourse is seen as a duality constituted by two dynamically interrelated levels: the surface level of communicative actions and the deeper level of discursive structures, recursively linked through the modality of actors' interpretive schemes. Within this broad view of discourse, an analytical approach based on rhetoric and hermeneutics was employed to analyze the discourses operating in the UK operations of People Associates (PA),[2] a global consulting firm focusing on people issues, in the context of PA's organizational change program that took place in the mid-1990s.

This study had three aims. First, to clarify the nature of "modes of discourse" (Giddens, 1984: 33) in organizational settings. Second, to explore how, if at all, modes of discourse in specific social settings are interrelated. Finally, the study aimed to explore the constructive potential of modes of discourse in their social and organizational context. Empirical analysis revealed three modes of discourse, which I have labeled the dominant discourse, the strategic change discourse, and the marginalized counter-discourse. As will be discussed in detail later, the dominant discourse is patterned in terms of enthymeme structures (rhetorical structures of argumentation that draw from the premises already held by the audience, in particular social contexts) that possess both normative and positive, action-oriented, elements. The strategic change discourse draws its legitimacy by being located in the structures and constructions of the dominant discourse, exhibiting a co-optive relationship with the dominant discourse. The counter-discourse, on the other hand, bears an antagonistic relationship with the dominant discourse. It is patterned by what it opposes but its

---

[1] This chapter is based on Heracleous (2006).
[2] The name of the organization and other related information is disguised.

opposition is weak and impotent in influencing its social and organizational context. These modes of discourse can be expressed as rhetorical enthymemes constituted of both relatively stable normative structures and flexible, action-oriented structures. The results suggest that the constructive potential of discourse is based primarily on its deeper structures and the consonance of surface communicative actions with these structures.

Empirical Research and Discourse Analysis Approach

Field Research

In early 1994, I set out to study the nature and constructive role of organizational discourse(s) in the context of organizational change. I collected the empirical data reported here between June 1994 and March 1996, and also conducted retrospective data gathering focusing on the organization's history and critical incidents, going back to the organization's founding in the United Kingdom in 1963. The philosophical commitments guiding the research program centered on interpretivism, the conviction that accounts of social life must consider the actors' own frame of reference and be adequate at this level of first-order meaning, and on a view of reality as intersubjective and socially constructed (Berger and Luckmann, 1966).[3]

I employed the methodological paradigm of ethnography with an action research or "clinical" element, a role approaching that of "the ethnographer as clinician" (Schein, 1987a), but with a more pronounced ethnographic rather than clinical element. I partly acted as a clinician since I was allowed access to the organization on the assumption that my involvement would "add value" to the organization change program under way. As I realized later on, this orientation was deeply ingrained in the organization's culture and the way members related to each other (for a detailed exposition of this aspect from a researcher reflexivity viewpoint see Heracleous, 2001). In this context, I offered periodic feedback to senior management regarding actors' views on the change process and any specific issues that actors brought up in this connection, with the understanding that

---

[3] These philosophical commitments were discussed in detail in chapter 2.

management could employ this feedback in more effectively managing change in the organization. The incorporation of a clinical element can enable the clinician to be taken "behind the scenes" by senior managers who seek advice, but could also constrain data collection from lower levels of the organization who perceive the clinician as an instrument of management, or "one of them" (Schein, 1987b). In this case, however, being perceived as a clinician in a clinicians' land proved to be an important facilitating factor in data collection from all levels of the organization.

Given the commitment to understanding the *'natives'* frames of meaning (Geertz, 1973), I employed the research strategy of a long-itudinal case study with an emergent, interpretive slant (for a debate on the different approaches to case study research see Eisenhardt, 1989, 1991 and Dyer and Wilkins, 1991). After initial correspondence with the company enquiring about access for the study, I was invited to its London headquarters for two separate interviews with senior management, after which I was granted access. Within the strategy of a longitudinal case study, I used the methods of in-depth interviewing, participant and nonparticipant observation, cultural audits through focus group sessions, use of informants, periodic descriptive surveys, and document analysis. I conducted a total of 104 interviews involving consultants, surveys and IT staff, support staff, and past leaders of PA. I triangulated the data within and across methods in order to increase the internal validity of the findings and discover within- or between-method divergences or convergences that could lead to new lines of inquiry. After I discerned the main cultural values and beliefs of the organization, my findings were circulated to all employees, who widely judged them to be representative of their organization, a key validating criterion of ethnographic research (Hammersley and Atkinson, 1995).

My initial analytical aim was to detect patterns and processes which could help to "make sense of what is going on in the scenes documented by the data" (Hammersley and Atkinson, 1995: 209–210). I was conscious throughout the research program of what Giddens (1993) calls the "double hermeneutic" in social science, and Van Maanen (1979) "first- and second-order concepts" in ethnography, aiming to align my understanding with the first-order concepts of the agents involved. In the context of a hermeneutic orientation, I did not take individual fragments of data as indicative of cultural features but interpreted them as part of a wider corpus of data. The data analysis was characterized by an iterative process of going back and forth from critical reflection to the data, and from part to whole, searching for key themes and patterns, and questioning, redefining, or buttressing with further evidence the themes and patterns identified (Kets de Vries and Miller, 1987; Thachankary, 1992).

Discourse Analysis Approach: Hermeneutics and Rhetoric

The discourse analysis approach I employed drew from the field of rhetoric (Aristotle, 1991; Gill and Whedbee, 1997) within the context of a hermeneutic orientation (Giddens 1979, 1987; Ricoeur 1971a,b; 1973a,b; 1983, 1997). Rhetoric and hermeneutics share close historical and conceptual linkages as well as a constructive view of language (Berger and Luckmann, 1966; Palmer, 1969). Rhetoric originally included the domains of moral education, philology, and interpretation of classical texts (Palmer, 1997). Principles of textual interpretation were then transferred from rhetoric to hermeneutics during the Renaissance, when rhetoric encompassed not only the *ars bene dicendi*— the art of speaking well but also the *ars bene legendi*—the art of reading well (Gadamer, 1997; emphasis in original).

A key insight in hermeneutics, as the art of interpretating texts, (Ricoeur, 1973a, 1997), is that meaning does not reside solely in the text but is conditioned by its context and the perceptions of the agents within that context (Palmer, 1969). As discussed in chapter 2, however, acknowledging the possibility of various textual interpretations does not necessitate a lapse to relativism, the resignation to the idea that there is no way to arrive at certain textual interpretations that are more valid than others (Phillips and Brown, 1993). For Ricoeur (1971a), for example, a text displays a limited field of potential interpretations as opposed to being a repository of potentially unlimited meanings. In line with this view, Giddens suggests that the interpretive validity of texts can be improved through ethnographic inquiry in the settings of production of the text, the intellectual resources the author has drawn on, the characteristics of the audience it is addressed to, the author's or speaker's intentions, as well as the practical knowledge involved in writing or speaking with a certain style for a particular audience (Giddens, 1979: 43; 1987: 106).

In line with the above, I approached texts as collections of communicative actions fixed in writing (Ricoeur, 1971b, 1973b), and analyzed interview transcripts, published documents, and observations as texts. I employed intertextual analysis, aiming to identify central themes in and across texts, explored the existence and extent of thematic unity (how central themes are interrelated in broader argumentations both within texts and intertextually), and searched for patterns in textual and ethnographic data over time (Barry and Elmes, 1997; Kets de Vries and Miller, 1987; Thachankary, 1992).

With regard to rhetorical analysis, I aimed to identify the rhetorical strategies that actors have consciously or unconsciously used consistently in PA. These rhetorical strategies act as structural features of discourse and can be discerned through the analysis of communicative actions of various speakers/authors, discussing various issues in different situational and temporal contexts. These rhetorical strategies most often take the form of enthymemes or argumentations-in-use. These enthymemes are not necessarily consciously evoked, being located in actors' practical consciousness (Giddens, 1984).

Enthymemes are rhetorical structures of argumentation. Traditionally, "whereas the syllogism was the most prominent form of logical demonstration, the enthymeme was its rhetorical counterpart. Enthymemes were thought of as syllogisms whose premises are drawn from the audience. They are usually only partially expressed, their logic being completed by the audience" (Eemeren et al., 1997: 213). Enthymemes, therefore, are not universally rational or true, but are so only within specific sociocultural contexts, depending on their conformity to the audience's existing beliefs and assumptions (Cheney et al., 2004). One way researchers can uncover taken for granted values and beliefs within particular contexts is through identification and analysis of enthymemes, and particularly their unstated and assumed premises (Gill and Whedbee, 1997). These values and beliefs can be seen as structures of legitimation that underlie agents' interpretations and (communicative) actions (Giddens, 1984, 1993).

Enthymemes whose premises are inculcated in agents in particular organizational contexts have been labeled "enthymeme 2" as opposed to "enthymeme 1" where the premises are drawn from broader societal and cultural contexts (Tompkins and Cheney, 1985), even though it would be difficult to distinguish neatly between these in practice. In line with an interpretive view of organizational discourse,

enthymemes have an important constitutive role in organizations, influencing agents' interpretations and actions (Cheney and McMillan,
1990; Cheney et al., 2004). Thus, I treated the research site as a
"field of institutionalized discourse" (Cheney and McMillan, 1990:
103) and endeavored to discover these institutionalized features that
I operationalized as organizational enthymemes.

In order to identify enthymemes in PA, I first searched for central
textual themes. I explored individual texts for central themes that
were explicitly stated or assumed, and then compared the results
intertextually to discover themes that transcended individual texts
and were present in several texts deriving from diverse sources and
produced in different situations. I then analyzed the interconnections
among these central themes and their functions in structures of argumentation. I then combined the findings of the first two steps to
determine enthymeme structures, following Fisher (1988). I finally
conducted intertextual analysis, relating findings from single texts
across several texts, moving from the single texts to the broader
discourses and vice versa. Throughout the process I utilized ethnographic data both as a resource for enriching textual interpretation
and as a form of triangulation with the textual data, in order to
improve the validity of textual interpretation and the enthymeme
structures structuring these texts.

Three Modes of Discourse at People Associates

Central Values and Beliefs at People Associates

My interviews with past leaders and document analysis indicated that
PA's early growth was characterized by conditions fostering the development of "thick" cultures. These conditions include a long history
and stable membership, absence of institutional alternatives, and fre-
quent interaction among members (Wilkins and Ouchi, 1983). Key
features of PA's culture included a strong client orientation, a perception that the "core business" of the firm was job evaluation, and also
high individualism and autonomy of consultants. The mythology of
the organization was replete with the figures of "lone rangers" and
"guidechart jockeys" who would individually "ride" in client organizations, conduct the job efficiently, and help to achieve record annual
sales for the consulting firm. The organizational structure was loose,

and subject to continuous incremental changes labeled "autumn man-euvers" in the organizational vocabulary, that did not pose a challenge to deeper, entrenched values and beliefs.

Although there are other subcultures in PA (in particular the sup-port staff and survey department's subcultures), it is the consultants' subculture that dominates. Its importance is indicated by the high number of its members, its potent influence on organizational deci-sions and actions, and its strong internal homogeneity. In terms of membership numbers, over two-thirds of PA's employees are consul-tants and many of the around one-fifth of employees who work in the survey and IT departments aspire to becoming consultants in the longer term, as ethnographic data have shown. In terms of influence on decisions and actions, leaders of the consulting subculture deter-mine PA' strategic direction and most internal organizational arrange-ments. Finally, in terms of homogeneity of the dominant consulting subculture, data on the recruitment process, observation of behaviors, and in-depth interviews indicated a highly homogeneous body of consultants. When interviewing new recruits and asking for surprising or puzzling features of PA (Schein, 1992), many marveled at how "everybody is so much like me."

The Dominant Discourse

I analyzed several texts in PA such as transcribed interviews, internal memorandums, reports of project groups, company publications, and Christmas speeches over a 5-year period (1991–1995) prepared and delivered by three different MDs. Two discursive central themes were discerned: *success*, or another variant such as being number 1, and *clients*. Success was constructed financially, and adding value to cli-ents was seen as the means of achieving success. These central themes were involved in implicit and more explicit enthymematic structures in which they functioned as goals or means. These central themes are part of an overall rhetorical strategy characterized by primary and secondary argument structures that fulfill normative and positive functions in their organizational context.

The core enthymeme identified takes a form of an argument where two premises jointly support a conclusion (P1 and P2 lead to C1). This conclusion (C1) then becomes the first premise (P1') of a sub-enthymeme which, jointly with a second premise (P2'), supports a

Table 7.1. Core Enthymeme Structure of the Dominant Discourse

Enthymeme Structure	Discursive Manifestation		Nature of Statement	
P1 + P2	P1	Our key goal is X	P1	Value stating desirable state of affairs
	P2	Y leads to X	P2	General belief of contingent relationship in normative domain
C1→ P1' + P2'	C1→P1'	Therefore, we need to take appropriate action to achieve Y	C1→P1'	General conclusion on required type or class of action
	P2'	Action Z leads to Y	P2'	Belief of contingent relationship in the action-oriented domain
C2	C2'	Therefore, we need to do Z	C2	Conclusion of required specific action to be taken

Source: Adapted from Heracleous (2006).

second conclusion (C2). Table 7.1 shows the core enthymeme structure identified, the main discursive manifestation of each element, and an explanation of the nature of each statement.

The structurational view of discourse, discussed in chapter 5, provides the theoretical grounding for this enthymeme pattern. P1 and P2 represent persistent deep structures of agents' discourses; these are the implicit, taken for granted, and usually unstated premises, acting as entrenched structures of legitimation in specific social contexts. These deep structures are continuously manifested in agents' (communicative) actions, residing in agents' "practical consciousness" (Giddens, 1984). Their main function is normative, acting to support or rebuke action-oriented argumentations which are more explicitly articulated in communicative actions (represented by P1', P2', and C2). The content of P2' and C2 is variable and can shift according to the situation. The communicative level enthymeme structures are thus not only flexible in terms of content but also patterned and entrenched in deeper discursive structures. These deeper structures function as structures of legitimation that are highly influential on actors' interpretations and actions. Analysis of PA's discourse indicated that X is the central theme of success (constructed financially), Y is the central theme of adding value to clients, and undertaking *strategic change* was the situational exigency that took the place of the flexible theme Z.

The central themes of success and clients, interrelated in a means–end relationship, dominated all the Christmas speeches given by PA's

MDs over a 5-year period. Such speeches are highly symbolic as they are delivered to the whole organization in a context where the MD recounts what is truly important to them and the organization. In addition, they are not for outside consumption, so comments aimed at managing the organization's image with outside stakeholders are helpfully absent from these speeches. In PA's case, three different MDs were involved over this period, which increases the validity of inter textual findings, as the texts did not originate from the same person and at the same time but in a sense from the "collective consciousness" of the highest levels of the organization.

Several other texts displayed the above themes. For example, the following is an extract from a report to senior management prepared in 1995 by the "expertise working group" that was charged with reviewing consultants' expertise development process and was led by a senior partner who was also a member of senior management. The following extract is a key part of the document as it in effect contains the legitimatory statement as to why managerial and consulting attention and scarce organizational resources should be diverted from other areas to the expertise area.

The purpose of the expertise area is to help grow the business:

> In the long term by developing client solutions which are not easily replicable by competitors and which represent value added to the client and therefore good margins for PA.
> In the short term/medium term by developing and upgrading client solutions and equipping/enabling consultants to sell and deliver.
> →The ultimate test of success will be for PA Consultants:
>
> – does it help me sell more?
> – at value added prices?"

This textual fragment is a microcosm of the dominant discourse's enthymeme structures, central themes, and their constructions: First, success ("the ultimate test of success . . .") is matter-of-factly placed as the ultimate objective of the whole endeavor. Second, success is constructed financially both for individual consultants ("does it help me sell more?") and for the organization ("the purpose of the expertise area is to help grow the business"). Third, clients are seen as the means to this success ("in the long term by developing client solutions . . . in the short term/medium term by developing and upgrading client solutions . . ."). Fourth, the expertise project, the surface theme of this textual fragment, occupies the place of Z in the secondary structure. This is flexible enough so that matters relating situational exigencies (the positive order) are located in it and legitimated by reference to the primary structure (the normative order).

A telling indication of the importance of the central themes of clients and success, and specifically financial constructions of success, could be seen in the organization's reward and evaluation system. This is a key organizational process in that it indicates what an organization values and what agents should attribute importance to. Interviews showed that consultants overwhelmingly believed that their success and promotion in PA was determined by whether they achieved their billing and sales targets. For example, a widespread view among consultants was that

... at the end of the day I think that PA will place more emphasis on meeting the targets than anything else. . . . I believe that my evaluation for the last year was based 100% on the extent to which I met my billing target, regardless of any circumstances which impacted on my ability to meet this target.

Referring to PA's efforts to broaden the evaluation criteria, another consultant expressed the broadly held view that

The performance management process is still very numbers driven. I mean, there's been a lot of talk about moving away from that, and the competency framework is useful in focusing more on behaviors, than just on numbers, just on outputs, but at the end of the day, you don't hit the numbers, you don't get a decent appraisal, irrespective . . . .

Targets were set at a very challenging level. Sales targets depended on one's seniority with more senior people having higher sales targets. Billing targets on the other hand were similar across the hierarchical spectrum, generally set at 185 days per year. Excluding weekends and holidays, this did not leave much time to develop client relationships, develop project proposals, sell projects, and carry them out; all while trying to develop one's expertise. This caused high levels of stress to consultants who knew that if they missed their targets for 2 years in a row, their job was at risk. To highlight this point, some consultants mentioned the example of colleagues returning to work after falling sick, without having made a full recovery, because they were concerned about meeting their targets. In turn PA's focus on billing and sales targets led to zealous guarding of one's client list, which constituted a potent power base in PA, a means by which one's success in the organization was attainable and sustainable.

In interviews, consultants reiterated how important it was to develop one's internal network so that one would be invited to participate in delivering projects to clients. The widely held view was that "it's down to who you know and how you manage your network." PA exhibited an internal market in this regard, and it was up to consultants to "sell" their skills and convince their colleagues that they could indeed deliver to a high level of reliability and quality. According to a consultant,

the other thing which is different from other companies is the sort of internal market . . . where you're basically selling yourself to your colleagues to get involved in a project. . . . Lots of freedom, but you're sort of, you name your price. . . . If I wanted to do something, if I'm desperately short of work I could price myself at half the time and am actually encouraged to do so in order to just get the numbers up.

It was particularly crucial for new consultants to develop their internal network and to be "taken under the wing" of a more senior person. One new consultant showed me her personal "positioning" diagram that she had developed and subsequently updated, which portrayed her particular consulting skills in relation to PA's "organizational effectiveness" consulting practice. In effect she had developed a visual representation that positioned her specific skills vividly in the broader context of PA's offerings, so as to improve the visibility and memorability of her position in PA's competitive internal market of consulting talent.

Thus PA's reward and evaluation system, and the related operation of the internal market, can be seen as a further microcosm of the discursive central themes of PA; the importance of clients as a means of reaching financial success, not only for the organization as a whole but also for individual consultants. Access to clients was determined by one's success in building their internal network, as well as by their existing client list, which was a potent source of power in PA. These organizational processes (reward and evaluation system and the internal market) ensured that the discursive central themes of clients and success penetrated both the agential and by extension the organizational levels, perpetuating their continuous reproduction through their recursive effects at the level of interaction.

Vivid examples of the effects on agents' action was consultants placing high priority to client demands above all else, sometimes neglecting their own expertise development, being possessive about their client list, and often treating support staff abruptly and insensitively. With regard to expertise development, an interesting example of the importance of clients is found in the following memorandum, sent by a senior director to the MD in 1994:

Consultant Training

Dropping out of booked courses because of client meetings/client pressures has once again become accepted practice. Consultants are treating course attendance as optional, and are:

1. Failing to meet their own development objectives.
2. Letting down their colleagues on the course.
3. Abusing the time of tutors who are also under client pressures.

If we can't manage this through the expressed values I suggest we do so through the measurement system.

How about?

1. People won't be accredited if they don't do the training. Then they won't be able to do the work.
2. If people cancel at less than a week's notice because of client commitments they can go to their commitment, but the billing goes to the tutor.

This example was a suggested remedy to what was seen as a growing problem, consultants placing their commitments with clients above the most important internal process in a knowledge organization, their own expertise development. A representative view in PA was, according to a consultant, "if a client says 'jump,' you jump!"

The importance of adding value to clients as a key legitimating factor for consultants' actions or inactions is illustrated by the following incident I observed in the corridors of PA's headquarters: Two female consultants, one a new recruit and the other an experienced principal consultant, met in the corridor. They had a short, friendly chat around work issues. At one point the principal consultant asked why the new consultant had not attended a meeting with a certain client which had taken place a couple of days earlier. The new consultant replied that she did not think that she could have added value, since she did not have experience in the particular topic of the meeting. The principal then replied that she would have actually added value if she had attended since she could have given a fresh perspective to the situation. This incident can be seen as a typical manifestation of the overall pattern, in which the new consultant's inaction is placed as Z in a variant form of the secondary enthymeme pattern:

P1   We need to do what it takes to enable value-delivery to clients (implicit premise)

P2   My going along to the meeting would not have enabled this because I do not have enough experience in the topic of the meeting

C   Therefore I did not go

The principal consultant's counterargument can be stated as follows:

P1   We need to do what it takes to enable value-delivery to clients (implicit premise)

P2   Your coming along to the meeting would have enabled value-delivery to the client because we would have had the benefit of a fresh perspective on the topic

C   Therefore, you should have come along to the meeting

Both the argument and the counterargument are acceptable in that social context because they are legitimated at a higher level by the primary structure, where adding value to clients is the means to reach the ultimate goal, financial success.

A further example of the importance of clients, and the impact of this focus on support staff in PA, is the first 1-day orientation program for support staff held during March 1995, which I observed. This program was set up partly as a result of my feedback to the organization that support staff did not feel adequately familiar with PA's client offerings and how they contributed to them. The afternoon session was structured as a "trial" of an imaginary PA consultant. The charge, coined by a senior director, was

that the defendant, a PA consultant, treated support staff in a way that failed to use their time effectively or showed respect for them and their skills, thus preventing PA from giving best service to our clients.

The judge, the counsels for both sides, and the jury were all secretaries; there was no doubt of the verdict. The defense of the consultant was half-hearted, the prosecution strong, and the deliberation of the jury unusually short and unanimous.

A key revealing aspect of the mock trial from a discourse analysis perspective is first, the nature of the charge and second, how it was legitimated. The charge was derived from my earlier feedback to senior management, based on interviews with support staff, that they generally felt unvalued and unhappy with the way many consultants treated them. The legitimation of the charge, importantly, was based on "preventing PA from giving best service to our clients," as opposed to several other possible legitimating factors (e.g that some consultants' inconsiderate behavior caused mental distress to support staff, or that it is ethically wrong to mistreat people).

The enthymeme and central themes discussed earlier constitute PA's dominant discourse in at least three senses: First, in terms of legitimatory power: if one's arguments and opinions are to be taken seriously by those in power, they must draw on the discursive structures and constructions discussed earlier. Second, in terms of fixing of spoken discourse as text: the overwhelming majority of written communications in PA exhibit this discourse. Third, in terms of diffusion: the majority of organizational members (consultants, surveys and IT staff, and some support staff) articulate their task-related thoughts and opinions in terms of this discourse.

The Strategic Change Discourse

I defined PA's strategic change discourse as the general body of texts that addressed the various issues related to the change process. Such texts included initial memorandums among senior directors about the need for change, the outcomes of planning sessions, handouts at employee consultation meetings, and internal organization change bulletins. The analysis of this body of texts did not focus on such surface issues as the specifics of the structural change, implementation details, or who would be responsible for what, but rather on the legitimatory statements for the change and its aims. This is a methodological direction arising from Giddens's (1993: 92) discussion of the rationalization of conduct as a "basic feature of the monitoring intrinsic to the reflexive behavior of human actors as purposive beings." To understand these rationalizations, I thus focused on textual fragments that displayed them.

Strategic thinking at the communicative level

At the surface communicative level, initial texts about the strategic change process were concerned with the long-term direction, structure, and processes of the organization. For example, initial internal memorandums among senior management discussed PA's evolution from a single product/service organization to portfolio integration, then the alignment of this portfolio with business strategy, the organizational implications of these shifts, and the critical success factors for sustaining this journey. A second focus for discussion was the changing patterns of PA's various consulting offerings, relating these to market trends and requirements, making strategic recommendations as to where PA should focus in future, and arguing for the need for radical change. Finally, texts focused on defining a vision and mission for the future, defining the main organizational changes required to arrive to that, the particular competitive advantages that PA should strive to achieve, the main internal processes that needed to be focused on, and the management of PA's image in the marketplace.

The outcome of these dialogues was that PA had to aim for cultural change (especially a shift away from individualism to teamwork); substantial growth in size through more intensive recruitment of consultants and selling of larger consulting projects; a more focused client relationship management process to increase the efficiency of consulting effort; increased breadth and depth of consultants' expertise; and integration of various distinct consulting methodologies.

As the intended strategic direction became clearer, later texts focused on more operational issues such as the required organizational design through business process mapping, critical success factors both for PA and for achieving the change, the responsibilities and membership of the change steering group and the change teams, action timetables, and the progress achieved over time.

The structural level of the strategic change discourse: Focus on success

Despite this diversity of content at the communicative level, at the structural level almost all internal communications posed explicitly or implied that success was the ultimate objective of, and legitimating factor for, the strategic change program. For example, statements such as "what underpins our success?" and "what are the factors most critical in sustaining the transformation, in the right direction and to achieve success?" were abundant. In a more subtle way, however, success was constructed financially in the strategic change discourse, in common with the wider, dominant discourse. Initial analyses of the market were not made in terms of market structure, competitor analysis, or client segmentation, but in terms of PA's previous, current, and projected revenues from each of its main offerings. Conclusions from these analyses focused accordingly on PA's revenue growth prospects, which were taken as the main objective of the strategic change program. As an analysis of internal memorandums indicated, at the senior management level, the need for strategic change was argued for in terms of market trends, but the focus was on the implications of these trends in terms of PA's revenue performance.

Rationalizations for the strategic change program thus overwhelmingly rested on financial success and revenue growth. Strategic change was seen as the means to revenue growth, and by implication to financial success, which would in turn satisfy all the stakeholders (support staff was not included in the discussion of stakeholders, which referred to clients, consultants, and partners of the firm):

Why are we doing this?
... We can only meet these professional and business needs if we grow in profitability to finance the necessary investment. We can only become more profitable if we concentrate on profitable consulting and that requires that we manage ourselves more purposefully.... The case for change:

Where are we going and why? Our strategic thinking over the last six months has developed to the extent that we know we need to grow.... Revenue growth is the only way to satisfy all our stakeholders....

Another text indicating financial constructions of success was a forward-looking statement written in 1994, and was a description of the ideal future of the organization:

Our culture is dynamic and so are our results. For example, in Europe our operating profit has grown from X million in 1994 to Y million in 1999. Our revenues have grown from X million to Y million. What underpins our success?

Thus, financial constructions of success pervaded the strategic change discourse, even though on rare occasions some texts displayed a double-loop awareness that the organization defined success solely in financial terms to the exclusion of other criteria. For example, a document referring to consultant evaluation cautioned that

Performance management needs to be more complex, to recognize different forms of "success", but sales and billing still dominates.

Focus on clients

The central theme of clients pervades the strategic change discourse. Clients are constructed as stakeholders "who need us to grow," as the focus of PA's mission ("we intend to be the premier consultancy for helping clients realize their strategy through people"), or as platforms where the individualistic behaviors of PA consultant were manifested; behaviors that needed to change. The main way in which the client theme is constructed in the strategic change discourse, however, is the need for a more differentiated focus on clients depending on the size of revenue they deliver to PA and on how to achieve this focus organizationally. Client differentiation was seen as a key lever for change in the early stages of the change process:

Through achieving greater focus on our key clients, rather than dissipating our energy by failing to understand and to provide a service to a vast number of so called client organizations. It will make better commercial sense and it will provide a higher level of service if we can differentiate.

The "principles underlying the change" were all focused on clients with the expected outcomes being more "interesting and profitable business":

The principles underlying the change should be borne in mind. They are to:

- give clarity of focus to different kinds of client so that we can waste less time trying to manage them all in the same manner,
- improve consultant allocation to clients and projects
- provide a better offering to our clients,

All of which is designed to increase the amount of interesting and profitable business for us all.

This differentiation of focus, depending on the extent of revenue that each client brought to PA, was expected to lead to further revenue growth:

To secure the growth we want, and to consult with clients in the way we want to, we must do three clear and straight forward things:

1. Key account focus: . . . We will therefore specify and then manage those key accounts that should secure us the largest revenues and most diversified work . . .
2. Client Service Focus: What of the other X thousand or more clients that PA has in Europe? The more important of these will also be managed by consultants but with a lower priority than the key accounts . . .
3. Expertise management: . . .

Clients were segmented in four groups, depending on the actual and potential size of revenue that PA earned from them: case accounts, key accounts, medium accounts, and small accounts, with the aim of moving clients progressively upwards. This segmentation was expected to lead to higher efficiency of sustaining and growing sales levels:

With a bit of focus like this, X or so consultants could be sustaining sales levels that it currently takes about (twice X) of us to produce . . . . The aim will be to move clients up through these levels, accepting that sales will fluctuate in the short term, and recognizing that it is a dynamic set of relationships with clients moving in both directions.

Sales growth was seen as important enough to have a special project on this area, and to devote an internal "change bulletin" solely to the progress of this project.

The organizational change process itself was legitimated as worthwhile and important, by allowing consultants working on change projects to charge for their time. In terms of the prevailing reward and evaluation process in which charging for one's time (billing to clients) was the key element of success, the organizational change process was now a client! Consultants could then contribute to organizational success by spending time in the interests of the change process, as well as to their individual success within the organization, by contributing to their billing targets. Allowing consultants to charge for their time when working on organizational change projects was symbolically potent because it drew its legitimacy from PA's reward and evaluation system, which embodied the discursive central themes of clients as means to (financial) success.

The strategic change process was thus constructed and legitimated as the means of achieving the ultimate goal of success (constructed financially), through a more effective focus on clients, which would enable higher sales to them. The strategic change theme occupied the

Table 7.2. The Location of the Strategic Change Discourse in the Dominant Discourse

Enthymeme Structure	Discursive Example		Nature of Statement
P1 + P2	P1	Our key goal is success	P1	Value stating desirable state of affairs
	P2	Higher sales to clients lead to success	P2	General belief of contingent relationship in normative domain
C1→ P1' + P2'	C1→P1'	Therefore, we need to do what it takes to achieve higher sales to clients	C1→P1'	General conclusion on required type or class of action
	P2'	Undertaking strategic change will lead to higher sales to clients	P2'	Belief of contingent relationship in the action-oriented domain
C2	C2	Therefore, we need to undertake a strategic change program	C2	Conclusion of required specific action to be taken

Source: Adapted from Heracleous (2006).

place of Z in the secondary structure and was legitimated through its conformance to, and co-optation by, the dominant discourse. Table 7.2 portrays the location of the strategic change discourse in the dominant discourse.

Thematic unity thus existed not only between the central themes of the dominant discourse (success and clients) but also between these themes and the strategic change theme. The particular form this unity took is a means–ends relationship. In the case of the primary structure this relationship is more implicit and located in actors' practical consciousness; in the case of the secondary structure it is more explicit and located in discursive consciousness (Giddens, 1984). The linkage between the two structures (C1 and P1') can be seen as an implicit premise, which is close to discursive consciousness but is most often left unstated since it is taken for granted by actors in this social context.

In addition, the means–ends relations involved are those that exist in the interpretive schemes of the actors in that particular context, and not necessarily those which hold more objectively. Rhetorical enthymemes, as Aristotle pointed out, are arguments at a lower level of probability (an apparent or seeming probability) than a logical dialectic (Rhetoric, 1:1:14, 1:2:6). These means–ends relations gain their apparent validity from the particular constructions of central themes in the dominant discourse. For example, if success were not constructed as primarily a financial affair, undertaking a strategic change program focused on achieving higher sales to clients would not have seemed such an appropriate course of action.

The Marginalized Counter-Discourse

A counter-discourse is also operating in PA, which does not conform to the discursive structures and constructions of the dominant discourse. It uses different channels, is concerned with different issues, has different functions, and derives from a different organizational group. Its relationship with the dominant discourse is one of opposition, albeit weak in extent and consequences. It acts as a coping discourse, helping to safeguard support staff identity against the assaults of the dominant discourse whose constructions of "success" attribute low status, worth, and priority to staff groups that are not in direct contact with clients, and are not seen to contribute to client sales and thus to PA's (financial) success.

The counter-discourse is concerned with commenting on support staff's view of their condition in PA. It is manifested in humorous images and captions sometimes created by support staff themselves, located in their personal space, on the walls in front of their desks and mixed with other images such as photographs of their loved ones and pets, holiday postcards, and functional data such as where the consultants they work with can be found on different days. The counter-discourse does not have any formal means of expression; it is not fixed in text (other than the scattered images in support staff's personal space); is not a collective, coordinated, or planned effort; does not contain potent criticism of the dominant group's actions or beliefs; and is certainly not effective in influencing the direction of strategic changes. In all these senses, it was the opposite of the organized resistance through humor that Rodrigues and Collinson (1995) found, which had been effective in a different context.

The counter-discourse shows in a "humorous" way support staff's reflection on their condition in PA and their dissatisfaction with it, and draws attention to issues support staff are concerned with but have no other means of airing. Several of these issues arose in my interviews with support staff during the initial stages of the change process and were fed back to senior management so that action could be taken to remedy them.

Support staff concerns included not feeling valued in PA, being given low priority, feeling dissatisfied with their salaries that they believed are in the lower quartile in the consulting industry, being expected to work overtime without extra pay (citing PA's inflexible approach to salaries in this regard), having no clear options for career development, and being treated in an inconsiderate and impolite manner by many consultants. In addition, they perceived their work appraisal process as too subjective, without a clear framework, and being based too much on the personal relationship between the support staff and their boss. Commonly used expressions in interviews were that support staff often felt like "part of the furniture," and were always the "last to know" about organizational or other changes, even about things that affected them personally. They felt that they did not know enough about PA's offerings to the market, and how their work fits in or contributes to these offerings. Support staff perceived a divide between them and consultants, a "them and us" situation. Many members of this group also wondered why their suggestions to senior management were never implemented or even taken seriously.

Vivid examples of consultants' inconsiderate treatment of support staff, for example, were given in the mock trial of the imaginary PA consultant that I had observed. After the charge was read, the first witness for the prosecution gave a damning testimony, describing an incident where a consultant gave her work without explaining clearly how it should be done. Then, the consultant wanted a changed version "for no good reason," and "couldn't understand how long it would take to redo" (half a day in the secretary's estimation); he then did not even say thank you when the revised work was delivered. The second witness gave a similar testimony. A client had phoned up wanting the consultant's report for use in a meeting. The secretary "covered up" for the consultant who was not around, and when he returned, he wanted the work done there and then, not realizing that the secretary had also other consultants' work to do. Even though she explained, the consultant did not understand.

Support staff in interviews mentioned examples of not only consultants' but also management's actions that they saw as telling of management's attitude toward them. One such example that left a deep impression on a secretary occurred during her annual meeting with her boss to discuss her performance review. During the review a consultant walked in the office wanting to speak to her boss about a client project. The boss immediately interrupted the review to speak to the consultant. To the secretary, her boss's response was a potent symbolic indication that the boss did not value her very much, since he was willing to interrupt their most important annual meeting, to speak with someone who came in unannounced and without an appointment, about something that in her view could have waited until after the review meeting was finished.

Later interviews and informal conversations with support staff, as well as company-wide surveys I conducted, revealed that the change process did not address their concerns, contrary to consultants' concerns which were being addressed through the institution of internal projects focused on these concerns. Even though dominant groups expressed their desire to get feedback on support staff concerns, and said that these were as important as consultant concerns, their actions and the allocation of resources indicated that support staff concerns were of low priority.

The third survey I conducted, for example, in February 1996, validated interview and informant data by showing that only 3% of support staff felt that the following concerns expressed around one and a half year earlier had been addressed: not feeling valued in PA (own ideas do not count, last to find out about things, insufficient and inflexible financial arrangements); inconsiderate treatment by consultants (poor workload planning, unclear accountabilities for resolving support staff concerns); and work appraisal (no clear framework, too subjective). Even less than that, 0% felt that the following concerns were addressed: insufficient knowledge of PA's offerings and how support staff contributes, and absence of clear options for career development.

The criticism of the dominant groups that the counter-discourse employs is of a kind legitimated by wider social conventions—satire. The penetration of this counter-discourse in the formal expressions of the dominant discourse, however, is negligible. The prominent monthly internal publication read by almost everyone, for example, is an instrument of the dominant discourse. Contributions of support staff in this publication are rare, involving mostly one's introduction to the rest of the organization when joining PA. There are no internal publications dedicated to support staff.

The satirical images used in the counter-discourse are both general, for example, humorously portraying professionally abused secretaries or portraying executives as egoistic and greedy, and specific to the particular situation of support staff. The themes of the more specific images are consistent with several of the concerns expressed by support staff in interviews. For example, there was an image of a cartoon character, Mr. Blobby, saying: "Blobby blobby blob! (Translation: I'm here to tell you about your pay rise!) Enough said." A second image of a dark tunnel had the following caption: "Due to current financial constraints the light at the end of the tunnel will be switched off." Another image showed an oppressed secretary literally under a huge thumb. Finally, another image showed a boss feeling distressed with work at 5:30 P.M. but with no apparent consideration for his secretary who is expected to work overtime without extra pay, has huge piles of work at her desk, and appears to want to go home.

It is interesting that management, the target of the satire, could see these images and identify the people who display them. In this sense humor and satire are more than "symbolic cloaks" which minimize the risk of managerial reprisals (Rodrigues and Collinson, 1995). In PA's case, they are openly used by identifiable individuals to express their task-related concerns and views on their condition in the organization. From a functionalist perspective of humor as a safety valve, the existence and content of this counter-discourse may be tacitly "accepted" by management because it functions as a steam-letting device, helping to enable the existing system and distribution of authority and resources to keep functioning without substantial disruptions. Another potential explanation for management's tacit "acceptance" through nonconfrontation may be that satire, a key discursive element of PA's counter-discourse is an indirect and subtle form of critique, a world apart from management's dominant discourse characterized by normative rationality, instrumentality, and teleology. The dominant discourse was thus faced with a different world, one it did not feel inclined or willing to engage with.

Modes of Discourse, Discursive Antagonisms, and Social Construction

Modes of Discourse and Interdiscursive Relationships

The aims of this research were first to explore the nature of modes of discourse in organizational settings; second to explore how, if at all, modes of discourse are interrelated; and third to explore the constructive potential of modes of discourse on their social and organizational contexts. Through addressing these questions, this research has aimed to respond to calls for greater clarity in the specification of the concept of discourse, as well as a deeper understanding of the constructive effects of discourse in social organizations (van Dijk, 1997; Grant, Keenoy, and Oswick, 2001; Keenoy, Oswick, and Grant, 1997).

This study has revealed an organizational field wherein a dominant mode of discourse forms an overarching structure where other discourses must be located if they are to be taken seriously by those in power and by the members of the dominant subculture. The findings suggest that one potentially useful interpretation of the nature of "modes" of discourse is that they are constituted of rhetorical enthymemes, of interrelated primary and secondary argument structures that enshrine the central themes of the discourse in terms of means–ends relationships, and which have both normative and positive effects on their social context. The secondary enthymeme structure is flexible in terms of content so that themes relating to situational exigencies can be located. Any additional themes that are located in this flexible secondary structure for the purposes of legitimation must also be co-opted in the existing means–ends relationships of the dominant discourse, if they are to be taken seriously by those in power and aligned with the powerful. The secondary structure thus functions at the positive, action domain and is located in actors' discursive consciousness, whereas the primary structure functions in the normative domain and is located in actors' practical consciousness.

Analysis of the strategic change discourse exemplifies the process of locating a situational theme in the secondary structure so that in this case the necessity and extent of strategic change argued for could be legitimated. The strategic change theme was linked argumentatively with the central themes of the dominant discourse and was consistent with their specific constructions. The strategic change discourse was thus subservient to, and located in, the dominant discourse.

The strategic change discourse also illustrates the existence of a wider rhetorical strategy in PA, which provides rules for "proper" argumentation in that context. This strategy has to be followed by actors in that context if they are to be taken seriously and is manifested in individual texts produced by different speakers or authors, discoursing about different issues, at different points in time and in different situations. The rhetorical strategy involved certain "rules" for proper argumentation in this social context, which are: First, to legitimate a certain course of action or inaction, locate it in the structures and constructions of the dominant discourse. Second, this can be done through implicit or explicit reference to its contributions to success and effects on clients. Third, follow the particular construction of these central themes in the dominant discourse; for example, talk of financial success and adding value or selling more to clients. Fourth, use both the vocabulary and style of the dominant discourse (in terms of style, your own texts should be imbued with teleology, instrumentality, and measurability).

Table 7.3 portrays key features of the three discourses in relation to each other.

This study, therefore, shows that discourses are not autonomous but linked with other discourses in cooperative or antagonistic ways (see Palmer and Dunford, 2002, for an extended discussion of the various potential relationships among discourses). PA's dominant discourse draws from wider contextual discourses, especially what du Gay and Salaman (1992) have referred to as the discourse of enterprise, emphasizing the "sovereign consumer" as the basis of organizational arrangements, as well as industry-wide concerns with "adding value" (Chatman and Jehn, 1994). The relationship between the dominant and the strategic change discourses in PA shows how one newly established, situationally prompted, and temporary body of discourse can draw from the structures and constructions of an overarching discourse; and how, in doing so, it seeks to legitimize itself and certain courses of action or inaction.

Discursive Antagonisms between the Dominant and Counter-Discourse

The analysis of PA's discourses has revealed a complex picture of the rule of a dominant discourse that is relatively stable at the structural level but flexible at the communicative action level where other discourses can be located (such as the strategic change discourse). It has also revealed the existence of a counter-discourse that lies outside the dominant themes and constructions of the dominant discourse, in this sense lending support to a dialogical rather than monological perspective on organizational discourse (Boje, 1995; Grant, Keenoy, and Oswick, 1998; Keenoy, Oswick, and Grant, 1997). This analysis has also aimed to address both the interpretive aim of understanding

Table 7.3. Features of the Dominant, Strategic Change, and Counter Discourses

Features	Dominant Discourse	Strategic Change Discourse	Counter-Discourse
Discursive elements	Enthymeme structures, central themes, specific constructions	Themes legitimated through the dominant discourse	Satirical images and captions
Channels of expression	Formal, extensive	Formal, extensive	Informal, scattered
Time scale	Long term	Temporary	Long term
Orientation	Normative, instrumental, teleological	Action oriented	Resistance through humor
Functions in social context	Communicative: Informing, coordinating, persuading; Constructive: Defining criteria of "success," allocating worth and value to org groups by reference to these criteria	Enabling organizational responsiveness to competitive demands, within lense of dominant discourse	Expressing dissatisfaction, letting off steam, safeguarding identity and self-worth

Source: Adapted from Heracleous (2006).

agents' worlds, and a critical concern with the effects of dominant discourses on disadvantaged groups (Mumby and Clair, 1997; Oswick, Keenoy, and Grant, 1997).

In this vein, an antagonistic relationship between the dominant and counter-discourses can be discerned, where the counter-discourse is shaped by what it opposes, being positioned against the central themes and constructions of the dominant discourse and its effects. In terms of its themes and constructions, the counter-discourse does not draw from the dominant discourse for legitimation because the very nature of the dominant discourse places support staff, the originators, and consumers of the counter-discourse in a disadvantaged position. Support staff receives low priority, as ethnographic data have shown over and over again, partly because of the nature and effects of the dominant discourse that stresses financial success, adding value, and achieving increased sales to clients. In terms of its existence, however, the counter-discourse is made possible by the effects of the very discourse it opposes.

From an organizational analysis perspective, this situation illustrates the argument that groups that can effectively enable the organization to respond to crucial contingencies have higher intra-organizational power (Hickson et al., 1971). In this case, PA's dominant discourse defines the perceived organizational contingencies and then attributes worth and power to those who can respond to these contingencies, the consulting staff.

From a critical perspective, however, the antagonism between the dominant and counter-discourses, the weak resistance of the counter-discourse, and the overarching effects of the dominant discourse are all illustrations of Foucault's view, drawing from Nietzsche, of discourses as the "will to power," or Habermas' thesis that "knowledge"-constituting interests take form in the medium of work, language and power" (1987: 313). Foucault, for example, suggested that "pure" or "value" free' knowledge was not possible because knowledge is subordinated to selfish interests and power relations (Foucault, 1977a). In this sense knowledge, and discourses portraying and producing such knowledge are by no means neutral or objective, but inherently and surreptitiously biased in favor of dominant interests, in this case illustrated by the nature and effects of the dominant discourse.

Power for Foucault, however, was not simply repressive, but had positive, productive, and seductive effects. People, in other words, may not simply feel dominated by power, but could be attracted to it and its effects such as the subjective identities it can offer through discourse (Foucault, 1977b: 119). In PA, for example, the constructive effects of the dominant discourse were desirable and attractive to both new consulting recruits and seasoned consultants, who enjoyed their consulting identity and the empowerment, status and autonomy that went with it. Many employees in the surveys and IT departments were also acutely drawn to the effects of the dominant discourse, seduced by the consulting identity, and aspiring to become consultants in future. The creation of an overarching discourse with pervasive themes and specific constructions in PA, as well as the projection of a seductive consulting identity, is a prime example of the exercise of power through concertive control (Tompkins and Cheney, 1985).

Support staff, on the other hand, perceived that they had no chance of ever becoming consultants, and feeling suffocated by the dominant discourse and its effects, were attempting to safeguard their identity and sense of self-worth through producing, and participating in, a courageous but weak counterdiscourse. Is there leeway for the dominant and counter-discourses to communicate within a context of constructive and cooperative dialogical exchange, for example, through the method of Socratic dialogue (Bolten 2001)? An effective dialogical exchange presupposes that the parties want to speak to each other, have a genuine interest in what each party is saying, and want to find common ground. While from a pluralist perspective (Morgan, 1986) this would be both possible and desirable, from a critical perspective a productive dialogue would seem unlikely. From a critical perspective the dice are already loaded; this discursive antagonism is imbued with power imbalances and surrounded by an ideology enshrined in the dominant discourse (Habermas, 1987: 311) that rationalizes and perpetuates existing power arrangements and attributions of worth.

Structural Discursive Features as Constructive of Social Reality

The potency of discourse to affect organizational processes and outcomes is well accepted (e.g. Maitlis and Lawrence, 2003; Palmer and Dunford, 2002; Vaara, Kleymanm, and Seristo, 2004), and one of this study's aims has been to gain a deeper understanding of this constructive potential. One finding is that the constructive potential of discourse is based primarily on its deeper structures and the consonance of surface (communicative) actions with these structures.

PA's enthymeme structures and central themes illustrate empirically the nature of structural features of discourse. Within particular social contexts, these features transcend individual texts, manifesting in a variety of situations and at different times. They are most often assumed and implicit rather than explicitly stated (Heracleous and Hendry, 2000). This research shows that discursive structures and constructions can be potent in constructing social reality in the following ways: First, they persist in the longer term and reside in actors' practical consciousness, informing their interpretations and actions. As discussed earlier, the central themes and constructions of the discourse were continually and recursively manifesting in agents' actions as well as organizational processes such as the reward and evaluation system and the internal market for consulting talent. Second, discursive structures and constructions (acting as implicit premises in organizational enthymemes) are inculcated in agents through socialization and experience in particular contexts, in the same way as cultural values and beliefs (but they are different from cultural values and beliefs, however, in the sense that they can be seen as perceptions of implicit means–ends relationships). Third, discursive central themes and their constructions take on the properties of normative devices for orienting action, where action is itself a symbolic affirmation (or potentially challenge) of the importance of these themes, as was shown earlier.

Conversely to field data that have shown tight consonances between discursive structures and constructions as discussed earlier, field data have also shown that if there are communicative actions that do not agree with the dominant discourse, such statements are not potent in constructing social reality. For example, the MD addressed the organization in a 1994 speech, and characterized all groups, including support staff, as stakeholders in the business in order to encourage them to identify with the future of PA and motivate them to change. Such comments were partly prompted by my earlier feedback to senior management that both consulting and support staff had certain concerns about the change process and more generally about the organization, and on the compelling effect of this data on a newly appointed MD to show concern for all groups in the organization. The MD's statements could not change the fact, however, that consultants get a much larger profit share and higher priority than nonconsulting staff, and everyone knew that the most significant financial stakeholders were the partners who own PA. The MD's statements, therefore, were not potent in influencing social reality because of two main factors: first, their disagreement with the structures and constructions of the dominant discourse; and second, the existence of contextual, extradiscursive conditions that also defined which stakeholder groups were seen as more important.

In sum, this research has shown that modes of discourse can be usefully conceptualized as rhetorical enthymemes constituted of relatively stable, normative structures and flexible, action-oriented structures; second, modes of discourse can interrelate through their deeper structural features and can have mutually co-optive or antagonistic relationships; and finally, the constructive potential of discourse is based primarily on its deeper structures and the consonance of surface (communicative) actions with these structures.

മ

Even though the concept of discourse can potentially have as many meanings as one cares to ascribe to it, I have endeavored in this book to present a series of analytically defined and theoretically informed approaches to understanding this concept, as well as employing it empirically in organizational settings, drawing on my own research over the last few years. My own underlying orientation has been an interpretive one, even with regard to studies with a functional, critical, or structurational slant. The analytical distinctions and assumptions underlying these streams have been discussed in some detail in the various chapters, but they are all made possible by the deceptively simple realization that language (or discourse, as composed of texts, composed of language) is not simply a conduit for transfer of information from one person to another; it is a constructive, shaping force that can extend beyond the interpersonal level, the group level, the organizational level, and even the societal level, to transcendent megadiscourses, that intermingle with local discourses and a plethora of perspectives, positions, and voices in struggles to define social reality.

Even though the constructive role of language now seems a simple realization, it took nothing less than the "linguistic turn" in the social sciences for it to be taken seriously. The task of the discourse scholar becomes an endeavor, in a reflexive manner, to make sense of the nature of discourses at the relevant levels they are researching, to trace in some detail and in a manner that is both valid and ideally additive to understanding the constructive potential of these discourses as actualized in social and organizational settings, and, when warranted, try to make a difference. The organization studies field has embraced the concept of discourse, becoming a home for a variety of multi-disciplinary studies of discourse in organizational contexts. This trajectory has only gained critical mass over the last decade, and its promise is still far from being fulfilled.

References

Aristotle. 1991. *On rhetoric*. G. A. Kennedy (trans.). Oxford: Oxford University Press.

Barry, D. and Elmes, M. 1997. Strategy retold: Toward a narrative view of strategic discourse. *Academy of Management Review*, 22: 429–452.

Berger, D. and Luckmann, T. 1966. *The social construction of reality*. London: Penguin.

Boje, D. M. 1995. Stories of the storytelling organization. A postmodern analysis of Disney as "Tamara-Land". *Academy of Management Journal*, 38: 997–1035.

Bolten, D. 2001. Managers develop moral accountability: The impact of socratic dialogue. *Reason in Practice*, 1 (3): 21–34.

Chatman, D. A. and Jehn, K. A. 1994. Assessing the relationship between industry characteristics and organizational culture: How different can you be? *Academy of Management Journal*, 37: 522–553.

Cheney, D. and McMillan, J. J. 1990. Organizational rhetoric and the practice of criticism. *Journal of Applied Communication Research*, 18 (2): 93–114.

Cheney, G., Christensen, L. T. Conrad, C. and Lair, D. J. 2004. Corporate rhetoric as organizational discourse. In D. Grant, C. Hardy, C. Oswick, N. Phillips, and L. L. Putnam (eds.), *Handbook of organizational discourse*: 79–103. London: Sage.

van Dijk, T. A. 1997. The study of discourse. In T. A. van Dijk (ed.), *Discourse studies: A multidisciplinary introduction*, vol. 1: 1–34. Beverly Hills, CA: Sage.

Dyer, W. G., Jr. and Wilkins, A. L. 1991. Better stories, not better constructs, to generate better theory: A rejoinder to Eisenhardt. *Academy of Management Review*, 16: 613–619.

Eemeren, F. H., Grootendorst, R., Jackson, S. and Jacobs, S. 1997. Argumentation. In T. A. van Dijk (ed.), *Discourse studies: A multidisciplinary introduction*, vol. 1: 208–229. Thousand Oaks, CA: Stage.

Eisenhardt, K. M. 1989. Building theories from case study research. *Academy of Management Review*, 14: 532–550.

   1991. Better stories and better constructs: The case for rigor and comparative logic. *Academy of Management Review*, 16: 620–627.

Fisher, A. 1988. *The logic of real arguments*. Cambridge, MA: Cambridge University Press.

Foucault, M. 1977a. History of Systems of Thought. In D. Bouchard (ed.), *Language, counter-memory, practice: Selected essays and interviews by Michel Foucault*: 199–204. Ithaca, NY: Cornell University Press.

1977b. *Discipline and punish*. London: Penguin.

Gadamer, H.-G. 1997. Rhetoric and hermeneutics. In W. Jost and M. J. Hyde (eds.), *Rhetoric and hermeneutics in our time: A reader*: 45–59. New Haven, CT: Yale University Press.

du Gay, P. and Salaman, G. 1992. The cult(ure) of the customer. *Journal of Management Studies*, **29**: 615–33.

Geertz, C. 1973. *The interpretation of cultures*. New York, NY: Basic Books.

Giddens, A. 1979. *Central problems in social theory*. London: Macmillan.

1984. *The constitution of society*. Cambridge, MA: Polity.

1987. *Social theory and modern sociology*. Cambridge, MA: Polity.

1993. *New rules of sociological method* (2nd edn.). Stanford: Stanford University Press.

Gill, A. M. and Whedbee, K. 1997. Rhetoric. In T. A. van Dijk (ed.), *Discourse studies: A multidisciplinary introduction*, vol. 1: 157–183. Thousand Oaks, CA: Sage.

Grant, D., Keenoy, T. and Oswick, C. 1998. organizational discourse: of diversity, dichotomy and multi-disciplinarity. In D. Grant, T. Keenoy, and C. Oswick (eds.), *Discourse and organization*: 1–13. London: Sage.

2001. Organizational discourse: Key contributions and challenges. *International Studies of Management and Organization*, **31** (3): 5–24.

Habermas, J. 1987. *The philosophical discourse of modernity*, Oxford: Oxford University Press.

Hammersley, M. and Atkinson, P. 1995. *Ethnography: Principles in practice* (2nd edn.). London: Routledge.

Heracleous, L. 2006. A tale of three discourses: The dominant, the strategic and the marginalized. *Journal of Management Studies*, **43**: 1059–1087.

2001. An ethnographic study of culture in the context of organizational change. *Journal of Applied Behavioral Science*, **37**: 426–446.

Heracleous, L. and Hendry, J. 2000. Discourse and the study of organization: Towards a structurational perspective. *Human Relations*, **53**: 1251–1286.

Hickson, D. J., Hinings, C. R., Lee, C. A., Schneck, R. E. and Pennings, J. M. 1971. A strategic contingencies theory of intra-organizational power. *Administrative Science Quarterly*, **16**: 216–229.

Keenoy, T., Oswick, C. and Grant, D. 1997. Organizational discourses: Text and context. *Organization*, 4: 147–157.

Kets de Vries, M. F. R. and Miller, D. 1987. Interpreting organizational texts. *Journal of Management Studies*, 24: 233–247.

Maitlis, S. and Lawrence, T. B. 2003. Orchestral manoeuvres in the dark: Understanding failure in organizational strategizing, *Journal of Management Studies*, 40: 109–139.

Morgan, G. 1986. *Images of organization*. Beverly Hills, CA: Sage.

Mumby, D. K. and Clair, R. P. 1997. Organizational Discourse. In van Dijk T. A. (ed.), *Discourse as social interaction*: 181–205. London: Sage.

Oswick, C., Keenoy, T. and Grant, D. 1997. Managerial discourses: Words speak louder than actions? *Journal of Applied Management Studies*, 6: 5–12.

Palmer, I. and Dunford, R. 2002. Managing discursive tension: The co-existence of individualist and collaborative discourses in Flight Centre. *Journal of Management Studies*, 39: 1045–1069.

Palmer, R. E. 1969. *Hermeneutics*. Evanston, IL: Northwestern University Press.

1997. What hermeneutics can offer rhetoric. In W. Jost and M. J. Hyde (eds.), *Rhetoric and hermeneutics in our time: A reader*: 108–131. New Haven, CT: Yale University Press.

Phillips, N. and Brown, J. L. 1993. Analyzing communication in and around organizations: A critical hermeneutic approach. *Academy of Management Journal*, 36: 1547–1576.

Ricoeur, P. 1971a. The model of the text: Meaningful action considered as a text. *Social Research*, 38: 529–562.

1971b. What is a text? Explanation and understanding. In D. Rasmussen (ed.), *Mythic-symbolic language and philosophical anthropology*: 135–150. The Hague: Martinus Nijhoff.

1973a. The task of hermeneutics. *Philosophy Today*, 17: 112–128.

1973b. The hermeneutical function of distantiation. *Philosophy Today*, 17: 129–141.

1983. On interpretation. In A. Montefiore (ed.), *Philosophy in france today*: 175–197. New York, NY: Cambridge University Press.

1997. Rhetoric-poetics-hermeneutics. In W. Jost and Hyde M. J. (eds.), *Rhetoric and hermeneutics in our time: A reader*: 60–72. New Haven, CT: Yale University Press.

Rodrigues, S. B. and Collinson, D. L. 1995. 'Having fun?' humor as resistance in brazil. *Organization Studies*, 16: 739–768.

Schein, E. 1992. *Organizational culture and leadership* (2nd edn.). San Francisco, CA: Josey-Bass.

1987a. *Process consultation*, vol. 2. Reading, MA: Addison-Wesley.

1987b. *The Clinical perspective in fieldwork*. Qualitative Research Methods, CA: Sage.

Thachankary, D. 1992. Organizations as 'texts': Hermeneutics as a model for understanding organizational change. *Research in Organization Change and Development*, 6: 197–233.

Tompkins, P. K. and Cheney, G. 1985. Communication and unobtrusive control in contemporary organizations. In R. D. McPhee and P. K. Tompkins (eds.), *Organizational communication: Traditional themes and new directions*: 179–210. Beverly Hills, CA: Sage.

Vaara, E., Kleymann, B. and Seristo, H. 2004. Strategies as discursive constructions: The case of airline alliances. *Journal of Management Studies*, 41: 1–35.

Van Maanen, J. 1979. The fact of fiction in organizational ethnography. *Administrative Science Quarterly*, 24: 539–550.

Wilkins, A. and Ouchi, W. 1983. Efficient cultures: Exploring the relationship between culture and organizational performance. *Administrative Science Quarterly*, 28: 468–481.

Index